SOUTHVIEW
TO
GETTYSVUE

From a Coal Camp to Olympic Podium,
to Courtside with Michael Jordan

To: THE HAPPY ENVELOPE
A GREAT CREW
THAT DOES INCREDIBLE
WORK!! ENJOY!!

BILL SCHMIDT

Olympian, Olympic Organizer, Sports Marketing Guru

NEWMAN SPRINGS PUBLISHING
320 Broad Street
Red Bank, NJ 07701

First originally published by Newman Springs Publishing 2022

ISBN 978-1-68498-445-9 (Hardcover)
ISBN 978-1-68498-447-3 (Digital)

Printed in the United States of America

MY LIFE'S JOURNEY

I shall be telling this with a sigh
Somewhere ages and ages hence:
Two roads diverged in a wood, and I—
I took the one less traveled by,
And that has made all the difference.

—Robert Frost, "The Road Not Taken"

Trust in the Lord with all your heart, and
do not lean on your own understanding.
In all your ways acknowledge Him, and
He will make your paths straight.

Proverbs 3:5–6

In memory of Helen P. Schmidt

A daughter of immigrants from Yugoslavia (Slovakia) who arrived in the United States in 1896, Helen was one of nine children. Born in 1912, married at eighteen years of age to a coal miner, she moved from McKees Rocks, Pennsylvania, to Southview, Pennsylvania, surrounded by in-laws.

Southview was a coal camp built by the coal company where you were paid in company script that could only be spent at the company store. She had very little formal education, gave birth to seven children, and was left to raise six children after her husband committed suicide at the age of forty-four. She was thirty-eight, and Bob and I were two and a half years old.

Older siblings quit school to go to work or joined the US Army to help support the family. There were three of us, my sister, Mary, and twin brother, Bob, who were at home being raised by this God-fearing woman who showed incredible common sense and a great work ethic.

She was generous, protective, and learned from her own school of hard knocks. We were poor, but I don't remember ever being hungry or lacking clothes. She worked cleaning individual homes after moving to Canonsburg, Pennsylvania, for $8–$12 a day, and her last job was as a custodial worker at Western State School and Hospital.

She dressed my twin brother, Bob, and I alike until we were seniors in high school. She ruled with a strong disciplined hand and put the fear of God in us. Her incredible strength, perseverance, will, and divine guidance and divine intervention defined us. For who we are and what we accomplished, we owe it all to our mother, Helen P. Schmidt.

CONTENTS

TESTIMONIALS

Bill's truly a pioneer. People forget that sports drinks were hardly a category—he defined it. He was very difficult, and that's a compliment. But you knew the dance would end with a deal. We used to pride ourselves on knowing everything about Gatorade's business, and he would sit down and know just as much—if not more—about the NBA.

—David Stern, Former NBA Commissioner

Bill has done more for the athletic training profession than any other single person. He elevated their importance, even within their own leagues.

—Tom Fox, Former Chief Commercial Officer for European Premier League Club Arsenal, CEO of Aston Villa and former President of the San Jose Earthquakes.

Bill had this gift of knowing sports inside out and realizing where the best opportunities would be. Like so many of Schmidt's initiatives, they are currently still around today.

—Hank Steinbrecher, Former Secretary General of US Soccer

He brought the importance of relationships to this business and turned it into an art form. I never had a conversation with Bill when he didn't ask, "What can I do for you?"

—Rick Welts, President, Chief Operating Officer, Golden State Warriors

Bill was a genius at developing relationships. Some people have relationships with all the commissioners and chairman, but he knew them and all the people in the trenches. I have never met a person in corporate America more well-liked.

—David Falk, Founder of F.A.M.E. and former agent for Michael Jordan

Bill comes from an individual performance sport, but you'd think he was a middle guard on an offensive line because he's able to build a good team around him quickly. He just has this vision. When everyone is heading right, he's always looking left, just to be sure.

—Peter V. Ueberroth, Former Chairman, Los Angeles Olympic Committee and Commissioner of Major League Baseball

Bill was one of the most charismatic and intimidating individuals I ever worked with. He had the strongest relationships at the highest levels.

—Steve Seyferth, Bayer Bess Vanderwarker Agency, Advertising Executive

Bill is one of the originators of sports marketing in this country. He was the one of the guys who first showed how you could use sports to get it done. The evidence of that is Gatorade's growth.

—Phil Marineau, Former President of Quaker Oats, President of Pepsi-Cola and CEO of Levi Strauss

PREFACE

Throughout my career participating in sports and in sports marketing, there were numerous times and individuals who said, "Bill, you need to write a book. Your life and life experiences would not only be inspirational but educational and motivational."

I was a competitor who had no coaching, no athletic scholarship offers from any universities, but I did have a dream—a dream I chased for almost twenty years. My dream was to represent the United States in the Olympic Games. It wasn't until the evening before the Olympic Finals in the javelin throw in 1972 that I thought I could win an Olympic medal.

My career in sports marketing started at a time before there was a definition or career path for sports marketing. I took advantages of opportunities where I clearly wasn't qualified. My work ethic, discipline, and focus that I had in the competitive arena carried over to my business career. I built strong relationships and became creative at times where I had no budgets, limited resources, and when individuals said I wouldn't succeed.

For a kid who was born in a coal camp in western Pennsylvania, one of seven children whose dad committed suicide, when he was two and half years old, it was a highly unlikely journey. It was filled with disappointment and setbacks, but that only made me more determined to succeed.

The coal camp was Southview. The upscale golf community where I now live is called Gettysvue. It was quite the journey, one that I know I couldn't have completed without the divine guidance from Jesus Christ, my Savior. I was never vocal about my goals or desires and never publicly voiced my strong religious belief. I was raised Catholic, and I knew the Lord was with me every step of the way.

Where I grew up—with my twin brother, Bob, and sister, Mary—defined us. The competitive relationship with my brother, Bob, made us both want to succeed. It wasn't that we thought we were better than anyone else; it was just that we wanted to prove ourselves. We did that by challenging each other every day in everything we did. I owe who I am and what I've accomplished to Bob for challenging me.

In my business career, I knew what I didn't know. I became a good listener and asked a lot of questions. I had no one that mentored me. From one of my first employers, I learned about hard work and doing the job the right way. As I moved through the corporate world, I established core strengths and learned something new from everyone I encountered.

I could focus on the objectives, establish a strategy, and get the job done. I was results driven. If I was told, "You can't do it," I found a way to accomplish it by thinking outside the box. I looked at things differently than most people. I was blessed with common sense and "street smarts." In addition, I had incredible intuition, and my first impressions never failed me.

The opportunities I had at Gatorade and the Quaker Oats Company I owe to Phil Marineau. He believed in me, trusted me, and supported me. We shared the best of times as we built Gatorade from $80 million in sales to $1.75 billion. We made Gatorade synonymous with sports and being there on the "Field of Play."

Gatorade wouldn't be where it is today without the athletic trainers. From the Professional Football Athletic Trainers Society (PFATS) to the Professional Baseball Athletic Trainers Society (PBATS), the National Basketball Athletic Trainers Association (NBATA), and the Professional Hockey Athletic Trainers Society (PHATS), they all supplied Gatorade with exposure during all their televised games. The National Athletic Trainers' Association (NATA) provided relationships with their twenty thousand members, which included high schools, colleges, universities, private practices, and clinics. The relationships I had with these individuals within these organizations were special and personal. I remain close friends with many of them.

My hope is that you are inspired, motivated, entertained, and learn something from the experiences I share.

CHAPTER 1

COAL IN MY VEINS

We are who we are, and our ancestry determines where we are born and how our lives are established. It doesn't necessarily determine where we end up or the journey that we take as our lives unfold. We make lifelong decisions as opportunities present themselves and as hardships and challenges occur.

My great-grandfather, Ludwig Schmidt, "Ludwig the Great," worked as a strongman in the circus throughout Europe. Otto von Bismarck, the first chancellor of the German Empire, had concentrated on developing "strongmen" before World War I. My grandfather, Louis Schmidt, was born in a small village near the German town of Oberammergau in the Bavarian region of Germany. It's a little ironic that I would compete in Munich, Germany, the capital of Bavaria, in 1972.

My grandfather came to this country aboard the ship SMS *Kronprinz Wilhelm der Grosse* in 1909. He came without his family. His wife, my grandmother, Mary Germoni Schmidt, was born in 1888 in one of the Czech republics. When he entered the United States, through Ellis Island, he settled in Imperial, Pennsylvania, working at the Cliff Mine.

In 1911, his wife, Mary, and children—Joseph, Mary, and Louis—arrived in the US and settled in Imperial, Pennsylvania. After living there for a year, they relocated to Cherry, Illinois. Cherry, Illinois, had been the site of one of the worst mining disasters in US history.

The Cherry Mine Disaster killed 259 miners on November 13, 1909. My grandfather was working on the Chicago, Milwaukee, and St. Paul Railroad in 1912, which was near Cherry, Illinois.

While living in Cherry, Illinois, the following family members were born: John 1 and John 2 (both died at or near birth), Julius (1914), and Rudolph (1916). Coincidently, my mother gave birth to her second son, named John, and he passed away two weeks after birth.

The entire family moved west with the railroad and lived in Salt Lake City, Utah, in 1919 and 1920. In early 1921, they moved to Longview, Washington, near the Oregon border along the Columbia River. Alfred Schmidt was born in St. Helens, Oregon, in 1921. They relocated to Goble, Oregon, for a short period of time, all while working on the railroad. In 1914, the family returned to western Pennsylvania and settled in McKees Rocks in 1925. Bill Schmidt (Uncle Willie) was born there later that year.

My mother's father, Juray (Georguim) Peremba, was born in Kamenica, Slovakia, December 24, 1871. At that time, it was ruled by the Austria-Hungary Empire. Her mother, Katharina Dija, was born in Dravce, Slovakia, on April 16, 1877.

They immigrated to the United States in the late nineteenth century, around 1890, and settled in Braddock, Pennsylvania. Braddock was known for its steel manufacturing plant, Edgar Thomson Steel Works, later known as United States Steel Corporation.

The 1890s saw a large contingent of immigrants from Croatia, Slovakia, Slovenia, and Hungary arrive in the United States. They were coal miners, farmers, and weavers. The coal fields and steel mills provided numerous opportunities for them. They settled in and around Pittsburgh, Pennsylvania. Coal and steel production was king, and coal companies and steel manufactures built camps to house this new work force along with a company store.

Katharina Dija and Juray Peremba were married on August 17,1896, and had their first child, a daughter, Anna, on June 27, 1897. Their second child, John, was born on October 28, 1899. They would move to another coal town, Moon Run, Pennsylvania, where they would have seven more children. Helen Peremba, my mother, would be born February 23, 1912, their seventh of nine children.

She would meet my father at a Slovakian social club and later marry him when she was eighteen years old. Her formal education was the sixth grade when she would quit school and work at a manufacturing job. There were no childhood labor laws at that time. Young male immigrants would be employed in the mines as early as six years of age and worked sixteen-hour days. Coal miners united under labor leader, John L. Lewis, and, through negotiations, strikes, and establishing a union, were able to change wages, working conditions, and age requirements in coal mining throughout the United States.

Lewis, after organizing the United Mine Workers Union, would later establish other labor unions through the Congress of Industrial Organizations (CIO) where he unionized the steel workers and many other industrial workers in the 1930s. My father marched with John L. Lewis in Washington DC in the 1930s. My dad would leave home to work various jobs to help support the family during the Great Depression (1929–1939).

My mother and father had their first child, George, born on April 29, 1931, in Moon Run, Pennsylvania. A second child, John, would be born in 1933 but wouldn't survive and died two weeks after his birth. They would go on to have two more sons while they lived in Moon Run, Pennsylvania, brothers Edward and Michael.

My father—with his brothers William, Julius, Rudolph, and their sister, Mary, along with their mother—moved their families to another coal camp—Southview, Pennsylvania. They would rent housing from the Pittsburgh Coal Company and work in the Montour #1 coal mine which opened in 1914. My sister, Mary, would be born in Southview in 1945, and my twin brother and I would be born in 1947.

My earliest memories had to be around the age of four. My father worked in the coal mines for a total of twenty-seven years. He was hurt in a cave-in accident and never went back into the mines. He suffered from black lung and depression. He committed suicide by hooking a hose up to the exhaust of his car. My brother, Ed, found him the next day. Years later, Ed would tell me that it wasn't the first time he tried to commit suicide. It was just the first time he succeeded. Ed was fifteen years old. Brother Bob and I were two and a half years old. We have no memory of him.

Our oldest brother, George went to work on the railroad. My brother, Ed, would lie about his age and enlist in the US Army. Our brother, Michael, who played high school football at Hickory High School in Hickory, Pennsylvania, would also quit school and eventually enter the US Army. They all quit school to get jobs to help support the family, my sister, me, and my brother still at home.

We would never want for anything, but we were poor, dirt poor, but we didn't know it. I remember going with my older brother, Mike, to the nearby railroad tracks where coal cars would be slowly moving up the tracks. I watched as he jumped one of the coal cars and started tossing lump coals out to the side of the tracks. I waited until he jumped from the train car and retraced his trail of coal. We gather it up in a wheelbarrow that I stood guard over. We then went back to the house to store it.

We went to a two-room school. In one room was grades one to four, and the other room was grades five to eight. Each row was a designated grade. Desks had inkwells, and one teacher taught in each room. There was also a cloakroom where we'd hang our coats and leave our boots. My brother, Mike, had the job of starting the potbelly stove on his way to high school. It heated both rooms.

This former coal camp had about fifty families. Some still worked at nearby coal mines after Montour mine #1 in Southview had closed. I remember my mother buying things at the company store. She didn't pay in cash. She signed a book, and we'd leave with some groceries. I realized years later she was buying things with a promise to pay it off. My older brothers helped, and Mom received some benefits from the miners as well as from my dad's immediate family who lived in Southview.

There was running water but no bathroom facilities. All the town's residents had outhouses. No matter what time of day or the time of year, you'd trek to the outhouse to "do your business." There was no toilet paper and no lighting inside. Somehow, there was an ample supply of *Sears and Roebuck's* catalogues for the job. I also remember in the summer, hucksters in trucks would cruise throughout town, selling vegetables. There was also the Fuller Brush salesman and the ever-present insurance salesman, preying on the poor. It was the only world I knew.

My mother and brothers never spoke of my dad. He "died." There was never any mention of suicide until I was in high school. I'd looked at the group Christmas photo of the family when we were two and noticed his gaunt face and dark circles under his eyes. There was a stigma attached to suicide, an embarrassment to the family.

My brother, Michael, was an altar boy at Guardian Angel Catholic Church. It was the only church in town. The Catholic church meant everything to these immigrant coal miners. It was the foundation that all family life was built around. It was their faith that led them to leave their country for the United States.

Given the age difference between Mary, Bob, and I and our older siblings, we weren't that close. Growing up, they had already left the house for jobs and military service. Brothers Ed and George would marry, but brother Michael wouldn't. Brother Mike would be home on leave and was extremely strict with us. We feared him. After completing three years of service in the US Army in the Corps of Engineers, he reenlisted. While he was an altar boy, the priests were trying to get him to commit to the priesthood. He had decided to be a priest, and at the last moment, before entering the seminary, he enlisted in the army.

During his second tour of duty, he suffered a nervous breakdown and was treated for schizophrenia. The treatment of the day was electroconvulsive therapy (ECT). These used electric current to elicit an epileptic seizure for therapeutic purposes. He was treated at a variety of Veteran Hospitals, receiving sixty-five treatments. When we were kids, we visited him and noticed his yellow nicotine-stained fingers from smoking four packs of cigarettes a day. My mother couldn't explain to us why he was there, and the doctors seemed to keep him medicated.

We later learned that he had been sexually abused by the priests while he was an altar boy—nothing my mother was aware of as she as a single mom and was trying to raise three kids, providing food and clothing. She raised us in a strict Catholic home. If we behaved badly, we'd have to kneel before a framed print of Jesus Christ praying in the garden of Gethsemane before his crucifixion. We'd prefer to be beaten with a belt.

I also learned that our dad was physically abusive toward our mother as well as her children. My brother, Ed, called him "mean." So here's a guy who worked in the coal mines all day, came home with dinner waiting for him on the table, got drunk, and beat the wife and kids.

I can't even imagine what that was like, other than hell on earth. I often wondered why he did that and why he made everyone around him suffer. We were spared. I know that our lives would have changed dramatically if we had grown up in that environment.

My brother, Michael, passed away in 2019. He had spent his last sixty years of his life in one mental facility or a halfway house, always supervised and sometimes under lock and key. At his funeral, I broke down. He had a shit life for sixty-plus years. I felt like I could have done something and that I let him down—a real feeling of guilt.

As numerous reports of the abuse of children by priests in the Catholic church was made public, I became angry. They not only targeted these children, they passed them around with other priests, and when their behavior was reported, they'd transfer these priests to other parishes where they would again prey on the innocent. It made me sick thinking about how my brother was abused and how the Catholic church covered it up. A week after his funeral, I quit the Catholic church, where I was a member and had supported for over twenty years. I was also their financial chairman for the funding raising campaign for the new cathedral in the Knoxville diocese.

I didn't lose my faith; I just left the Catholic church. They say we should forgive. I'm not there yet. I know someone said, "Animosity is the poison we drink in the hope that the other person dies." I'm still drinking.

To say that the Schmidt household was dysfunctional would be an understatement. My mother raised us and moved us from that former coal camp to Canonsburg, Pennsylvania six miles away. She bought a house for $3,000. She worked cleaning houses, and on

Saturday mornings, we'd pick up government surplus food at a distribution center in town. We received cheese, dry milk, and powdered eggs. Again, we were poor, but we didn't know it.

Everyone in Canonsburg knew Helen Schmidt. They knew her as a hard worker and someone who donated to those more needy than her and her family. She was amazing. Bob and I are identical twins, and she dressed us alike until we were seniors in high school. Our sister, Mary, quit school in her sophomore year. Bob and I are the only ones in our family to graduate from high school.

We learned the importance of hard work and getting an education. We both have advanced degrees from college. Bob lacks just his dissertation from receiving his PhD. Some would say that all we wanted was a chance. We also learned that you could only count on your brother and only on yourself to make changes in your life.

Canonsburg, Pennsylvania, was a great place to grow up. With a mother who was absent due to her working every day, the Town Park provided us with a place to go and grow into adulthood. There were sports programs and coaches that provided a male influence in our lives. For that, Bob and I will always be grateful. When I made the United States Olympic Team in 1972, they established donation toll road stops where individuals donated to help send my mother and my wife, Nikki, to Munich, Germany.

When I returned from Munich, after winning my Olympic bronze medal, the town threw a parade. Two months later, they held a "Bill Schmidt Testimonial Banquet" in my honor. It made my wife, mother, family, friends, and community proud.

My mother had just one request of me. She was working as a custodial worker, washing walls and cleaning at Western State School and Hospital. It was a facility for physically and mentally challenged children. Sometimes, she literally scrubbed and cleaned feces off the walls. Now I would do anything for this woman. Without her guidance, discipline, and life's lessons she taught us, we wouldn't have survived. Her one request: bring my Olympic medal to the school and throw the javelin for the kids.

I showed up in my competition uniform with my Olympic medal and javelin in hand. While I warmed up, she showed off the medal to her coworkers and the kids who had lined the grassy field outside the hospital. I took about a dozen throws while everyone screamed on each throw. This event was covered by the local newspaper, and the smile on my mother's face appeared front page and center in the next day's paper. I've never seen her so proud.

So the natural strength I have I owe to my great-grandfather, "Ludwig the Great, the Austrian circus strongman," and my generosity and the love of people from my mother. But rest assured, the work ethic and desire to succeed, it's because I have "coal in my veins" and the culture of surviving.

CHAPTER 2

YOUTH EXPERIENCES DEFINE US

As kids, we'd host and conduct competitions in our backyard at our second house in Canonsburg, Pennsylvania. My mother informed us early in our life, "You don't need friends. You have a twin brother, play with him."

As we got older, we ventured out, feeling a need for independence, and developed friends. Maybe it was the desire for new competition. After all, I was competing against this guy who looked just like me, moved just like me, and was as intense as me. It planted the seed of the need for competition and the "will to win."

These "backyard games" would include high jumping over a rope, throwing a bowling ball, and pole vaulting with a clothes prop. The rope used in the high jump was loosely attached so when touched by missing the height, it would fall off the wooden poles it was lying across. The bowling ball we found under a neighbor's porch. We asked if we could borrow it, and they gave it to us. A clothes prop is what was used to support a clothesline that had the weight of wet clothes being dried outside. It was our pole vault pole. It was a flat four-by-one inch of wood. Splinters were very common.

Dennis Pettrone, a new friend, had weights at his house, so we competed in weightlifting. We awarded medals in the various disciplines. There were four of us competing, so there were four medals—gold, silver, bronze, and tin. I guess the tin medal was the equivalent of today's participant trophy, but nobody wanted it. It was more of a joke. There were no real medals, just the acknowledgment of receiving them.

As a single mother who worked each day cleaning homes, my mother looked for activities that would keep us occupied. There were three of us at home, Bob and I and our older sister, Mary. My oldest brother, George, had quit school to work with the railroad company, laying railroad ties. Brother Ed, the next oldest, quit school, lied about his age, and joined the US Army. My mother signed his induction papers because he was underage and needed parental consent. He would later fight in the Korean War. He was later stationed in Japan where he played baseball.

Bob and I have no memory of our father, Louis Schmidt. He committed suicide when we were two and a half years old. No one talked about suicide due to the stigma attached to it at the time. When asked about our dad, we said, "He passed away after a mining accident." My mother never spoke to us about what type of husband or father he was.

Years later, I would ask my brother, Ed, as well as my mother about my dad. The picture they painted was that of a coal miner who drank heavily and beat the hell out of my mother and my siblings. My brother, Ed, described him as a mean man. I can't imagine what it was like growing up in that environment. I'm certain that my life would have been different had he lived.

In this "inquisitive period" of my life, I also asked about my siblings and their relationship with our father. I learned that my oldest brother, George, had been beaten constantly by my dad. He also called him *Dummkopf,* which in German means dumb or stupid. I have no memories of George living at home. I do remember working with him in his grass-cutting business. I also remember when George and Ed would show up at my mom's house at the same time, and they would always get in a fight. Mom always threatened to call the police. When I asked my mother about Michael, she said the priests had convinced him to become a priest. He was an altar boy, and they influenced him in more ways that my mother could ever imagine. He later moved into the priest's residency but later joined the army.

It's only been later in life and with the publicity about the abuse by the priests in the Catholic church that we realized that Michael had been abused by the priests, plural. He was targeted, passed around, and raped. His condition in life and his experiences in the army, in my opinion, related back to those days of abuse.

My mother, ever blindly loyal to the Catholic church, never acknowledged this behavior by our local priests. She was a single mother of six kids, trying to provide food and clothing to her family. Having a son as an altar boy was considered somewhat of an honor in this coal mining community. In addition, the priests were viewed as a father figures and someone to look up to and admire.

Because my dad committed suicide, by the laws of the Catholic church, he could not have a funeral service at the church. As was the case in these small coal camps, the deceased was viewed at his home in a casket with flowers, etc. over a two-day period. I have no memory of this.

So when asked about my religious beliefs, I'm considered a "cradle Catholic." When pressed on the subject, I say with a brother who was abused by the priests, a mother who suffered at the most difficult time dealing with the suicide of her husband, and the church's view of my divorce, the Catholic church failed us at that time we needed them the most. I believe that Jesus Christ never failed me in my life. I give him all the praise and glory for all that I've accomplished. His divine guidance and intervention have made me who I am. My mother raised us with the fear of God, but I have come to know the love of God.

My sister, Mary, was the only girl among six boys. My mother said my dad denied that he fathered this child. This was his German male-driven ego that females were inferior and he could only father the superior male species. My brother, John, born after George, lived only two weeks. From what my mother described, he had thin tissue near his lower back. I can only assume it was spina bifida. She told me that it was in the shape of a fist. She also told me that Dad had beaten her during that pregnancy.

Mom moved us from Southview to Canonsburg, Pennsylvania, when we were in the third grade. She, at the time, was dating a gentleman named Bob Cook. He seemed like a great guy. He treated Mom great and would take us on Sunday drives. We learned how to pick wild mushrooms in farmers' fields and riding in the back of a car was a real treat. Mom loved to dance, and they would go dancing every Saturday evening. We had babysitters those Saturday evenings that Mr. Cook would pay for. He was the first real male influence in our life. He was the reason my mother left Southview. He said, "Helen, you need to get these kids out of this town." Now, to this day, I'm not so sure it was to be closer to him as he lived in Canonsburg. Either way, it was an event that would dramatically change our lives forever. He'd take us to a variety of events and cookouts, hosted by different social and ethnic clubs. On several occasions, he'd ask us to go by his last name. No problem for me. Hot, good food, and plenty of it. I assumed later that they were company picnics, put together for employees only and their families. Bob Cook passed away from throat cancer within two years of us relocating to Canonsburg. I always thought Mom was going to marry him.

My older brother, Ed, taught me how to long snap a football for punters. I had no experience, and for that matter no size, but I would start to play organized sports in the seventh grade. My first experience in sports was going out for Little League Baseball in Canonsburg. Up until that time, we had only played at Curry Field in pickup games. A variety of aged boys in the summer, and we'd play from sunup to sundown. The field was only a five-to-eight-minute walk from our house.

Of course, Bob and I both tried out for Little League. There were several local teams, and there would be the usual throwing, hitting, and fielding opportunities to showcase one's skills. There was also a local rule that if you pick one brother on your team, you had to pick both brothers. No teams picked us, so we were relegated to Tee Shirt League. This gave everyone the opportunity to play if you didn't make Little League. I always felt we were both good enough to play, but no team wanted to take a chance on both of us. We weren't that good. In Tee Shirt League, we both played. I played for the Yankees and Bob the Giants. Fun in organized sports would keep us both busy and Mom happy.

Each and every Saturday morning, my mother required us to attend catechism at St. Patrick's Church in Canonsburg. She was Catholic and she raised us as Catholics. The Catholic nuns taught the classes and they were very strict. If you were disobedient, they'd slap you on the hand hard with a ruler. I had friends who went to Catholic school, but we were too poor to pay for it. But I liked school. I'm not saying I was good at it, but it guaranteed me a hot lunch.

It was after one of these Saturday morning classes that a friend invited us to attend a YMCA sponsored dodgeball event at the Chapel Gym at the Canonsburg Junior High School. Of course, we couldn't go without asking permission from our mother. We asked, and she said no. She had no idea what YMCA meant, but it wasn't Catholic-related, so no way. The following Saturday, we attended the weekly event and didn't tell her.

At this weekly event, the captains, the two best players, would draw up sides and play dodgeball for about two hours until noon. Now being that Bob and I had never played there before, no one knew what level or talent we had. This was also the first time either of us played dodgeball. We were the last two players picked. After playing for several weeks, Bob and I became the best and ultimately captains and picked the sides. I also came to realize at this early age, I could put "mean" velocity on the ball, making it hard to catch, and it hurt when it hit you. It was early, but the experience helped me realize that I could throw anything!

BILL SCHMIDT EARLY LIFE, FAMILY, HISTORY

SMS Kronprinz Wilhelm der Grosse, the German passenger ship that my grandfather arrived in the United States in 1909.

Montour Mine #1 at Southview, circa 1927. Gene P. Schaeffler collection.

Brother Michael, Bill, brother Ed, Bob and sister Mary, in our backyard in Southview. Bob and I were about 2 years old.

Me and Bob celebrating our 3rd birthday.

Celebrating Easter in our Southview backyard. Back
row, Brother George, Helen P., brother Ed, home from
the Army. Front row, Bob, Bill and sister Mary.

Christmas Day, 1949, we were 2 years old. Back row, dad, (Louis Schmidt), brother Ed, mother (Helen P.) Front row brother Michael, brother Bob, Bill and sister Mary.

Me and Bob in second grade. We're together on the right, second row.

Me and Bob spending the day at Town Park, Canonsburg, PA.

CHAPTER 3

IS CHICKEN FRIED STEAK CHICKEN OR STEAK?

My dream was to compete in the Olympic Games and represent the United States of America. Now someone born in a coal camp with little or no male influence, this was a steep hill to climb. It was a challenge, to say the least. I remember the first time I said it out loud. It was always in my head, but saying it meant making a commitment, one that I had no idea how to get there and, on the other hand, the kind of training that was necessary to make it a reality.

When I was growing up, I had the best competitor ever, my twin brother, Bob. We competed in everything. We played baseball, football, and threw anything for distance. As a ninth grader, I was the track manager. I didn't compete. I just handled the duties required. I lost the keys to the locker room behind a wall, and Joe Gowern, the coach, literally had to remove the wall to retrieve the keys. My managerial days were over. My next year as a sophomore, I went out for the track team. Joe Gowern would factor into my future as well as my career of throwing the javelin.

As a sophomore, I weighed 150 pounds and stood five feet and ten inches tall. I had gained almost thirty pounds from my freshman year. Not a beast but a significant improvement over the previous year. I went out for football, as did Bob. We practiced every day but never made it into any of the games. Bob tried out for the wrestling team, where he really found his niche.

I needed to do something in the spring, and track fit the bill, pun intended. I threw the shot, discus, and javelin. I also tried pole vaulting, high jumping, and hurdling. That's what's great about track and field—there's something for everyone. I had no real technique training or any idea of how to throw anything. I had a good arm and I could throw, so the javelin would be my discipline of choice. My sophomore year, I threw 156 feet. I didn't win anything, but I had a lot of fun competing. This was also the year I measured off 280 feet and thought, *My God, how could anyone throw a javelin that far?* In hindsight, I guess I should have measured off 300 feet.

My junior year, I made a conscious decision to change how I gripped a javelin. I gripped the javelin between my index finger and my middle finger of my right hand. No one told me to do it that way. I just did it. My junior year was less enjoyable, and I believe I threw 165 feet.

In my senior year, I went back to the grip I used as a sophomore and gained some consistency and reached 184 feet toward the end of the season. My best friend, Chuck Benedict, who was the real athlete in high school, played football, basketball, and in track, he threw the javelin and ran the high hurdles. We also played baseball together through the Colt League and American Legion Baseball.

In the Western Pennsylvania Interscholastic Athletic League (WPIAL), they had one competition where three individuals would total their best distances and award places and medals accordingly. In addition to Chuck Benedict and I, Richard Golden was our third thrower. We finished second to Butler High School whose best thrower happened to be the quarterback on their football team, Terry Hanratty. Terry would later play football at the University of Notre Dame and lead them to a National Championship. He was drafted by the Pittsburgh Steelers and would win two Super Bowls as a back up to Terry Bradshaw. Bradshaw was also a javelin thrower in high school in Louisiana. He set the national high school record his senior year, throwing 245 feet.

After winning the District Championship, it was later that weekend that Joe Gowern and I attended the Big Four Meet in Morgantown, West Virginia. It was West Virginia University, the

University of Pittsburgh, Penn State University, and Villanova. Each school had its areas of success. WVU and Villanova were known for their distance runners, and Pitt and Penn State were known for their field athletes. It was the first time I saw a javelin thrower throw over 240 feet. It was awesome. Penn State had three great throwers, Skip Krombolz, Lennart Hedmark, and Jim Stevenson. Jim Stevenson would go on to win the NCAA Championships in 1966 with a throw of 258 feet and 5 inches. Hedmark was a Swedish thrower who later concentrated on the decathlon and would compete in the Olympic Games in 1968, 1972, and 1976.

Joe Gowern, now my head coach, introduced me to the head coach of Penn State while we were on the field after the javelin completion. We had a brief conversation, and the coach asked me, "How far have you thrown?"

I said, "About 184 feet."

He said, "There are some guys in the eastern part of the state throwing over 200 feet."

I answered, "I'm going to throw over 200 feet." I did the next weekend, 204 feet and 4 inches to be exact, a new school record at my high school. Penn State never offered me a scholarship, but I used that as motivation. No javelin thrower from Penn State *ever* beat me in a competition.

The WPIAL Championship was on a Saturday. My senior high school prom was on the day before. I took Nikki O'Hare, whom I'd been dating my senior year. We double-dated with Dennis Svitek and his date, Carolyn Stutts. After the dance at the high school, we went to the Holiday House, a dinner club, until one o'clock in the morning. There was no alcohol, just dinner and entertainment by Ray Anthony and his All Star Band.

I didn't get any sleep that Friday night, and Chuck Benedict picked me up the next morning in his Volkswagen Beetle. I held the javelins through the sunroof as we drove to the meet. The individuals who finished in the top two spots would advance to the state meet the following week. I was tired so I purchased a product called NoDoz to try to keep me awake and to supply some energy. After the prelims, I was in first place with a throw of 201 feet, 5 inches. This was my second time throwing over 200 feet.

In the finals, an individual passed me with a throw of 202 feet. Joe Gowern came over to me to say, "They take two to the state meet." Later, with their last throws of the competition, three other individuals beat my throw, and I finished fifth and didn't qualify for the state meet.

My javelin career at that point appeared to be over. I had no interest from any college or university in the Pennsylvania area. The University of Florida reached out to me and offered a scholarship that included covering most of my tuition that was packaged with a work study program that would get me close to covering almost all my cost of an education. I knew that I could work at a summer job to supplement what they had offered. Within a month, they rescinded the offer. They had decided to offer the scholarship to another thrower from another state who had thrown 224 feet. Couldn't fault them for that.

I decided it was time to pursue a college career, and I enrolled at Point Park Junior College in downtown Pittsburgh, Pennsylvania. I'd commute each day to and from the school by bus. It was about fifty miles each day. My brother, Bob, and I were the first to graduate from high school in our family. He had enrolled at Clarion State where he received a wrestling scholarship. This was new territory for both of us.

In high school, I wasn't the greatest of students. I was enrolled in the college preparatory program but didn't apply myself and had about a C average. I graduated 201st out of a class of 383. At Point Park Junior College, I enrolled in sixteen hours of classes that included German, US History, biology, English composition, and general math. This was considered a full load. Now my study habits didn't improve, so it shouldn't have been a surprise that I did poorly. I say it was the fact that I missed some classes and spent too much time in the Lords and Ladies Billiard Parlor across the street from the college. I was efficient in billiards, but my college career suffered. I barely passed three classes and failed two. I was readmitted for the next semester but on academic probation.

Now some say that college isn't for everyone, and it was no shame to get a job and start working. In this area of western Pennsylvania, there were the coal mines or the steel mills. There were also two companies in my hometown of Canonsburg that were the main employers, the Pennsylvania Transformer Company and the Canonsburg Pottery. I decided to work for a small company with five employees that were metal and wood fabricators. I was collecting a paycheck and living at home with my mother.

One client of this small company manufactured horse trailers and vans. The shell of the vans were delivered to them, and they would customize the interior with wood paneling. It was steady work, and the owner had started the business by building one van for himself, then someone liked it and asked if he could build one for them. It was custom work, and the purchasers were affluent as horses are expensive to own. He eventually was the largest selling brand of horse vans in the country. The Shah of Iran even purchased one of his vans. His name was Frank Imperatore.

As I worked for this small fabricator, Frank Imperatore noticed my work ethic and hired me with the approval of my current employer. As I worked for Frank Imperatore Vans, I learned every aspect of his process on manufacturing horse trailers. He'd order the cabs from either Dodge or International with the chassis attached. He'd then transport them to Thiele Body Company in Windber, Pennsylvania. Thiele was started in 1901 when they produced horse drawn wagons. They evolved to manufacture dump bodies and vans for a variety of companies. They would then be transported back to Canonsburg where the interiors were installed and outfitted.

As I worked for Frank Imperatore, I learned various life lessons in working the right way, your word is your bond, being conscious of your work, and the attention to detail, skills that would later define my career. He was the first real male influence in my life.

While I was working for Frank Imperatore Vans, Joe Gowern, my high school track coach, continued to search for colleges and universities that needed a 200-foot javelin thrower. At the time, he was more committed about me going to college than I was. I did have that desire to compete and prove myself. I just needed an opportunity.

Joe reached out to me one day after work and said he had a school that was interested in having me "walk on," which meant they weren't offering me a scholarship. They were just giving me an opportunity. That's all I needed to hear. The school was North Texas State University in Denton, Texas. I never heard of the school. I did learn that their javelin thrower and school recordholder was Calvin Bowser, and he was from Butler, Pennsylvania. He had graduated, but they had numerous athletes from western Pennsylvania on the track team.

I was excited and knew this was an opportunity that I had to pursue. Given my poor academic performance at Point Park Junior College, I was admitted under "scholastic probation." I could enroll, but I had to make good grades that first semester. So I was off to Denton, Texas, to chase a dream and prove myself.

Frank Imperatore was excited for me. He presented me with two new Samsonite suitcases for my trip. This would be my first time on an airplane as well as my first time traveling out of state.

I flew out of Pittsburgh to Love Field in Dallas, Texas. Upon arrival, I had instructions to catch a Trailways bus to Denton, Texas. When I arrived at the bus station in Denton, an elderly gentleman met me and introduced himself as "Pop" Noah, the track coach for NTSU. He drove me to the campus and got me moved in at the athletic dorm. I had two other roommates, and we shared a room that was twenty-by-twelve feet. We each had a small closet, and the floors were polished concrete. The Quadrangle of four dorms were built in the 1950s.

I was welcomed by the track team, most of whom were on some type of scholarship. Not only was I not on scholarship, a walk-on, I was a "Damn Yankee." I had to take the jokes and started to process where I was and where I would be for the next four years.

My grades that first semester were good enough for me to be removed from scholastic probation. I couldn't workout with the team, but I was able to get paid by applying for "work study."

It was a work program where you received a nominal hourly fee for doing specifically outlined jobs. I worked in the admissions office processing entrance applications. I found the work to be educational and informative. Now I wasn't involved in the selection of who or whom would be admitted to NTSU. I just listed basic information from the applicants' admission forms and summarize it on the form the administrators supplied.

There was a variety of information that surprised me. I noticed that one individual had graduated fourth in his class. As I read further, there were only eight in his graduating class. He also played football, and because of the limited enrollment, his school played in a league where they played seven-man football, not enough athletes to field the usual eleven-man team. Texas was full of surprises for me.

On Sunday nights, the cafeteria was closed. I was invited to join a few teammates for dinner. I didn't have a car, so I loaded up with them, and we headed out. My experience in eating out was limited to McDonald's or Bob's Big Boy Drive-In. I also had limited resources meaning cash.

When we arrived at the restaurant, I had calculated how much money I had, and that would determine what I could order. They were quick to suggest the chicken fried steak. I thought, *Is that chicken or is that steak?* It was my first dining out experience in Texas. It became my favorite meal. When the waitress came back and ask me if I wanted more iced tea, I thought, *I don't have enough money to order another iced tea.* I later learned that refills were free. To say I was naive was an understatement. On some Sunday nights, I'd purchase a ten-pack of breaded steaks and a loaf of bread. I then cooked them in an electric skillet in my room and sold them for $1 each.

Fall of my freshman year was my first time away from home on my own, establishing my lifestyle, and imposing self-discipline. I was bored but tried to stay focused on grades and adapting to college life. I played football in the common area of the four housing dorms and played quarterback. Everyone was impressed as to how far I could throw a football.

I decided to enter the intramural wrestling tournament. I was six feet tall and weighed 191 pounds. I signed up for the 190-pound class division and signed the entry form that was on the wall in the gym.

When I arrived at the gym on Saturday morning, I noticed my name was in the heavyweight division. When I said I signed up for the 190-weight class, they said I was the only one who signed up for that division, so they moved me to the upper division.

So, as I looked at my bracket, one guy weighed 276 pounds, another 255 pounds, and the last guy weighed 236 pounds—not what I had in mind when I signed up. Now I wrestled my twin brother all the time, but if I didn't beat him or pin him early, he'd wear me out and win. I thought that would be my default strategy. In addition, the three-period matches would be only one minute each, not two minutes. That favored me. I also decided to wear the Clarion State football jersey that my brother gave me. I guess I thought I'd psych out a few competitors. I needed help.

My first match was with the six-foot, five-inch, 276-pound football player. We started in the up position, and I wouldn't lock up with him. I stalled the whole minute of that first period. People were booing me, but I was running for my life. The second period, I won the coin toss and chose to be down. This meant I was on my hands and knees, and he had one arm around my waist and the other on my elbow. When the official yelled, "Wrestle," I did a quick kick over, caught him on his back, held on for dear life, and pinned him. He quickly jumped up and tried to reengage, but the official held him off, thank God.

I ended up winning all my matches by pins, and the last guy I beat, for the championship, was a New Jersey State champion in high school. I was always quick, and I used that to my advantage. I thought, *Damn, that was a great Saturday morning, and I was the intramural heavyweight wrestling champion at North Texas State University.* But more importantly, I survived.

I couldn't compete that freshman year, and a few track athletes who were members of a variety of fraternities encouraged me to sign up for "Rush." It's the formal process where you visit with selected fraternities to see which ones interested you and which ones were interested in you. You would then receive an invitation to pledge from one or more of the fraternities.

I was extended an invitation from Sigma Phi Epsilon, a national fraternity headquartered in Richmond, Virginia. I, along with twenty-eight pledge brothers, spent the semester learning about the fraternity, gaining social skills, learning how to dress, communicate, and function in an environment that was totally foreign to me. It was also the best structure that provided me an education that would round out my college experience and provide me with a skillset that would be forever beneficial to me. There was no physical hazing, just more of the mental challenging type. The fraternity experiences provided me my social education and social growth.

I came back to NTSU my sophomore year with a partial athletic scholarship as a full member of the track team and a member of a fraternity. I spent the summer working and improved my wardrobe, and Frank Imperatore surprised me with a stereo system as a going back to college gift. Life was good.

My first meet that sophomore season, I equaled my high school best—204 feet, 4 inches. I went on to throw over 200 feet in seven of eight meets. My best for the season was 219 feet, 2 inches. I placed second at the Kansas Relays and sixth at the Drake Relays.

It was "Pop" Noah's practice to meet with each track athlete at the end of the season and evaluate their season going forward. He said I had a good year, and he'd keep me on my partial scholarship. I felt I deserved a full out-of-state scholarship. He said if I wasn't happy, I didn't have to come back. I then said, "What do I have to throw to get a full out-of-state scholarship?" I thought he'd say 230 feet. He said 240 feet. I decided to come back, like I had a choice in the matter.

I came back my junior year and opened the season with a throw of 210 feet in muddy conditions. The next week, after rainstorms and muddy conditions, I threw 242 feet, 2 inches. It was a new meet record. I raced over to Pop and said, "Is that good enough for a full out of state scholarship?"

He said, "Yes, for next year."

I competed in sixteen track competitions that season. I won seven of them, and in two of them, I set meet records. Three meets in a row, I set NTSU school records. I won the Missouri Valley Conference with a new meet record in Peoria, Iowa. They had defined the throwing area in streamers. I threw over the streamers in setting the meet record. I qualified for the NCAA Championships in Knoxville, Tennessee.

As I was the only person on the team to qualify for the post-season events and the championships, Pop, his wife, Bernice, and I traveled together in Pop's car. It was a family thing. I realized I was competing for Pop. I loved to see that smile on his face when I won. I loved that man and Bernie. It was family.

I had an incredible year competing. I established a new personal best. I broke the school record three times and established a new school record at 253 feet, 1 inch, an improvement of 33 feet, 9 inches. An improvement year over year of ten feet is considered average. To say my improvement was phenomenal is an understatement.

What was the main reason for this improvement? I did a lot of film study of the world's best javelin throwers. I noticed that regardless of their size, they did one thing in common. In their last crossover, they accelerated off their left foot on the penultimate and got into the air before driving into their plant foot. Now this was loop film, and my designated throws coach, Don Hood, would hold the loop as I ran the film machine. Don's specialty was the pole vault. He admittedly knew little about throwing the javelin. I also started a weight training program. NTSU didn't have weights. They had a universal machine that had a variety of stations.

I returned my senior year, focused and more determined. I intensified my weight workouts and my lower body leg training. My stadium stair regiment had greater purpose and took on more meaning. My classroom courses had advanced, and competition of my degree in business management with minors in psychology and personnel management was near completion. The university had constructed Kerr Hall, and I took up residence there. I had moved out of the fraternity house and focused on training, leaving no time for a social life.

On Friday, February 6, 1970, in a practice meet in Lewisville, Texas, I threw 272 feet, 1 inch. I had improved almost twenty feet in my first competition for 1970. Pop had threatened to take the javelin away from me. He didn't want me to peak too early. I had changed javelins. The best javelin throwers in the world were throwing 90-meter rated javelins. I had been throwing an 80-meter rated one. I also had a new pair of javelin throwing boots. My freshman year, I competed, wearing football spikes. I loved those white boots.

They were light and made me feel faster. Pop was quick to point out the added cost of the javelins as well as the shoes. He provided me with the necessary equipment for me to be the best. I was still coaching myself.

I went on to set six meet records, winning twelve of sixteen competitions. I won the Texas Relays, Drake Relays, and was second at the Kansas Relays. I threw over 260 feet five times. I won the Missouri Valley Conference Championship with a meet, stadium, and school record and placed sixth in the discus to help our team win the conference team title. I won the California Relays on my last throw, beating the American record holder, setting a new meet record that was set by Jorma Kinnunen, the world record holder from Finland the year before. I was elected team captain and had established a new school record at the California Relays with a throw of 280 feet, 7 inches, an improvement of 27 feet, 6 inches, over the previous year.

I did sustain an elbow injury on my throwing arm on that throw. I was still able to rally to finish second at the United States Track and Field Federation Championships and second at the NCAA Championships, throwing over 260 feet and winning All-American honors. I lost to Bill Skinner from the University of Tennessee on both occasions. He was almost ten years my senior. I didn't think the age difference mattered until I was twenty-eight years old, competing against collegiate-level people. The maturity mattered and made a difference.

I have to say that my collegiate career as a javelin thrower was extremely successful. I was a 204-foot javelin thrower who walked on at North Texas State University and won a full scholarship, elected captain of the track team, and improved almost eighty feet with no coaching.

Pop Noah, when he took the team out to eat after track meets, would say, "Eat like you competed." We would always eat at Morrison's Cafeteria. To Pop, everyone was always a freshman, regardless of your class rank.

He would say to me, "Freshman, forget that chicken fried steak, have a real steak."

CHAPTER 4

WINNING THE LOTTERY

Monday, December 1, 1969, was a day that changed many lives for those males born between January 1, 1944, and December 31, 1950. It was the first Vietnam Era Draft Lottery conducted by the US Selective Service. Up until this time, local draft boards in local communities conducted reviews and classifications of all males eighteen to twenty-five years of age. Deferments were granted based on health, college enrollment, marital status, conscience objector, hardship and surviving sons or brothers. In my town, the draft board was made up of three individuals who literally determined your future. I was never aware of any cases where my draft board was influenced by an individual or family member.

It was widely assumed that a draft board could be influenced if your family had wealth. The phrase "If you have dough, you won't go" captured the essence of the time.

As a college student, I had a 2S deferment. All males in college had that status while enrolled or until they graduated or dropped out. I remember a few friends who constantly monitored their grades and hours enrolled to maintain their 2S status. Without a college deferment or other deferments, a status of 1A meant you were eligible for the draft and would be notified to report to an induction center for a physical. This usually meant induction and two years of mandatory service and, at the time, a certain trip to Vietnam.

Now you had choices once you were notified for induction. Some individuals enlisted in the National Guard. This normally fulfilled your military obligation and kept you from going to Vietnam. The National Guard most often had a waiting list, and your local draft board wouldn't wait. Others decided to enroll in their choice or branch of service with a longer commitment, four to six years. If you were drafted, the term of mandatory service was two years with a reserve status of four years. You could be called back after two years, but it was highly unlikely. Because of the unpopularity of the war, some decided to avoid the draft altogether and headed to Canada. They were called "Draft Dodgers."

For me, there were few options. Being in a single parent household and with a mother of six, I never pursued the hardship deferment. My older brothers both enlisted in the US Army. One fought in the Korean War, and the other built airfield runways in Guam with the Army Corps of Engineers. As for avoiding the draft by moving to Canada, that was *never* an option. My dad and his family had emigrated from Germany when he was six. His brother, Rudolph Schmidt, enlisted in the US Army and was in four invasions. He fought the Germans in Normandy and was shot by a German sniper on June 8, 1944. He was evacuated from Normandy to a military hospital where they performed surgery and put a metal plate into his head. He lived to be almost seventy years old.

I felt proud, if called on, to serve my country as my brothers and my uncle Rudy did. Many before me fought, sacrificed, and died for the freedoms we have today and that were provided to me. If drafted, I would embrace the responsibility and proudly serve. I also knew that being drafted, I probably would be in the infantry. That meant I certainly was going to Vietnam.

So on this Monday evening in December 1969, I was headed back to my dorm room to listen to the broadcast of the Draft Lottery on the campus of what was then North Texas State University (in 1988, it became the University of North Texas), located in Denton, Texas. It was a great school known for its music school and historically a teacher's college. I was a walk-on athlete and eventually earned a full scholarship my senior year.

There were a few well-known athletes and musicians who had attended UNT. In football, "Mean" Joe Greene, Abner Haynes,

Cedric Hardman, Ron Shanklin, golfers Don January, Billy Maxwell, musicians/singers Pat Boone, Norah Jones, Bobby Fuller, Roy Orbison, Don Henley, Meat Loaf, Tom "Bones" Malone, Jeff Coffin, and personalities Dr. Phil McGraw, Phyllis George, Joe Don Baker, and Bill Moyers.

The enrollment was a little over twelve thousand when I attended there in 1966–1970. It was a tumultuous and historical time in the United States, and my experiences there helped shape me as an individual and educated me to the world outside of Southview, Pennsylvania, where I was born and Canonsburg, Pennsylvania, where I was raised. It opened my eyes to the world and helped define who I would become.

When I arrived at the dorm, they had already drawn the first twenty numbers and dates. Now, having a twin brother who was also in college with a 2S deferment and was attending Clarion University in Clarion, Pennsylvania, I assumed that he was also listening to the broadcast. In describing what the moment was like, a nationally televised event that literally every male eighteen to twenty-five years of age waited to hear about one's destiny. It was like being in the Roman Coliseum and waiting for the "thumbs up, you live" or the "thumbs down, you die," all in a number that, ironically, was the date you were born and was now determining if you would die. Maybe it sounded fair on the surface, but it certainly was cruel and borderline inhumane.

The 1960s were very political times, not only for the Vietnam War but also for cultural changes as well as Civil Rights protests. As a high schooler, I played hooky only one day of my entire high school career.

I looked forward to attending every day, not so much for the schedule of classes but for the hot lunches that were served in the cafeteria. My mother commuted. She took a bus to clean houses in an affluent town about fifteen miles away. She'd earn $8–$12 per day. She was amazing. Just a sixth-grade education, but she kept us in clothes and put food on the table. We were poor but didn't know it. My mom would go to the US Government Surplus Distribution Center and get powdered eggs, flour, and cheese once a month on a Saturday. I now know that was food for the lower-income families in our town provided by the US Government Welfare Department.

Again, we never thought we were poor. My mother would buy us clothes before the start of each school year at Sears and Roebucks or Montgomery Ward's. Being a twin, Mom dressed Bob and I identical until we were seniors in high school. She was a single mom whose husband committed suicide and left her with six kids—five boys and one girl. Bob was the sixth child, and I was seventh. An older brother, John, had died two weeks after birth.

That hooky day was Thursday, November 22, 1962, the day that John F. Kennedy was assassinated in Dallas, Texas, at Dealey Plaza. I was already watching television when Walter Cronkite, on CBS, interrupted the program. I was glued to the television and watched the whole day's events unfold. It was history happening, being reported as it happened, and I had a front row seat, a day I will never forget. It had to be as shocking to me as to those that heard about the Japanese attack on Pearl Harbor on December 7, 1941.

While I was attending North Texas State University, the Air Force ROTC offices were bombed. Muhammad Ali visited our campus, speaking to about 500 people in front of the Administration Building. Our track coach advised us not to attend. I did. I remember walking around "The Champ" as he spoke about the Vietnam War and advocating African-American pride and racial justice. I was amazed at how big he was, six feet, three inches tall and a neck that was huge. He was "The Greatest." I may have been one of five White people there.

While I was competing at the Texas Relays in Austin, Texas, in April of 1968, Martin Luther King was assassinated in Memphis, and Bobby Kennedy was assassinated on June 6, 1968, in Los Angeles, California. It was as if the whole world had gone crazy. It was the most uncertain of times.

As I listened to the Draft Lottery Numbers being called, I was told that if your number was close to 200, it was doubtful that you would be drafted. The numbers reached 125, and I still hadn't heard my number. As the lottery continued, guys who had early numbers were already returning from a beer run to Dallas and were shouting and shit-faced. Their future had been decided; they were going to be drafted.

As the numbers got to 150, I was holding out hope and declining to drink with the drunks. The numbers got to 200, and I was feeling pretty good. At the time, way back in my mind, I thought, *I hadn't heard those first 20 numbers* but didn't focus on it. The numbers got to 250, and I thought I was going to be safe.

As the numbers drawn were now at 300, that feeling of being diagnosed with cancer came over me. I was now really focused on those first twenty numbers that I hadn't heard. So as 365 and 366 were called, it became evident that I was in the top twenty. Meanwhile, a guy down the hall was 366 and was celebrating and being as obnoxious as hell and drunk. Now, remember, there was no way to check the internet or your cell phone. I did the next best thing. I called my twin brother. "Hey, Bob, so what number are we?"

He replied, "Sixteen." We both knew our fate had been determined.

About three months went by when I received notification to report to Dallas, Texas, to the military induction center for my draft physical. I was still in classes at North Texas, and I along with some other college students, as well as males in the general population, boarded a bus in Denton, Texas, for the trip to Dallas, a city I had never visited, and wishing I wasn't on this "cattle bus," on my way to the penultimate step before being drafted into the US Army.

Physicals are physicals, all completed and done. The group was nineteen-to-twenty-year-olds in great health and in the prime of their life. As I tell the story, I took my physical that day with one Charles E. Greene. He failed his physical. "Too big for standard army uniforms." I passed my physical. Charles E. Greene was drafted by the Pittsburgh Steelers in the first round, and I was drafted by Uncle Sam's US Army in the first round. "Mean Joe" Greene went on to a Hall of Fame career and to win four Super Bowls as a member of the Pittsburgh's "Steel Curtain" defense.

In the late morning, around lunch, they gave us a break and told us to be back in an hour to board the bus back to Denton. Being the induction center was in the middle of downtown Dallas, and it was a weekend, I decide to stroll through the downtown area. As I entered the center of town, I noticed this large Hertz sign over this building. I realized it was the Texas School Book Depository Building, and I was in Dealey Plaza where JFK had been assassinated. My mind quickly flashed back to that Thursday in November 1962. I walked the entire plaza and viewed it from every angle. I also imagined what it was like that day. I really didn't have to imagine it. I was there as I viewed it as it unfolded six years earlier. I was numb.

At the time of the 1968 Draft Lottery and before my induction into the US Army on September 20, 1970, all the dots hadn't been connected on my timeline. It was only the start of a plan that would shape my life forever. As many who looked at their draft numbers and knew they would be drafted, our lives were planned, and we would eventually end up in the Vietnam War. Sure, my number was "16," but as my life and army career played out, *"I won the lottery!"*

CHAPTER 5

BREAKOUT PERFORMANCE IN MODESTO

Competing in the Olympics was always a dream of mine. It was fueled by a 1951 movie, *Jim Thorpe—All-American*. Burt Lancaster played the role of Jim Thorpe. It was also the movie that inspired me to throw the discus, not the javelin.

My Olympic dream may have started early, but my competitive career didn't start until I was in the ninth grade at Canonsburg Junior High School. I decided to go out for the track team after being its manager the year before. That career ended quickly after I lost the coach's set of keys behind the wall in the Chapel Gym. They were lying on the top of the mats, padding the walls under the basket. The track coach, Joe Gowern, was also the woodshop teacher. He removed the mats with a crowbar and hammer and was able to retrieve the keys. This enabled Coach Gowern to unlock the locker room and let the athletes dress and go home. The whole scene was embarrassing, and the gym looked like a construction zone. Coach Gowern would play a significant role in my javelin career and life when he was my coach in high school.

My dreams were big, but I wasn't. In the seventh grade, I weighed ninety-seven pounds. By the ninth grade, I weighed 120 pounds. The Schmidt twins, although small in stature, never missed practice and were hardworking. In my sophomore year of high school, I weighed 150 pounds and graduated weighing 175 pounds, standing five feet and ten inches tall.

Not the physique of an of all-neighborhood athlete let alone that of an All-American. I would later win a full scholarship after being a walk-on as well as All-American honors at the University of North Texas, realizing both of those dreams. I was six feet tall and weighed 220 pounds.

In all the form charts, the prognosticators *never* picked me to make the 1972 Olympic Team. After winning the US Olympic Trials in 1972, I wasn't given any chance of finishing in the top ten, let alone winning a medal. The USA hadn't won a medal of any kind in twenty years. In 1952, at the Olympics in Helsinki, Finland, the USA finished with a Gold and Silver with Cy Young and Bill Miller. They beat the Finnish favorite, Toivo Hyytiainen, in his own backyard. Other American male javelin throwers to medal in the history of the games were Steve Seymour, a silver medalist at the London Olympics in 1948, and Eugene Oberst at the Paris Olympics in 1926, where he won the bronze medal.

On May 23 of 1970, at the California Relays, I had my first exposure to the best competitors in the United States. Up until then, I was winning collegiate competitions at the Texas Relays, Drake Relays, as well as the Missouri Valley Conference Championships. Great competitions and great competitors, but this was in California with the nation's *best*. I looked forward to the completion, and so did my seventy-year-old head track coach, Winton "Pop" Noah. Historically, the California Relays produced world records and some of the best results in the world in track and field. That's why ABC's *Wide World of Sports* television crew would be there to broadcast live.

I was also excited because I invited my uncle, Alfred Schmidt, his wife, Eunice, and their son, Alfred Jr., and daughter, Malia, to visit from Sacramento to watch me compete. We hadn't seen each other for almost twenty years. He was my dad's youngest brother. There were six boys and one girl in his family, the same number in mine. They knew nothing about my current javelin career and, quite honestly, were not really prepared for what was about to happen. They didn't understand the scope of the meet or the level of competition.

My early thoughts about the competition was that it would be a great test for me not only how I'd competed but how I handled the pressure. I was also curious and excited for the challenge. I would later draw on this in-meet experience in later competitions as well as in my business career.

Now I had a different mindset than most when it came to my fellow competitors. I didn't like them. I didn't want to get to know them. I didn't want them as friends. Sure, I'm certain they were good people, but I wanted to "kick their ass." I wanted to dominate them.

Scheduled to participate in the javelin were Mark Murro of Arizona State University the American record holder and US Olympian 1968; Frank Covelli, former American record holder and US Olympian 1968; Bill Skinner, a thirty-one-year-old thrower from the University of Tennessee; Larry Stuart of the Southern California Striders; and all the post collegiate throwers from the West Coast.

The meet record in the javelin had been set a year before by the world record holder from Finland, Jorma Kinnunen. He won the silver medal at the Olympics in Mexico City in 1968 and set a new world record in 1969.

The day came. I was confident and ready. There were eight throwers. You had to be "invited" to participate. As Pop Noah mentioned on numerous occasions, "This will take funding that isn't in the budget." I believe they promised us lodging and a per diem for meals.

Any throw over 260 feet in the javelin is considered "world class throwing." All the competitors on this day had personal bests that exceeded 260 feet previously or during the current year. My best throw until this day was 272 feet, 1 inch. This was a packed field. The spectators were in for quite the competition.

My confidence showed in my early throws. You get three throws, and then the top six leading throwers advance to the finals where they receive three additional throws. Then they throw in reverse order. The leading thrower in the prelims will be the last thrower in the finals.

It was a great day for me. All of my throws were over 260 feet, and after three throws, I was leading the competition at 267 feet. I was dominating the competition. It was now time for the finals where I'd throw last. I continued to lead the competition, going into the sixth and final throw for each of us.

I remember thinking, *If the sixth thrower didn't beat me and the others did, the worst I could get was fifth. When the fourth place person didn't beat me and the others did, the worst I could finish was third.* Sounds moronic, I know. So it's down to the second best thrower, Mark Murro, the American record holder and me. I'm still in first place. Mark was an exceptional competitor. I use to tell people, "This guy threw with his hemorrhoids"—total body all-out effort. He was also on the 1968 USA Olympic Team in Mexico City, no stranger to big-time competition.

On his last throw, Mark came down the grass runway and released a great one, 270 feet, 3 inches. He took the lead. As I was walking toward the runway for my last throw, I thought, *You did pretty good today against this world class competition. Second place isn't embarrassing and you competed well.*

When I got to the back of the runway, and while collecting my thoughts for my final effort, I thought, *Hey, dumbass, he's only three feet in front of you.* My competitive juices were flowing now. I came down the runway confident as hell, planted my left leg, and "let it fly." The public address announcer commented, "That's a long throw for Schmidt, and it appears he's taken the lead on his last throw."

The throw measured 280 feet, 7 inches. It also broke the meet record of Jorma Kinnunen of Finland of 270 feet, 11 inches. An ABC staffer ushered me to the interview area for my *Wide World of Sports* debut. Ralph Boston, the Olympic long jump champion, conducted the interview. It was happening so fast. It was surreal. At the end of the day, this javelin thrower born in a coal camp, who never competed at the state meet, and was a walk on college athlete, had just beaten the best in the US, and the world had to take notice.

Now my Uncle Alfred and his family had no idea about the competition, so the excitement of the meet, the dramatic finish, and the TV interview put them in an euphoric state of being. As for me, I felt a little "pop" in my elbow on that last throw. I incurred an elbow injury, but this was one of my "best days of my life," and I wasn't going to let a sore elbow take away from the excitement and glory of this competitive win.

CHAPTER 6

TESTING THE INTERNATIONAL WATERS

With an injured throwing elbow and the cloud of being drafted into the US Army and going to Vietnam hanging over my head, thoughts of making the Olympic team in 1972 seemed remote at best.

After my regular season was over, I was selected to compete in the World University Games in Turin, Italy. The World University Games was from August 26 through September 6, 1970. Fifty eight nations competed in nine sports. There were 2,080 competitors and eighty-two events. It would be my first opportunity to compete against the best in the world and to test my ability to compete on the international stage. Stan Huntsman was the head track and field coach for the USA team. He would later play a key role in my career after my competitive days were over. It would also be the first time I traveled outside the United States.

Nursing that right elbow injury, I competed poorly. In fact, USA was dominated by the Russians in most every sport. Later, I discovered that most of the Russian athletes were in the military and not in universities. The javelin throw was won by Miklos Nemeth from Hungary with a throw of 268 feet, 10 inches. Jozsef Csik, also from Hungary, finished second. I would compete against these two Hungarian javelin throwers in Munich at the Olympics and get my revenge.

The javelin competition was over on September 2, and with the track competition ending September 6, and my first time in Europe,

I along with three other athletes decided with the permission of Coach Huntsman to tour Europe by train. Actually, he said, "If you don't meet our international flight in Brussels that is the connecting flight to the US, we'll leave you!"

So the four of us pooled our money, bought train tickets, and boarded a train. I led this group that included Dave Murphy, a shot-put and discus thrower, from the University of Southern California; Chuck LaBenz, a 1,500-meter runner from Arizona State University; and Don Warren, a triple jumper from Northeast Louisiana State. We were in for an adventure and excited about the unknown.

For two days, we traveled through the Alps, France, Switzerland, Germany, and Belgium. We never slept. We bought wine, cheese, and sandwiches. We loved the various short stops and customs checks as we crossed various international borders. College kids enjoying an experience of a lifetime.

We arrived really early in the morning in Brussels. We hadn't showered or shaved in two days. We loaded ourselves into a taxi at the train station and headed for the airport to meet our team for a flight to New York. Upon arriving at the airport, we located the nearest men's restroom, stripped to our underwear, and proceeded to do an all body wash in front of the sink basins. We had saved clean pants and shirts that we changed into after the body wash.

We proceeded to the Pan American ticket counter to check in. Before departing Turin, Italy, Coach Huntsman gave us our airlines tickets to use, assuming we were able to meet them in Brussels. So here we were, clean, dressed and ready to surprise our fellow teammates who hadn't seen us in two days.

We checked in at the ticket counter, and because we didn't use the ticket flight segments from Turin to Milan to Amsterdam, we were upgraded to first class and assigned seats in the upper level lounge of the Boeing 747, a fact we didn't share with the team until we boarded. Irony of all ironies, they didn't expect us to make the flight, and we ended up in first class for the flight to New York with great food and unlimited drinks. It did help ease the pain of a poor performance at the games.

My other international competitive experience came after I was drafted into the US Army in 1970. After going through basic training at Fort Dix, New Jersey, and infantry training at Fort Polk, Louisiana, I was assigned to Fort MacArthur in San Pedro, California. There I would practice and train with other soldiers competing on the army track team. It was common knowledge among the group that you had thirty days to "make it" or you're back to your home unit or off to Vietnam. Real motivation in its truest form.

There was exceptional talent among the thirty or so active army athletes stationed and training at Fort MacArthur. There were two other javelin throwers—Bob Wallis, a graduate of West Point, and Mike Lyngstad from the University of Montana. Both of these throwers were talented and would provide me with all the competition I needed. The team was coached/managed by Ralph Higgins, legendary track coach from Oklahoma State University. Ranking officer was Mel Pender Jr., Captain and Gold Medalist on the US Olympic 4 x 100 relay in Mexico City in 1968. We didn't have to wear army uniforms or engage in any military duties, drills or responsibilities. We all knew what we had to do, and if we didn't perform, we knew we were headed back to the regular army.

After competing in various meets in California throughout the 1971 season, I qualified to represent the USA in the World Military Championships (CISM) in Turku, Finland. Now Finland is considered "the Mecca" for javelin throwing worldwide. It's their national sporting event. In the United States, we give our kids baseball gloves. In Finland, they introduce their children to throwing the javelin. In addition, they've won more Olympic medals in the javelin throw than any other country in the history of the Olympics.

I discovered the Finnish method of throwing the javelin while in my sophomore year at North Texas State University, now the University of North Texas. Although Pop Noah was the head track coach at NTSU, there wasn't a throws coach. Don Hood was an assistant coach, but his expertise was in the pole vault. Coach Hood learned along with me. I shared my findings and research, and I used his eyes to look for certain elements in my throwing. We did have a Polaroid sequence camera that provided me instant feedback. There were no written daily workouts for me. I did what I thought was necessary to improve based on my findings. The "Finnish Method of Throwing the Javelin" became my Bible. I also watched endless hours of 16mm loop films of the top javelin throwers throughout the world.

So in August of 1971, I'm off to compete in the World Military Championships in Turku, Finland, more recently dubbed "The Military Olympics." Now most of the world's best athletes were in the military. It also goes without saying that the Eastern Bloc countries had historically had their best athletes in their military. If you researched most of the biographies of the USSR athletes, the occupation listed was "military service."

The games, CISM (Conseil International du Sports Militaire), had an opening ceremonies as well as a parade of nations. There were eighty-two nations competing in twenty-four different sports. Track and field or athletics as it is known worldwide is one of the most popular and provided the largest number of competitors.

My elbow was still causing me some issues, so when I arrived in Finland, my throwing sessions consisted of low effort throws, working on technique, not distance. It was fall in Finland, and the weather was a little chilly at times. I didn't want to reinjure my arm, but I did want to compete well and represent the US Army and the USA.

The competition was intense. I felt no pain and won the competition on my last throw, throwing 270 feet. I also set a new world military record for the event. The former record holder was Klaus Wolfermann from West Germany. His name will be forever etched in stone following his performance a year later at the 1972 Olympics in Munich.

At the closing ceremonies of the World Military Championships, I was chosen to carry the US flag in the Parade of Nations. It was a time I'll never forget. Not only had I competed in Finland, the javelin throwing Mecca of the world, but I had set a new world military record in doing so. I was also honored not only to represent my country but honored to carry its flag.

CHAPTER 7

SO YOU WANT TO BE
IN "SPECIAL FORCES?"

To say I was a "longshot" to make the 1972 USA Olympic track and field team is an understatement. Although I had placed second in two National Collegiate Championship meets in 1970, I finished poorly in the USA/AAU Championships, the one that included all javelin throwers in the USA, not just collegians.

On my longest throw of the season at the California Relays in Modesto, California, I injured my right elbow. Upon returning to Denton, Texas, the doctors had confirmed that I had stretched the tendon in my right elbow. Good news was that it wasn't a tear. The bad news, I couldn't throw across the room without pain.

I was afraid my season was over. My physician treated me with a cortisone injection directly into my elbow, and I rested the arm and didn't throw in practice. The NCAA National Championships were in Des Moines, Iowa, and I wanted to compete for a national title. I had competed twice in Des Moines this season and won both times. Once was the Drake Relays, and the other was the Missouri Valley Conference Championships where I set a new conference record and we won the Conference Championship.

After some discussions with my orthopedic, it was determined that I couldn't do any additional damage to the elbow if I threw. There was still this issue with the pain that wouldn't let me compete at 100 percent. My effort with the pain was around 50 percent, and those results wouldn't justify me even attending the championships.

My physician did give me an option. He said I could go to the meet, warm up, and see how much pain I could tolerate. If it hurt too much, I could take an injection of xylocaine from a vial he provided along with the necessary syringe. It scared the hell out of me. He instructed me on how and where to administer the injection. I would need a teammate to "do the deed."

In the prelims, I warmed up and felt extreme pain in my elbow. I solicited a teammate to give me the shot. It worked. I led the qualifying round but still had to compete in the finals the next day. Joe Gowern, my high school coach, had surprised me and drove from Canonsburg, Pennsylvania, along with my brothers, Bob and Ed. This would be the first time family or friends had seen me compete. Now there wasn't any post competitive soreness or reaction to the injection. It enabled me to compete with no pain, no damage, plain and simple.

The finals were the next day, and I knew my routine—warm up, and if there was pain, have someone administer the shot. In warming up, I felt the pain and decided to have my teammate give me an injection. I went on to throw well and finished a close second to Bill Skinner from the University of Tennessee. Bill was a thirty-one-year-old ex-welder who'd taken up the sport on a bet. He was an imposing figure at six-foot, six inches tall, and 260 pounds. In winning All-American honors, I had realized my dream from that Jim Thorpe movie I watched years ago.

The next week was the United States Track and Field Federation (USATF) Championships in Wichita, Kansas. It was a one-day competition but still a National Championship. I decided to compete along with one other college teammate who had qualified in his event.

This was back-to-back weekend competitions, and I knew what to expect as well as my routine. I never felt any danger to myself, and the injections were approved by my physician. In addition, this was not any performance-enhancing drug (PED).

I was familiar with the routine at this point. Warm up, pain, injection. Well, I did warm up and I did have pain. Bring in the needle. I finished second again to Bill Skinner.

The last National Championship meet was the AAU Championships in Bakersfield, California. I was the only athlete from North Texas State University, now University of North Texas, to qualify. So it was "Pop" Noah, and I headed west for my last national championship effort in 1970.

It is usually very hot in Bakersfield, California, in June. The meet was scheduled with a twilight start, and the javelin competition was around 7:00 p.m. I would be competing against the same individuals from the past two weeks with the addition of the post collegiate throwers. This was, after all, the US Championships.

As I warmed up in the infield, I felt the same pain that plagued me the previous weeks. I had my vial of xylocaine and syringe at the ready. The only thing I didn't have was a teammate to administer it. Pop was a seventy-year-old man, and I didn't expect him to deliver the shot. As I reflect back, I don't believe I ever told Pop about my injection treatments.

So here I am, in pain and relief at the ready but no one to deliver on the solution. I certainly couldn't have any stranger administer my shot. So with the vial and syringe in my shoe bag, I found a porta john and decided to do it myself.

Well, the portable toilet was dark, no lighting, and I had to fill the syringe and inject myself at the exact location into my elbow. I looked for a mirror, but the only reflective mirror was a six-inch square of stainless steel on the wall, meant to be a mirror. It was not the best of conditions, and I could identify with a "crack" addict shooting up.

So, after doing the deed, I went out to compete hoping that I made the injection in the right location, and like the last two weeks, compete without pain. Well that was *not* to be.

I went back warming up and started to feel a little numbness in my hand. It was my turn to throw but I could barely grip the javelin. I assumed I injected the nerve in my elbow. Long story short, my middle finger, my ring finger, and little finger on my right hand were all numb. I competed, but it was a disaster. Nobody could understand my poor performance but me. I swore then to never take or administer a shot again.

I would win a national title eight years later at the 1978 USA National Track and Field Championships with a throw of 276 feet, 8 inches, beating Bob Roggy who threw 272 feet. "USA National Champion" has a nice ring to it.

In 1971, I was in the US Army, preparing mentally to be deployed to Vietnam as an infantry soldier. I was prepared to do what my brothers and uncles had done before me: defend our freedom when called upon. I had finished basic training at Fort Dix, New Jersey, and was finishing advanced infantry training (AIT) at Fort Polk, Los Angeles, in early January 1971.

When it was obvious that I was going to be drafted into the US Army, I searched for information regarding the US Army track program. I went to the local recruiting office. I said to the sergeant, "I'm going to be a college graduate in June, and my draft lottery number is 16. What are my options?"

He said, "Number 16, you are going to be drafted, that's certain. We also like college graduates, they last longer in Vietnam."

I then said, "I am interested in Special Forces."

His face lit up.

"I want to compete on the army track team."

He said, "You mean Special Services." He then asked me to leave.

Before reporting for basic training, I learned that I had to apply for admission into the army track program. I secured the appropriate forms, filled them out, and forwarded them to the office of Special Services, US Army, in Washington DC. I came to learn that a Mr. George Wilson was a GS-19 in charge of administering the program. GS meant he was a civilian, Government Service, with a 19 rank, a man who would determine my career and life while I was in the US Army.

CHAPTER 8

WHAT DID YOU DO IN THE WAR?

Following my victory and World Military record in Turku, Finland, I flew back to the United States on a US Air National guard C-130 Transport. The crew was from the West Virginia National Guard. The assignment gave them the opportunity to log their necessary air miles for the year. We left Turku, Finland, and spent the night in Reykjavik, Iceland. We were confined to our military quarters. Many of us wanted to go down town and "see the sights," but that wasn't going to happen. We boarded our noisy aircraft early in the morning of the next day.

We flew hours before we landed and refueled in Gander, Newfoundland. We had to stay on the plan during refueling but wanted to "touch ground in Newfoundland." After a few hours, we took off for Andrews Air Force Base in Camp Springs, Maryland, a suburb outside of Washington DC. Air Force One uses this facility as its home base. We then boarded our commercial flights to our designated duty stations across the United States.

My destination was Fort Ord, California, near Monterey Bay, California. It seemed like a great place to be stationed. It was a basic training center for newly drafted and enlisted personnel as well as advanced infantry training. The United States was still engaged in the Vietnam War, and the base was training our next wave of soldiers to fight.

The military assigns you with a specific code, an MOS, your Military Occupational Specialty. This is based on your area of military training and education classes within the service. My MOS was 71H, or as they say, "71 Hotel." That meant I was a Personnel Specialist.

Now when you're drafted, the army assigns you to a position where they have a need. They also train you to function in that position. When I was drafted and entered the US Army on September 20,1970, 95 percent of those drafted ended up in the Infantry in Vietnam. At the time, the most undesirable MOS was 11B or 11 Bravo or 11 Bush. If you graduated from basic training and were assigned to AIT, advanced individual training, with an 11Bravo MOS, you could start packing your bags. You were headed to Vietnam after training.

I passed a draft physical in Dallas, Texas, during my junior year of college in 1969. Upon returning from the World University Games in August of 1970, I received a notice to report for a pre-induction physical at the US Induction Center in Pittsburgh, Pennsylvania. I was to report to the Draft Service Center in Washington, Pennsylvania, and board a bus with other inductees.

The usual procedure was that after you received your draft notice and took your physical, you had two weeks before you had to report for duty. That gave you a chance to go home, say goodbye to family and friends, then report. In my case, they used the previous exam that I passed two years earlier as an immediate induction. After passing another physical in Pittsburgh, Pennsylvania., I would immediately report to duty.

I left that day, knowing that I was probably not coming home. A large number of draftees took advantage of that two-week "family Farewell time" to make their way to Canada. That was never a choice for me. If called on, whether I agreed with the war or not, I was called to serve and would serve my country. My two older brothers served in the US Army. My older brother, Ed, fought in Korea. Two of my uncles fought in World War II.

So I boarded the bus in Washington, Pennsylvania, to Pittsburgh, feeling like a man going to the gallows. The uncertainty was excruciating. I knew I was in good health, and my newly completed physical proved it.

I then boarded another bus with all my new inducted companions who, like me, were sworn in and now headed to basic training at Fort Dix, New Jersey. Pittsburgh, Pennsylvania, to Fort Dix, New Jersey, is almost six hours of driving time. Traveling on the Pennsylvania Turnpike, one of the worst roads in America, made the trip even more miserable.

During the induction process, you take numerous aptitude tests. If possible, the army wants to utilize any skillset that you may have to their benefit. Now unbeknownst to me, I tested high in two specific areas, leadership skills, and language efficiency.

When our bus arrived at Fort Dix, it took no time to realize, "You're in the army now." We were all being shouted at to shed our civilian clothes, get in line for our haircuts, and issued military clothes and uniforms. It's the walk of shame with the addition of being treated like subhuman beings. Now a six-hour bus ride with individuals from around your hometown area will make you relate and bond. There's a certain comfort knowing someone who's a new friend will be going through this ordeal with you. This would be ten weeks of training unlike none of us had ever experienced.

So I was surprised when I was told to report to another area and leave the group that I had spent the entire day with since Pittsburgh. I walked into another room and was informed that I was selected to attend a Leadership Academy. The sergeant in charge made it clear that we would be attending classes for two weeks, and we'd cycle into another group when we graduated. We also were told that we would be platoon sergeants and be in charge of four squads and about fifty training cadets. A curveball for sure, but I came to expect the unexpected while in the military.

Our routine was intense. It was like attending Officer Candidate School condensed into two weeks, classes that focused on the skills necessary in developing and leading men through ten weeks of intense basic training. Men that came from different socioeconomic backgrounds with various educational experiences were to be led by me through one of their most physically challenging times of their lives. I learned the most important element in molding men was to establish discipline and be an example to your men. They came first. I already came to miss the guys from the bus trip. My role had changed, and I hadn't any control over my life in any way. The army would now tell me what to do and when to do it, 24-7.

After an incredible twelve weeks of training and leading a group of forty-nine men through ten weeks of basic training, I graduated with the Fourth Platoon, Echo Company, Fifth Battalion, Third Brigade. We were trained by Drill Sergeant Rodgers and Second Lieutenant Lynskey.

After a series of interviews and additional tests, I was name "Trainee of the Cycle." This meant that I graduated first in my class of 1,200 cadets, an honor that I certainly didn't expect but one that I was proud of. I also weighed 191 pounds, the lightest since my freshman year of college. Good fighting weight for a soldier but not for throwing a javelin.

One of my interviews was for the Old Guard, the army's official ceremonial unit and escort to the president. They are widely known as the group that stands guard at the Tomb of the Unknown Soldier, 24-7, 365. The interview went really well until I mentioned that I would be training for the Olympics, and according to Special Services guidelines, I would receive one hour a day out of my regular army schedule to train. They abruptly closed their notebooks and thanked me.

While I was competing in college, I heard about the army track team. It was assumed you could apply, and if you were good enough, you would be selected. I thought my competitive resume spoke for itself. I was a little naïve about the process but felt certain I would qualify. So I received the appropriate paperwork and submitted it for evaluation.

Over halfway through basic training, I was contacted by George Wilson, a gentleman from Government Services located in Washington DC. It was his responsibility to review applicants who had applied for Special Services, validate their application, and make a recommendation. I was told that they were currently validating my performances and that I was under serious consideration.

On the last day of training, the graduates are given their next training assignment, advanced individual training (AIT). You fall out for formation, receive your orders, and ship out the same day to your new assignment. My morning assignment was 11B, and I was headed to Fort Polk, Louisiana, for advanced infantry training. Not what I wanted to hear 11 Bravo, training then off to Vietnam. I called Mr. Wilson in a panic. He said, "Be patient. Report to your assignment, your orders will follow." So I packed my duffel bag and headed south.

I was told on numerous occasions, "Never volunteer for anything in the army." When I reported to Fort Polk and my platoon, I was just one of the men and wasn't in any leadership role. One early morning at formation, the sergeant asked for volunteers for food servers. I heard "food" and raised my hand. So every morning before the three-mile run, hundred-yard low crawl, the sergeant would say, "Food servers, fall out." I never had to participate in those early morning physical training exercises. My morning activity consisted of serving bacon to a soldier, then eating two slices myself. This was repeated after five to ten soldiers were served. I gained back half the weight I lost in basic training in about a month.

As AIT moved through the eleven-week process, I stayed in communication with Mr. Wilson in Washington DC. He was very informative and continued to say, "Be patient." At the sixth-week mark and after being told by my sergeant I couldn't attend church services on Sunday, I was doing guard duty and guarding a specific command center when I experienced something that was extremely sobering. On the wall were maps of Vietnam villages that were replicated on the grounds at Fort Polk. Reality slapped me in the face. I was headed to Vietnam at the conclusion of my training. It was then I decided to pay particular attention to all the elements of the training because it could save my life.

The last week of training was a bivouac operation. You dressed up in jungle fatigues, carried BB guns, and got very little sleep while doing military exercises in the thick forests of Louisiana. There were booby traps, trip wires, and other devices meant to intimidate as well as replicate the challenges in Vietnam. The reality hit me that it wouldn't be me that got myself killed but the mistake of another that would. I confirmed in my mind then if I were going to Vietnam, I wouldn't return. That was the attitude I needed so I wasn't looking over my shoulder every minute of the day. That's how I would survive and return.

With but the AIT graduation left to go, I reached out to Mr. Wilson. "I've been patient, but in the next two days, I'll graduate and head to Vietnam. I'm prepared to go, but if the orders change and I'm in Southeast Asia, it will be more difficult to get me back to the States."

The next day, orders came down from Washington DC and changed my training schedule. I was to enter clerk typist school and proceed on an individual self-paced program where upon graduation, I'd have the MOS of 71H, clerk typist, a new career path for me in the army. I could still be sent to Vietnam, but this gave me the opportunity to be stateside while my orders to report to the army track team came through.

As they say, "Nothing goes as planned." I moved through clerk typing program quickly and expected to graduate the next day. I decided to make a bold move. At a phone booth on base, I called the adjutant general's office. This is the office that administers and carries out orders for all servicemen regarding their next assignments. I reached a young serviceman on the line and started a conversation.

I said, "This is Captain Davis, and I'm calling about Private Schmidt's orders."

He responded, "Do you have Private Schmidt's Social Security number?"

I said, "Just a minute." I then rattled off my Social Security Number, and he said, "Yes, I have Private Schmidt's orders. He's been assigned ninety days TDY (Temporary Duty) to the Military Language School in Hawaii."

I then asked, "What about after the ninety days?"

He said, "Private Schmidt will then be assigned to Saigon, South Vietnam."

I then asked, "When does Private Schmidt ship out?"

He responded, "Tomorrow."

Now I was initially excited about ninety days in Hawaii, but I felt the further I go west and out of the USA, the more difficult it would be for me to get back to the army track team when the orders did come. So I called Mr. Wilson. "Sir, I'm thinking about going to Hawaii for my next assignment, but after ninety days, I'll be assigned to Saigon, South Vietnam."

He said, "How do you know?"

I explained my story, and he said, "Hang tight." The next day, my orders were changed, and I was to report to Fort Ord, California, immediately.

I reported to Fort Ord, California, and was assigned as a clerk processing orders for the military court. I handled all the files for the US servicemen who were incarcerated in the post's stockade. Most were charged with a variety of crimes and awaiting discharge from the US Army. The range of discharges were either general or undesirable, and in some cases, very few, honorable. I did receive an hour a day to train off the duty roster.

A month later, my orders came through, and I was to report to Fort MacArthur, California, on a TDY assignment and given the opportunity to compete for a position on the US Army track team. It was now up to me as to how successful I would be and if I made the USA Olympic Team.

By the way, I stayed in touch with George Wilson throughout my career and sent him a Christmas gift every year until his death. When I did speak to him, I thanked him for the opportunity he gave me and the faith he had in me. He would respond, "Yes, we might have given you the opportunity, but you did the hard work and succeeded on your own."

Chapter 9

The Army Provided Me an Opportunity

While being stationed at Fort Ord, California., I was reassigned to Special Services from my assigned position of Personnel Specialist. My days of processing US servicemen for court martial or discharge were over. It was challenging for me when looking through an individual's file, in some cases where the soldier had made a minor mistake or bad judgment, and see how that escalated to major charges during his service. I remember someone in our company saying, "There is no justice in the Uniform Code of Military Justice." Their opinion, not mine.

The transition was easy. I had the help of an individual who showed me the ropes. Mike Lyngstad, in addition to being in Special Services at Fort Ord, was also a highly talented javelin thrower. He was leaving the US Army, and I was entering my last year of a two-year term. He was great. Very personal, highly motivated, and liked by everyone. So when he exited for civilian life, I moved into his slot.

Mike, in addition to his daily routine, worked the scoreboard for company level flag football games, and during basketball season, the scoreboard and the official stats. Now the beauty of these jobs were that you got paid. The amount would be $5 a game and playoff games for $10. They had budgeted game expenses and were willing to pay for your services. These were always night games and didn't conflict with any of my other military duties. As for my other military duties, Special Services meant you provided the services that were necessary for the US servicemen to be active in sports after duty hours. These football and basketball games were essential for maintaining morale and let soldiers be active and blow off some steam.

Now, remember, I was drafted into the US Army. They told me what I was going to do and when I was to do it. In this situation, I filled a need and did my job. My routine varied depending on whether it was football season or basketball season. There were normally four games each evening. Uniforms were provided, and they were checked out to each team captain and returned at the end of each game. Jerseys were soiled with sweat and sometimes dirt and blood.

I shadowed Mike Lyngstad until he left the service. I didn't get paid while doing it, but I learned what was expected and how to perform the necessary tasks. I was ready and willing to sacrifice my "free time" to make some money. When I first entered the US Army, the monthly pay for a Private First Class was around $200. There was an additional stipend paid if you were married, which I was. It came close to $300 a month, and I sent my whole paycheck to my wife and lived off the added income from these games.

I would be picked up by a Filipino civilian in the morning and off to pick up these soiled uniforms and take them to the Quartermaster, the laundry services for the base. My new Filipino friend's name was William Villalobos. He was retired military and now worked in Special Services. He was always laughing, making jokes, and cutting up. He was my boss, and we all reported to Roger Jellison, the civilian in charge of all sporting activities and sports facilities on the base. Now with twenty thousand to thirty thousand soldiers on base, there were numerous sports and facilities to manage.

After doing laundry service, Villalobos and I would head back to our offices at one of the small office areas on one of the parade fields that was also a football field. There would be a graduating basic training class at the end of every two weeks. We would then stripe off one to five of the football fields. We used a framed box that would be spaced every yard as a five-yard marking system. We'd use this rigged apparatus to put down all the hash lines on the sidelines as well as the two sets down the middle of the field. Pretty elaborate process, but the base took their flag football seriously.

Later in the afternoon, Willy and I would return to the quartermaster to retrieve the laundered jerseys and take them back and sort them by color and numbers for use that evening. Tough duty, I know.

I would meet another individual at these football games who was a referee and worked mostly every game. He would also work as an on-court game official for the basketball games. He was great at what he did, whether on the field or on the court, and commanded the highest respect from all the participants. They might have not liked the call, but they did respect him. Army rank meant nothing during the games.

His name was Mike Satarino, a University of Notre Dame graduate who taught at a Catholic high school in Dallas, Texas. He was a good-looking Italian guy who kept us all laughing. He lived off base, and we'd sometimes watched Monday Night Football at his home. We did watched *Brian's Song*, the movie about the Chicago Bears running back, Brian Piccolo, and his teammate, Gayle Sayers, at Mike's place. None of us would ever admit having watched it as the scenes of Brian suffering through cancer and the bond between him and Sayers made us all weep. Years later, while I was at Gatorade, I reconnected with Mike. He was now the principal at the school. I invited him and his wife to be my guests at the NBA All-Star Game that was in Dallas. If was great to connect with an old army buddy and have a great laugh.

Now no matter what your rank, everyone in the army had to pull duty on the "Duty Roster." This was a posted list of the individuals in groups that were responsible for tasks that included guard duty, KP (kitchen police), and burial detail.

With guard duty, you reported early evening, dress in fatigues and with spit-shined boots. You'd fall in formation, be inspected, and board a deuce and a half (a two and a half ton truck) with about twenty troops and head out to a barracks. There would be two-hour shifts on and four hours off. Your detail location for the two hours could be at an ammo dump, a road overlooking the seashore, and various building locations around the base.

For KP, you'd report at 3:30 a.m to the mess hall where everyone ate all their meals. It was a long day that lasted until usually 6:00 p.m.

We did everything from preparing food, scrubbing pots and pans, mopping and cleaning the floors, and any other tasks that the mess hall sergeant wanted done. He also loved the fact that he had complete control over all these college graduates.

Burial detail is exactly what it is. The Vietnam War was still taking casualties, even though the war was winding down. We would assemble in the morning in full military dress, and only the best dressed and polished were chosen to escort the bodies of our brothers at graveside ceremonies in the San Francisco Bay area. Reality struck a chord with me. I'm doing what I thought was a nonessential job, and these guys were dying over there.

Now when I first returned to Fort Ord, my name didn't appear on the duty roster. I was also at this time getting an hour a day to train and prepare for the upcoming track season and try to qualify for the Munich Olympic Games. Many of my fellow soldiers made comments about me not being on the roster. One friend said, "Schmidt must have a profile." That meant that an individual had a physical condition that "prohibited them from standing long periods of time and heavy lifting." I didn't volunteer to be on the duty roster and never denied that I was physically fit to perform any duties.

Several months went by, and finally, someone asked the obvious question. "How can Schmidt be training for the Olympics and have a profile?" What they didn't know was that by not being promoted, because I was on temporary duty for so long, seven months, I wasn't on anyone's promotable list. I wasn't going to argue about wanting a promotion, knowing that would trigger me being added to the duty roster. When asked, I joined the duty roster from that day forward. I did embrace it and that made people think I was a little crazy. To me, it was all about attitude and how you approached specific duties that other soldiers hated.

It was early in January of 1972, and the United States was cutting our resources in Vietnam. Soldiers were being offered "early outs." You could immediately be honorably discharged and go home. I was offered this package but declined. My fellow soldiers again thought I was a little crazy. I felt that I had a place to live, food to eat, and hopefully a few more months of TDY when track season came around. This was my routine, and it worked for me. In the civilian world, I'd have to find a job, train on my own, and pay my expenses for travel to competitions. Also, if you took the early out, you were more likely to be called up for active service in the US Army Reserves.

In February of 1972, the US Army selected an indoor track and field team of individuals to report to the United States Military Academy at West Point, New York, to train. This was a temporary duty assignment (TDY) for one month. These athletes would also be close to New York City, host of numerous indoor meets. It made perfect sense. What didn't make sense was that I was selected and assigned for TDY at West Point, and there's *no indoor javelin* at any of these meets.

Ralph Higgins, our US Army track coach, honored my request for the assignment. I'm certain that my winning the World Military Championships (CISM) in September of 1971 in Turku, Finland, and setting a new world military record helped in his decision.

West Point and the US Military Academy is a special place. I was honored to serve my country but excited to be stationed at a place with such historical significance. I love history and West Point, and the surrounding area provided many history lessons. This institution graduated some of the greatest leaders in American history. This was indeed "hallowed ground."

My training at West Point was twice a day—two hours in the morning and two hours in the afternoon. I scheduled my own training and met our team members each session. What was unique about my training at West Point was that at least three times a week, I worked out with the long jumpers and triple jumpers. The US Army team had two exceptional competitors in these events. Ron Coleman was a world-class long jumper, and Henry Jackson was a world-class triple jumper. Their workouts consisted of running, sprints, strides, and bounding drills. I had incorporated some of this in my workouts, but not to the level or to the extent that the jumpers had in their workouts.

This month of training I know laid the foundation for me making the US Olympic Team in July of 1972. I will always be thankful to Ron Coleman and Henry Jackson for their patience and help.

It was now March of 1972, the TDY assignment at West Point was over, and I was assigned TDY to Fort MacArthur, California, to not only try to qualify for the US Army outdoor track team but also begin my quest to qualify to make the 1972 Olympic Track and Field Team.

CHAPTER 10

MY OLYMPIC DREAM VERSUS REALITY

I finished my 1971 throwing season on a high note, winning the World Military Championships (CISM) in Turku, Finland. I established a new world record for the event, surpassing the record set by Klaus Wolfermann of West Germany. Remember that name as it will factor in the Olympic javelin finals and one of the greatest Olympic javelin competitions in Olympic history.

My throw was 270 feet, and I had the twenty-third longest throw in the world in 1971. I finished ranked ninth in the USA, not what most people would consider Olympic potential, let alone Olympic medal contender. The USA could qualify and send their three top throwers, and to say I was a "longshot" is an understatement. I would not let this deter me from my Olympic dream and my goal of making the USA Olympic Team. The "experts" had their opinion, and that's what I used as motivation.

The Olympic qualifying distance in the javelin was 80 meters or 262 feet, 5.5 inches. You had to have thrown that distance in order to even qualify for the Olympics. Oh, you also had to finish in the top three at the USA Olympic trials and finals over two days in July in Eugene, Oregon. I knew what I had to do and put a training program in place over the next three months, centered around weight training, running, and throwing as well as a competitive meet schedule that I needed to be challenging and successful.

My goal for March was to throw 250-plus feet. At my first meet on March 25, I threw 266 feet and won the competition. It was a meet between the US Army Track team and the University of Oregon at Bakersfield, California. I won my first meet of the season and exceeded the Olympic qualifying standard all in one day.

My goal distance for the month of April was 260–265 feet. I wanted all my meets to exceed the Olympic javelin qualifying standard. At my meet on April 8, I won but with a less than spectacular throw of 243 feet, 7 inches, twenty feet below the Olympic qualifying standard. The throw sucked! The grass turf was loose, and a win is a win. At least that's what I told myself.

My next meet of the season was at Long Beach, California, on Sunday, April 16. My winning throw was 262 feet, 10 inches. I had a great consistent series, and my winning throw met the Olympic qualifying standard. The next day, I traveled home to Muse, Pennsylvania, to visit with my wife, Nikki, family, and my high school coach, Joe Gowern.

I hadn't seen Nikki since Christmas. After about six days home, I returned to California and Fort MacArthur. My schedule set for the remainder of season, I kept training and preparing mentally for the challenges of the next two months.

My last meet in April was Saturday, April 29, at Mt. Sac Relays in Walnut, California. I won the competition with a throw of 265 feet, 4 inches. It was also over the Olympic qualifying standard, and I had three other throws that exceeded the standard. I also reached my minimum goal for the month of April of 265 feet. I was accomplishing goals, winning, and in my mind, moving closing to realizing my Olympic dream.

It was now May 1972, and my goal range of throws for the month was 265–270 feet and win! My next meet would be Saturday, May 13, at the West Coast Relays in Fresno, California. I won the meet with a throw of 265 feet on my last throw. Great competition with all my throws in the 260-foot range. I was now being consistent at a high level, which normally means a long throw in the near future.

I normally competed in back-to-back weeks and then took off a week or two. My next competition was at the Bakersfield Invitational in Bakersfield, California, on Saturday, May 20. I won first place with 265 feet, 8 inches. In winning, I also beat some of the USA Olympic hopefuls in the javelin. I was winning, and my throwing was very consistent. That was to change the next week at the California Relays in Modesto, California. It was my third meet in as many weeks, but I had a great history of throwing in Modesto and wanted to compete.

Well, compete…not so good. I finished in fifth place with a subpar throw of 248 feet. *Not acceptable!* That wouldn't make the USA team, and at fifth place, I'd be at home and not in Munich, Germany.

I took time off to visit home with Nikki, my wife, and friends over Memorial Day Weekend. I returned to Fort MacArthur, California, for the final push for the USA Olympic Trials, July 1–2. It was June 1, and the trials were one month away.

On June 7–8, the Inter Service Championships were held, and I won the javelin competition with a throw of 267 feet, 8 inches. The Inter Service Championships included all competitors from all branches of the service. The US Army had another javelin thrower, Bob Wallis, a West Point graduate who had thrown 260 feet. This competition was on Wednesday, and I was scheduled to compete on Saturday at the Kennedy Games in Berkley, California. This was very close for back-to-back competitions, but the Inter Service Championships were required. After all, I was in the US Army full-time.

I competed on Saturday and won the Kennedy Games with a throw of 266 feet, 10 inches. This was my second meet in June, and I had beaten a "number of Olympic hopefuls." I had actually moved up in the USA rankings to "outside chance of making the US Olympic Team." I had also set my distance goal for the month of June to 270–275 feet. I was getting close.

The AAU National Championships were in Seattle, Washington, June 16–18. The National Championships had little effect on the USA Olympic team selection process, but you were competing for a national title.

I led the qualifying round on Thursday with a throw of 268 feet, 6 inches. These throws don't carry over and count for the finals that were to be held on Saturday, June 17. The finals were won by Fred Luke with a throw of 277 feet, 4 inches. He was a local competitor and graduate of the University of Washington. Finishing second was Milt Sonsky of the New York Athletic Club (New York AC) with a throw of 263 feet, 9 inches. This was the first time Milt had competed outside the New York area. He lived in Brooklyn, New York. Finishing third was John Kaveny who was from California and threw 257 feet, 1 inch. I finished fourth at 256 feet, 2 inches, and fifth was Cary Feldmann another University of Washington thrower at 253 feet, 1 inch. Sixth place was a former University of Maryland thrower, Jack Bacon, at 251 feet, six inches.

After the competition, I said, "Holy shit, if I finish fourth like this at the US Olympic trials, I won't make the USA Team!" That was reality! No dream realized. I had a little over two weeks to right the ship.

All athletes competing today have a staff to support their training physically and mentally. I never had a javelin coach. I was self-taught and self-trained. As for the mental training, at the start of the year in 1972, I began to read *Psycho-Cybernetics*, a book by Dr. Maxwell Maltz. It became my Bible. I'd read it every day and focused on the mental aspects of positive thinking, visualization, and "letting your success mechanism work for you." One of the key learnings was to "*relax* and let your success mechanism work."

In my barracks room on base, I had a huge "Relax" in masking tape on the wall. My thoughts, *If I could relax, I've done all the necessary training to win.* It was mental preparation and mental training that came to serve me well.

The qualifying round of the javelin at the US Olympic trials was on Saturday, July 1. I took one throw and led all qualifiers with a throw of 266 feet, 2 inches. That was also above the Olympic Qualifying distance of 262 feet, 5.5 inches.

Many "favorites" did not make it through the qualifying rounds. The top favorites starting the year and, based on their performances in 1971, were (1) Cary Feldmann; (2) Bill Skinner; (3) Russ Francis; (4) Mark Murro; (5) Sam Colson; (6) Fred Luke; (7) Mike Lyngstad; (8) Frank Covelli; (9) *Bill Schmidt*; (10) Larry Stuart. Mark Murro was the current American record holder and a member of the 1968 US Olympic Team that competed in Mexico City. Frank Covelli was the former American record holder and also competed in the 1968 Olympics as a team member with Mark Murro. Bill Skinner was a two-time USA Champion and whom I finished second to at two National Collegiate Championships in 1970. All great competitors, and all of them presented a formidable challenge.

The next day, Sunday, July 2, would determine my dream being realized or, as some predicted, "The reality is that Bill Schmidt will not make the US Olympic Team." I felt, and so did Dr. Maltz, that I controlled my own destiny. Time would tell.

Sunday, July 2, I went to church early that morning and tried to control my anticipation and nervousness as I looked forward to the finals. I just kept repeating the one word on my dorm room wall: *Relax.*

At the finals, I didn't get off to a great start. My first throw was 230 feet, 4 inches. Again, I tried to relax. Each thrower has three preliminary throws, and then they take the top eight throwers and they get three additional throws. None of the qualifying throws from the previous day carried over. It came down to who was the best on that day, and the top three throwers would make the US Olympic Team and represent the United States in Munich, West Germany, at the 1972 Olympics later that summer.

My second throw was 257 feet, 4 inches. It was an improvement, and I was in third place. That was no guarantee that I'd finish third, and there was always improvement anticipated for any or all of the throwers.

Fred Luke was leading, and Milt Sonsky was second. On my third throw of the preliminaries, I fouled. It wasn't a long throw, so I just stepped over the foul line on purpose. I would receive three additional throws as would all the top eight finalists. My fourth throw and first throw in the finals was 265 feet, 1 inch. I moved into second place behind Fred Luke. Milt Sonsky improved to 267 feet, 10 inches, and took the lead. My second throw in the finals was 251 feet, 1 inch, no improvement. On my last throw of the competition, and the last competitor to throw, I threw 270 feet, 6 inches, and *won the 1972 US Olympic trials. I made the US Olympic team and was headed to Munich, West Germany, to compete in the 1972 Olympics!*

Those Olympic dreams started in the backyard as a kid with my twin brother, Bob, and were nurtured in high school. I did hold our high school record in the javelin at 204 feet, 4 inches, but I never qualified for the Pennsylvania State Meet. I was a walk-on athlete at the University of North Texas where my sophomore year I threw 219 feet, 2 inches.

I knew I was going to improve. In fact, I was a little cocky. I knew I was going to be good. Now 219 feet is far from being good. I said to my head coach, Pop Noah, "I'm going to be good."

He said he'd keep me on scholarship. He also said, "If you aren't happy, you don't have to come back to school."

I asked him, "What do I have to throw to get a full scholarship?"

Thinking it would probably be 230 feet, he said, "240 feet."

I accepted the challenge. My first meet my junior year, I threw 242 feet, 10 inches. I ran over to him and said, "Is that enough for a full scholarship?"

He said, "Yes, next year."

I improved to 253 feet, 1 inch, that year and threw 280 feet, 7 inches, my senior year, getting second at the NCAA Championships and winning "All-American" honors.

I loved competing for Pop Noah and the University of North Texas. It changed my life by providing me an opportunity to prove myself. All I wanted was a chance, and they gave it to me.

I was an US Olympian and was proud to represent my country, my family, my university, and my hometown.

Dream realized!

CHAPTER 11

OLYMPIC BOUND...
JAILBREAK TO HISTORY

After winning the US Olympic Track and Field trials in the javelin on my last throw on Sunday, I had a photo shoot with *Sports Illustrated* on Monday morning, then headed home to Canonsburg, Pennsylvania. Tuesday would be July 4th, and Canonsburg had one of the biggest parades and fireworks displays in Pennsylvania.

I met with a variety of friends, family, media, and local politicians. I had somewhat celebrity status and couldn't pay for a drink or a meal. There was great excitement in my small town, and everyone expressed congratulations and good wishes for me at the Olympics in Munich, West Germany.

On July eighth, I decided to visit the University of North Texas as well as my friends in Denton, Texas. UNT was *the* school that gave me an opportunity to walk on as a track athlete and feed my quest to compete in the Olympic Games. I met with Pop and Bernie Noah, my UNT track coach, and his wife. They, along with my fellow track members, were my family. During my junior and senior years, Pop, Bernie, and I would travel by car to various meets around the country.

All of the postseason track meets were either by invitation or you had to have met a qualifying standard in order to participate. I went with Pop to the Rotary Club luncheon while in Denton, Texas. During my senior year, I would be his guest on numerous occasions.

I knew he was proud of me then, and now that I made the Olympic Team, he was busting at the seams with pride.

I also visited with Jack Wheeler, a vice president at UNT who had been influential in my early campus days at UNT. I first met him when I was freshman, and I was working in a program that was called "Work Study." I wasn't on scholarship and had to work to pay for my tuition, room, board, and books. Jack Wheeler was the dean of students, and this program fell under his administrative responsibilities. You were limited on the amount of hours you could work, and usually, it was two to four hours a day. Although I wasn't on scholarship, I still worked out with the track team every afternoon for two to three hours.

Jack Wheeler took notice of my work ethic as well as my background, family, and my dreams. He was a great male influence. Later in my freshman year, I pledged Sigma Phi Epsilon Fraternity. This was also Jack's fraternity, and he was active and influential in the ongoing business of the fraternity and their role of "building men." The fraternity taught me how to dress, converse, and develop my social skills. It also gave me the opportunity to interact with other college males outside of the track team.

Jack Wheeler would later be Grand President of Sigma Phi Epsilon, a national office position. He also served as Vice President at the University of Texas Southwestern Medical School in Dallas, Texas. He was a lobbyist in Austin, Texas, during the governorship of George W. Bush. He was influential and highly respected. He, too, took pride in my accomplishments and some credit. He deserved it.

I flew back to Pittsburgh on July 14 and trained for five days before reporting to the US Track and Field Olympic assembly site at Bowdoin, Maine, on July 20. It would be the first time since the USA Track and Field trials concluded in July that the USA had assembled its team in its entirety. It was a great time to meet my team members and train with them.

There were six members of the team that were also my US Army team members. They were Jeff Bennett, decathlete, Thomas Hill, 110 high hurdler, Arnie Robinson, long jumper, myself, javelin thrower, Ken Swenson, 800 meters, and Tim Vollmer, discus thrower. We were all proud to represent the USA and to serve in the US Army. Three of us would go on to win Olympic medals.

On July 28, the entire USA team left for Portland, Maine, where we would depart for Oslo, Norway, our next training site. We landed on Saturday, July 29, and settled in for almost two weeks. The idea was to train and get acclimated to the time zone difference.

My first day of training in Oslo started with a morning run of 2.5 miles, my usual morning run. I was scheduled to throw in the afternoon. The track facility was exceptional. The infield was pristine with the grass being manicured to perfection and a synthetic runway.

The discus throwers and the javelin throwers were working out at the same time and throwing from the same end of the facility. This required coordination between the groups, and we would wait to throw at the appropriate sequence so as not to interfere with the others efforts.

I noticed that after each discus thrower's effort, a man would enter the throwing sector, throw some grass seed in the divot made by the discus, and then tap it down with his foot. He carried the seed in what looked like a carpenter's waist belt. I had never experienced this in any place I had trained or competed.

My warm-up routine was etched in stone. After a half mile warm-up jog and stretching, I began to loosen up with the javelin with small short throws from a standing position and then move back to a five-step approach. These initial short throws were to set the javelin position and throw through the point. The next phase of my warm up was a longer run up, seven steps, and really "hitting the point." These were hard low throws but through the point, going no higher than twenty feet off the ground. These were usually in the 220-foot range. All the while, the discus and javelin throwers were alternating our throws, and it was working out harmoniously.

As I waited my turn to throw in the sequence coordinating with the discus throwers, I also waited for the groundskeeper to fill the discus divot and move to the far end of the throwing sector. I started my approach and threw an explosive effort, driving through the point. As the javelin left my hand, I tracked the flight and noticed immediately that the groundskeeper had moved back into the sector and that my javelin was tracking directly at him as he walked toward me. I let out a scream, "Look out!" He looked up, and at that point, my javelin had hit him in the lower abdomen. He fell to his knees and pulled out the javelin.

I raced out to his side, and medical staff immediately attended to him. It seemed that his pelvic bone kept the javelin from continuing through him. I thought if he had taken one more stride, the javelin would have entered his chest cavity, and that would have caused real damage if not death. This event caused quite the commotion at our first day of practice in Oslo. An ambulance showed up immediately on site to take the individual to the hospital for treatment. As traumatic as this incident was, I decided I needed to continue my workout. I gathered my thoughts, refocused, and continued to throw.

It turns out the "groundskeeper" I speared was actually the promoter and financial head of the facility. I met him a month later in Munich after my competition. He came up to me and introduced himself as the man I speared in Oslo. He showed me his puncture wound and said that he had sustained no internal damage and that he was now "famous" for having been speared by an Olympic Bronze Medalist, and he wore the puncture wound like a badge of honor.

On Wednesday, August 2, I had my first meet since winning the US Olympic trials. I threw 263 feet and finished third. Bjorn Grimnes of Norway won the competition with a throw of 277 feet, and Miklos Nemeth of Hungary finished second with a throw of 276 feet. It was exactly one month until the qualifying rounds in the javelin would start in Munich, Germany.

After another week of training in Oslo, I traveled to Pisa, Italy, to compete on August 11. I threw 258 feet, 3 inches, in the meet at Viareggio, Italy, and felt good about my win but not overly excited about the distance. I had better speed and threw through the point with more body torque.

On Saturday, August 12, I flew to Munich, West Germany, and took up residency in the Olympic Village along with over 7,000 athletes from 122 countries. I was assigned a room with two other athletes: Jeff Bennett, a decathlete, and Fred Luke, a javelin thrower.

I knew Jeff quite well, but Fred had been a despised competitor of mine that I had no interaction with throughout the season. Fred was a great guy that I got to know and respect. It was my approach mentally that I hated my competitors and wanted to beat them all. With Fred, we actually had throwing sessions together that were quite productive.

Living and training in the Olympic Village was surreal. Every day was a dream. It was an education meeting the various athletes from all over the world competing in various sports. There was no pressure in training because, according to the "experts," I had little to no chance of being here in the first place. As for winning a medal, "unthinkable."

On Thursday, August 24, I competed in a pre-Olympic Meet, throwing 260 feet, 8 inches, and finishing second to Klaus Wolfermann who threw over 285 feet. Klaus, competing in his native country, West Germany, or the Federal Republic of Germany, had established himself as a medal contender. I had established myself as a 260-foot javelin thrower from the USA and nothing more.

On Saturday, August 26, 1972, the Games of the XX Olympiad opened, and the most memorable Olympic Games in history, for a variety of reasons, good and bad, had begun. We waited hours in a holding area in our white team blazers and red slacks for our turn for the opening ceremonies and the Parade of Nations. It gave us an opportunity to meet other US athletes and cherish the moment.

One strange thing I noticed was that a few athletes had newspapers tucked into their blazers and slacks, and I couldn't figure out why. Well, after taking our place on the infield and as the opening ceremonies unfolded, those who had the newspapers, took them out just prior to the release of the thousands of doves. It then became apparent that these athletes had attend previous Olympic Games opening ceremonies.

The doves were released, and the athletes held the newspapers over their heads. I don't know if it was the shock of being released or being cooped up for a long period of time, but the doves secreted all kinds of green and white excrement from their bowels. There were unsightly spots on those white blazers as well as other countries uniforms. I managed to avoid this aerial bombardment, no damage to the my white blazer. I would later donate my opening ceremonies uniform to my high school, Canon-McMillan High School in Canonsburg, Pennsylvania. I hoped that it would inspire other students to "dream big" in whatever they aspired to do.

The Munich Olympics were the best organized, technologically innovative games, and supported with the best facilities of any Olympic Games up until this time. New timing and measuring devices had been utilized to improve scoring as well as results.

Notable performances included:

- Mark Spitz, USA, winning seven gold medals with seven world records in swimming.
- Frank Shorter, USA, winning an Olympic gold medal in the marathon.
- Dave Wottle, USA, winning a gold medal in 1,500 meters.
- Dan Gable, USA winning a gold medal in wrestling.
- Olga Korbut, USSR, gymnast, three gold medals, one silver medal
- USSR Men's Basketball Team, gold medal, controversial win over USA

There were a variety of unexpected events at the Munich Olympics, none possibly more confusing than the USA 100-meter sprinters not showing up for the quarter finals. They were actually in the ABC Broadcast Center and were watching what appeared to be their race. ABC officials quickly got them in a car and raced to the Olympic Stadium. Too late for sprinters Eddie Hart and Rey Robinson, they were disqualified. Robert Taylor was able to compete and did qualify for the finals. He won a silver medal in the finals, finishing second to Valery Borzov of the Soviet Union.

The Americans would win revenge in the 4 X 100 relay with all the USA sprinters competing. They set a new world record of 38.19 and won the gold medal.

As for the disqualifications of Hart and Robinson, the USA sprint coach, Stan Wright, said they were following an outdated schedule of events from months earlier.

When we arrived in Munich, our designated coaches responsible for the javelin throwers met with us at our first training session. They openly said they knew nothing about the event but that if we needed anything to let them know. Not what you'd expect at the Olympic level, but I never had a javelin coach in high school, college, or currently in the US Army. So no big deal for me. Now administratively, that was different.

Mark Murro, the American record holder in the javelin and who competed at the 1968 Mexico City Olympics, probably gave me more information about competing at the Olympics than any coach or track administrator. He said, "You're at the stadium, throwing at 9:00 a.m. in the morning to qualify, and that's not ideal." So I started throwing in the morning to get used to it.

On the eve of the javelin throwing qualifying round, September 1, we had no meeting with our coaches or given any instructions. Transportation center was in the lower level of the Olympic Village, and that's where we would secure transportation to the Olympic Stadium. Although there were three javelin throwers on the USA Team, we didn't coordinate our training, workouts, or any scheduling of any kind. Although Fred Luke was my roommate, we probably trained together only once during the entire time in Munich.

Saturday, September 2, 1972, Men's Olympic Javelin Qualifying

The Olympic javelin qualifying distance was 262 feet, 6 inches, or 80 meters. They put a line out at 80 meters, and you have three attempts to throw over it. When you do, you automatically qualify for the next round on the next day. During my 1972 season, I felt very comfortable throwing that distance and rarely missed it.

I got up early that morning and didn't coordinate my schedule with Fred Luke. I grabbed a light breakfast and was ready for the day. My warm-up routine before throwing was an hour. Qualifying for the first group of two was at 10:00 a.m. I needed to be there, warming up by 9:00 a.m. Pretty simple, be on your way.

I figured that transportation to the Olympic Stadium for the competitors would be on a closed route on an athletes only bus or van. Take about twenty minutes, thirty max. I headed to the basement transportation area with those thoughts in mind. Shouldn't have to worry about transportation, just get prepared mentally for what was my goal that morning—qualify!

I arrived in the transportation level and started searching for the vehicle that was to get me to the stadium. I looked for buses with markings and vans as well. I tried to communicate with the people there that I needed to get to the stadium and fast. Time was not my friend, and I was thinking about my teammates, Eddie Hart and Rey Robinson, who missed their races the previous day. I thought about going outside the Olympic Village and securing a taxi but that would cost me precious time.

Now Eddie Hart and Rey Robinson were medal contenders, and when they missed their quarter finals round, that was big news. Now me, a 260-foot throwing non-medal contender who wasn't expected to even make the US Olympic Team, missing his event would be news, but not big news.

In a moment of sheer survival and panic, I decided to run to the Olympic Stadium about three miles away. I could see the Olympic Tower adjacent to the Olympic Stadium, and time was running out. My morning training always started with a run, but none had the significance of this morning. I was now within my one hour warm-up routine and wasn't at the stadium. I still had to check in for my event.

I arrived at a security gate next to the stadium where I could gain access to the warm up area and where I could check in. I arrived forty minutes before Qualifying Group 1 was to begin. The two security guards saw me quickly approaching and cut off me entering. I told them I was competing in the javelin and needed to gain access as well as check in. In my panic, I also blurted out "*Speerwurfer*," which was German for spear thrower.

They blocked my entry and said I was too late to check in. What? All the training, sacrifices, and dreams gone in that instant in that one sentence. What was I to do? The one guard had no sooner uttered that sentence when survival instincts kicked in.

I did a "*jailbreak*." I knocked down both guards and raced to the entry area of the stadium, not knowing whether I could gain entry or if I would "be captured." Purely instincts and adrenaline.

I reached an area when Group 1 had finished their warm up and were ushered into a small room. I followed the group. There were twelve of us, and it felt like we were caged gladiators getting ready to face our fate in the arena.

Each thrower has a run up in throwing the javelin. The distance of the run up varies with each thrower, and there's a point during the run where he starts his crossover steps and throws. I was very precise about my run up. I started at a distance of 102 feet, 1 inch, from the foul line, and my crossovers started at 46 feet, 6.5 inches from the foul line. Now you didn't always have a measuring tape, so you'd measure your steps by laying the javelin down and measuring by lengths. In addition, you'd have markers that you would place at these two points. Ideally, you could see the crossover mark in your peripheral vision and move quickly into the throw.

Group 1 competitors in this small room made no eye contact with any other thrower within the group—a real "Get your game face on" moment. We were led out of that room to a ramp down to the ground level. The moment entering the stadium with over 90,000 spectators cheering was one of the most memorable experiences of my lifetime. Normally, when competing, you don't hear the crowd. You're too focused on the task at hand to be influenced or distracted from what you need to accomplish. To say I was distracted was to put it mildly. I was hearing my name throughout the stadium, "Let's go, Schmidt!" Now we're in West Germany, and Schmidt is a very common name. They could have been calling the beer vendor for all I know. Distracted nonetheless.

As we headed down the ramp, some of the competitors raced toward a small box container near the throwing area. I walked over to it, and it had contained small markers that you were to use to mark your steps. Now it's ideal to have markers that you can easily see from the other competitors markers and the surface of the throwing area.

When I got to the box, there was only one set of markers, and they matched the color of the throwing area surface. I thought, *This day is not going well.*

My fellow competitors had warm-up time at the practice area as well as having had the opportunity to throw. My entire warm up was my run to the stadium and my "jailbreak sprint" from the security guards. Definitely not ideal.

Now in Olympic competition, they provide the implements, an assortment of javelins from a variety of manufacturers were there. You just had to jockey into position to retrieve one when it was returned after being thrown. There are also little nuances between all javelins, but they all meet standard specifications. If one that was thrown looked like it had a great flight to it, you tried to get that one.

The completion begins. It's throw 80 meters in three attempts or go home. Fred Luke was in Group 1 with me and on his first attempt. He threw 266 feet and qualified. On my first attempt, I came down the runway, stutter stepped at my marker, and threw 245 feet. I couldn't see my transitional marker from the others or from the color of the surface. When they call your name, there's a clock stationed near the runway that you can see, and you have ninety seconds to complete the throw or it's a foul and doesn't count.

I decided on my second attempt I'd have Fred Luke stand near where my marker was outside the runway. Fred was over six feet tall, and I could surely see him. As I'm in the lane and they called my name, they announced that all those throwers who have qualified assemble to the right to exit the stadium. I watched from the back of the runway as my six-foot-four marker walked out of the area. Second effort, again, I stutter stepped—247 feet. Not good. On my third and final attempt to qualify, I decided to lay my jacket near my marker. I'd definitely see it.

They called my name. I'd got ninety seconds. I was in the back of the runway, getting mentally prepared for this throw, when an official came over and dragged away my jacket. Damn—*not good.* I came down the runway and threw. It measured 78.96 meters, 258 feet, 10 inches. I hadn't qualified! It sunk in hard. I finished fifth in

Qualifying Group 1 and below the qualifying distance. I thought, *Not the Olympic experience I had trained and hoped for.*

I found my way into the stands and stationed myself in one of the entryways so I could view Group 2 qualifying. There was still a chance that if twelve throwers didn't throw over 80 meters, they would add throwers up to twelve.

As I sat there in fifth place, simple math told me that if more than seven throwers threw further than me, I wouldn't make it to the next day. If they had more throwers throw the qualifying 80 meters, all of them would go on to the next day, even if that exceeded twelve. I looked at Qualifying Group 2 warming up. It consisted of the current world record holder, European Champion, and eight other throwers who had thrown further than me.

As I looked at the field, an individual who could barely walk was pushing a wheelchair with another individual in it and went by me. It was like reality slapped me in the face. *Schmidt, how could you be so worried about how you did in this stupid competition when neither of these guys can walk?* I left the stadium at that point and went back to my room at the Olympic Village. Things were put in perspective.

When Fred Luke returned to the room from the stadium, I said, "How'd I do?"

He said," You finished tenth." That meant I lived to fight another day.

That evening, I met with Fred Luke and Milt Sonsky, my fellow javelin throwers. We had all qualified for the next day, a surprise to some but not us. I went through the list of the twelve throwers and stated that Janis Lusis from the USSR and Klaus Wolfermann from West Germany were in a class by themselves. Of the remaining seven throwers, not counting us, were national champions, former world record holders, and a handful of guys who had longer throws than us by ten to fifteen feet. I said, "One of us could win a medal." In my mind, I was thinking it was me.

Sunday, September 3, 1972, Men's Olympic Javelin Finals

The next day, I was at the Olympic Stadium early, first guy to the box of markers, focused and ready to compete. I didn't hear the spectators and was going to have fun. I honestly didn't keep track of who was in what place or the distances of the other throwers. I just threw.

After three attempts, they take the top eight throwers and they get three more throws. I didn't notice that I was in third place, behind Lusis and Wolfermann. I was also a little over three inches in front of Hannu Siitonen, the Finnish phenom and Finland's national champion who was in fourth. I wasn't aware of that at the time. I just knew I got three more attempts, and no American had done that since 1952. Fred Luke also qualified by being in eighth place. We both had made history but weren't aware of it at the time. As we continued competing, Wolfermann continued to improve. On his fifth attempt in the finals, the mostly German crowd started to shout his name. "Wolfermann! Wolfermann!" They continued, and the entire stadium 90,000 spectators were in sync. Klaus Wolfermann was really motivated by this as he started his run. At the point where he released the javelin, the crowd went totally silent. You could hear a pin drop.

With the new measuring and electronic devices, the throw was measured and immediately shown on a rotating board. His throw was 90.48 meters. It was a new Olympic record, and he had moved into the lead. Lusis had the lead from his first throw of 88.88 meters and improved to 89.54 meters. Klaus was close at 88.40 meters until that throw. The crowd went wild.

Janis Lusis had one throw remaining. I remember having been told of his performance at the 1968 Mexico City Olympics where on his last throw, he stopped, went back, and started over and won the gold medal on his last throw. That's with the ninety-second effort time limit.

It's now Janis Lusis's time to throw. They called his name, the clock was running. He moved into the throwing lane and started his run. Before he threw, he stopped abruptly and started all over again. I've never personally seen any athlete improve nor had a great throw after an aborted throw. Janis went back in the lane and started over. I know he had to be conscious of the time. He came down the lane, let go of the javelin, and it took off. It was a great throw. It seemed like it took a while for the officials to show the distance on the rotating scoreboard.

Now remember, Wolfermann's throw was 90.48 meters. They flashed the distance for Lusis—90.46 meters. Less than a half inch between the two, and Wolfermann won. I realized that I had one more attempt. I thought I had one throw to win this. I reached back, and as normally happens, trying harder doesn't necessarily mean success. It was a terrible throw that I fouled on purpose.

The competition was over. I was the first American male javelin thrower to win an Olympic medal in twenty years, after Cy Young won gold and Bill Miller won silver in 1952 at the Helsinki Olympics. What a day and what fun and success.

History made with a jailbreak by a walk-on athlete who didn't compete in his state meet and who wasn't expected to make the USA Olympic Team, let alone win an Olympic bronze medal. *Dreams do come true!*

BILL SCHMIDT COMPETITIVE/
OLYMPIC EXPERIENCES

Winning on my last throw at Modesto, 280 feet 7 inches.

Winning the US Olympic Trials 1972 in Eugene, OR on my last throw.

USA Olympic javelin team,1972. Bill Schmidt,
Milt Sonsky and Fred Luke.

Competing in the 1972 Olympic Finals in Munich

1972 Munich Olympics, Medal Ceremony. Bill Schmidt, USA, Bronze Medal, Klaus Wolfermann, Federal Republic of Germany, Gold Medal, Janis Lusis, USSR, Silver Medal.

Competing for the Pacific Coast Club, Kennedy Games, 1983 winning throw 283 feet 2 inches.

While competing in Italy, someone bet me I couldn't lift this car.

CHAPTER 12

JAVELIN THROWER OF THE DECADE—THE 1970S

My collegiate javelin career was over after the 1970 NCAA Championships in Des Moines, Iowa, where I finished second with a throw of 262 feet, 11 inches. In addition to having won All-American honors, the meet was significant in that my brothers, Bob and Ed, were there to see me compete. Joe Gowern, my high school coach, was also in attendance. It was the first time any of my family members and Joe Gowern would see me compete.

I knew with certainty what the future would hold for me. Based on our—me and Bob's draft lottery number 16—the military would be in our future. I would receive a notice to report for a pre-draft physical in the third week of September. Meanwhile, I was selected to participate in the World University Games, scheduled in Turin, Italy, at the end of August.

Although I was throwing at 70 percent, I decided to attend the competition in Turin, Italy, in late August and early September. My elbow was going to hamper my performance, but the experience of competing against the top javelin throwers in the world was an opportunity I couldn't pass up.

The World University Games in Turin, Italy, or known as the VI Summer Universiade, had fifty-eight nations, over two thousand athletes competing in nine sports from August 26 through September 6, 1970. It was the Olympic Games for university students around the world.

Miklos Nemeth, from Hungary, finished first, throwing 268 feet, 8 inches. His countryman, Jozef Csik, would finish second at 263 feet, 5 inches. I would finish sixth with a throw of 247 feet, 10 inches. Although my throwing effort was subpar, the experience of meeting other athletes from other countries was the greatest education I could have. I would later beat Miklos and Jozef in the Olympic competition in Munich in 1972.

I remember seeing and later meeting my first Russian athlete. My first reaction was one of hate. After all, there was Sputnik, the Cuban Missile Crisis, and Nikita Khrushchev, more than enough reasons to hate them. I later met a Russian water polo player. After a few conversations about our events, family, and education, we both left feeling less hateful and realized we had more in common than we ever thought. Big difference in politics and religion for sure but two individuals who shared the same desires for a better life for ourselves and our families.

In my second year in the US Army, I was stationed at West Point Military Academy, New York., after a short stay at Fort Ord, California. For the US Army team, we trained at Fort MacArthur, California. There were six of us from the US Army team that made the US Olympic Team. They were Ken Swenson, 800 meters; Jeff Bennett, decathlon; Tim Vollmer, discus; Thomas Hill, high hurdles; Arnie Robinson, long jump; and myself, in the javelin. Three of us—Thomas Hill, Arnie Robinson, and I—would each win a bronze medal at the Munich Olympics in 1972. I threw 270 feet, 6 inches, in winning the US Olympic Trials, and 276 feet, 11 inches, to win the bronze medal. Klaus Wolfermann from West Germany won the gold, and Janis Lusis, from the USSR, won the silver.

In 1973, I joined the Pacific Coast Club after I entered the University of Tennessee with a graduate scholarship. In addition to my training, I coached the javelin, the decathlon, and was the academic adviser. In addition, I oversaw recruiting. Stan Huntsman was the head coach.

I had five meets in the USA with a personal best at the Kennedy Games of 283 feet, 2 inches. The Pacific Coast Club was a group of athletes with Tom Jennings as its manager. Most of the team members were Olympic athletes, Olympic medal winners, and world record holders. The decision was made that the Pacific Coast Club athletes would not be competing in the AAU Championships but would be competing in Europe instead. While in Europe, I averaged over 262 feet in 6 meets with a best of 267 feet in Innsbruck, Austria, losing to Klaus Wolfermann who threw 267 feet, 5.5 inches. I ended 1973 with a rank of #10 best javelin thrower in the world and #4 in the USA. I was ranked seventh in world in 1972 and #1 in the USA. In 1975, I finished sixth at the US National Championships with a throw of 253 feet, 10 inches.

In 1975, I again competed in the World University Games that were held in Rome, Italy. I competed well, finishing second with a throw of 263 feet, 1 inch, winning the silver medal. Gheorghe Megelea, from Romania, won the gold with a throw of 267 feet, 5 inches.

In 1976, I decided to relocate to Cupertino, California. I moved in with John Powell, 1972 Olympic teammate and world record holder in the discus. Also living with Powell at his condo were shot-putters Brian Oldfield and Jesse Stuart. There were no dull moments at the condo.

I started the season slow. I had three finishes over 240 feet and two over 250 feet. To say it was a subpar year would be an understatement. I finally threw 263 feet, 3 inches, at the AAU National Championships and finished third and qualified for the US Olympic trials held in Eugene, Oregon, later in June.

I felt certain that it would take a throw of 270 feet to make the 1976 US Olympic Team. My current season indicated that I had to have a seasonal best to make the team. Training was going well, and I knew I would be competitive when it counted. I arrived in Eugene, Oregon, the day before the qualifying round. Eugene was a comfortable place for me to throw. I won the US Trials in 1972 on my last throw.

I was in the first flight of qualifying and was ready to throw. I was relaxed, coming down the runway, and released the throw. When it was measured, it was 282 feet, 1 inch—a new US Olympic trials and Hayward Field record. The old Hayward Field record was 272 feet, 11 inches. I bettered it by almost ten feet. It was also only a foot off my best throw ever of 283 feet, 2 inches. It surprised many people, but not me. I knew I'd be ready, but this first day of qualifying throws wouldn't carry over for the second round the next day. That evening, I went to the movies to relax. I had a restless night but still felt relaxed the next day. I was ready.

It usually took me forty-five minutes to warm up. I'd be ready both physically and mentally at that point. Now, at the Olympic Games, when they say the competition starts at noon, there's a competitor on the runway ready to throw at 12:01 p.m.

The javelin throw was scheduled to start at 5:45 p.m. on Sunday, June 27. I say that because at 5:15 p.m., the officials notified us that the high jump competition was running late. Now you'd normally say, "What would that have to do with the javelin competition?" Well, Hayward Field had a unique setup where the high jump utilized a portion of the javelin runway. They started their competition at 3:30 p.m., and two hours into it, they were still competing.

They returned to announce to the javelin throwers that the high jump would be running later by one hour. Now the positions for the US Olympic Team for the high jumpers had been determined, the top three make the team, but they continued to jump. At this point, I had warmed up, cooled down, and warmed up again. As I mentioned, this is not what occurs at an Olympic Games. Strike it up to poor planning by the scheduling committee and the layout of the competition site, the fault of the rules committee. Either way, I had a subpar early season but a great throw the first day of qualifying. I just wasn't ready for over an hour delay in the start of the competition, mentally or physically.

In all of my major competitions, I could always reach back for that final effort that would put me in first place or at least in contention. This one time, I reached back and had nothing left in the tank. I finished seventh with a throw of 259 feet, 9 inches. Sam Colson won it at 276 feet, 2 inches; Richard George at 269 feet, 9 inches; and Tony Hall at 267 feet, 8 inches.

I left the next day to fly back to San Jose, California, without making the US Olympic Team. I had one of the top ten throws in the world that first day but now was headed back to Knoxville, Tennessee. That was a long drive back with plenty of time to think. Think about the previous days of competition as well as my future in throwing the javelin. My wife, Nikki, stood by me while I chased my dream. We'd have to discuss what was next.

I decided to acquire my teaching credentials and started teaching in the Knoxville city schools. I was an accounting teacher and coached girl's cross-country and boys track and field at Central High School. It was challenging work, and it challenged my workouts. After teaching each day and working out, I felt no desire to go home. It was selfish, and our marriage suffered. We separated in 1977, and the divorce was final in early 1978.

I was renting a two-bedroom house on Oak Ridge Highway that had electric heating in the ceilings. It was very inefficient. I gave my wife all the furniture and bought the box spring and mattress from her so I'd have something to sleep on. I had stacked cardboard boxes taped together that were my dressers for my clothes. I started to work out more intensely. I was fueled by my failed marriage and focused on training and competing.

My first meet of the year in 1978, at the Florida Relays, I won with a throw of 263 feet, 4 inches. I knew the training would pay off. I won at my next meet but only threw 250 feet, 8 inches, but I did win. I competed poorly at the Tom Black Classic in Knoxville, placing fourth with a throw of 246 feet, 1 inch.

My last competition before the AAU National Championship on June 9–10 at UCLA Drake Field would be in Memphis, Tennessee, on June 4. I drove with Eve Beyer, a friend, to Memphis the night before the meet. I awoke the next morning, located the throwing area, and proceeded to warm up. My first throw was 266 feet, 7 inches; the second throw was 263 feet. The third throw was 250 feet. My fourth throw was 253 feet. I felt in great form, and the throws were effortless. I fouled on my fifth throw but finished the competition with a 260-foot, 5-inch throw.

Now I had a great series of throws, and the closest competitor was at 196 feet, finishing second. When you have a strong series of throws, you can usually expect good results, if not a personal best. I knew that I was ready to throw in the US Championships.

I arrived in Los Angeles on June 8 and stayed at the Holiday Inn Tower in Westwood, near the UCLA campus. I awoke the next day and competed in the qualifying round. On my first throw, I threw 258 feet, 9 inches. I took only one throw and finished second in the qualifying round. These throws don't carry over for the next day.

I slept great that night and spent the day watching television for about three hours before the finals. I watched a black and white movie, *Gunga Din*, from 1939. It starred Carey Grant, Douglas Fairbanks Jr., Victor McLaglen, and Joan Fontaine. I laughed and enjoyed the movie. It kept my mind off the finals.

On my first throw of the finals, I threw 267 feet, 11 inches. I was leading. I fouled on my next three throws, but Bob Roggy, the young stud of the young US javelin group, took the lead with a throw of 272 feet, 6 inches. On my next throw, I took the lead and won the National Championship with a throw of 276 feet, 9 inches. It felt so good. I had been close several times, but this confirmed my legacy.

I finished out 1978 with a win in Toronto, Canada, at the Guardian Games, with a meet record of 270 feet, 1 inch. At the USA versus the USSR meet, I finished fourth with a throw of 264 feet, 4 inches. The USA had beaten the Soviets for the first time in a dual meet since 1969. USA-119, USSR-102.

At the Pre-Commonwealth meet in Edmonton, Alberta, I finished and tied for second and took third place, throwing 254 feet, 8 inches. I did compete at the National Sports Festival in Colorado Springs and threw 256 feet and finished seventh. I wasn't training. I was just throwing. I was exhausted.

I flew to Taipei, Taiwan, Republic of China, and competed in two meets. In Taipei, I threw 263 feet, 8 inches, for first place and a meet record. The next day, I traveled to Kaoshiung, Taiwan, where I won but threw only 245 feet. My last competition for the year would be in Tokyo, Japan, at the Eight Nations meet. I finished in sixth place and was ready to end the long season. I was ranked second in the US rankings. Not too bad for a thirty-one-year-old javelin thrower.

In 1979, I finished third at the National Championships and felt in prime shape to make another run at the US Olympic Team in 1980. I was on the Board of Directors of TAC, which replaced the AAU as the governing body of track and field. At a board meeting in February of 1980, it seemed certain that the USA was going to Boycott the Moscow Olympics. I continued to train, but with no real goal of competing in Moscow, I just went through training and meets uninspired. I retired at the end of the 1980 season.

Track and Field News, "the bible of the sport," honored me by naming me "Javelin Thrower of the Decade" for the 1970s in the United States.

I had a great career, sure, some losses, but I wouldn't change a thing. And as for not making the 1976 US Olympic team, I wouldn't change the selection process. I'd still want whoever was the "best that day" to go.

I'm humbled by my accomplishments and specifically proud of having won the bronze medal at the Munich Olympics in 1972, the last American male to have won a medal since 1952, over seven decades.

CHAPTER 13

THE WORLD'S FAIR
KNOXVILLE? HOW?

World's Fairs are governed/supervised by the Bureau International des Expositions (BIE) in Paris, France. They regulate the classes of exhibitions, bidding, frequency, size, as well as the duration.

The BIE recognized and awarded the 1982 World's Fair to Knoxville, Tennessee. It was recognized as a "Specialized Exhibition" or a "Specialized Expo." Expo it was and considered a category three World's Fair at that time.

Knoxville's World's Fair was formally known as the Knoxville International Energy Exposition with the theme "Energy Turns the World." It was constructed on a Louisville and Nashville Railroad switch yard and depot that had about fifty sets of track, roughly seventy acres. That was all eliminated, except for one set of tracks which were open and ran during the off hours of the fair.

Over 11 million people visited the fair that opened May 1, 1982, and ran through October 31, 1982. Over twenty countries and eighty corporations participated, and the Sunsphere, a 266-foot steel structure with a five-story gold globe on top, was constructed as the Fair's Park theme structure. It still remains today as part of the skyline of Knoxville.

The fair was projected to return a surplus of $5 million. A season pass was $100 (presold for $60), daily ticket $9.95, group rate $8.95 with the AAA rate of $5 and $6. Additional revenue was generated through sponsorships and licensing agreements. There was an

"Official Car, Official Coffee, Official Camera, Official Popcorn, Official Luncheon Meats," and so on. Although there was sponsorship/involvement by Stroh's and Anheuser-Busch breweries, there was also a "World's Fair Beer."

When seeking sponsorships of "Sports at the World's Fair," I contacted all the beer breweries in the United States. I thought I had one, maybe two that were extremely interested. With the NFL Exhibition game, the NBA exhibition game, and a few other events that had sponsors linked to their appearances, it was a great portfolio of marquis events.

As is the case in any competitive category—and believe me, none were more competitive than the beer category—they played off of each other's interests and strategies. In the final analysis, they felt that the six-month run of the fair was a short-lived event, and most of the sporting events had little or no television appeal.

When it came to the soft drink category, the local Coca-Cola distributor, a family owned business, was involved, but it was not going to include sports at the World's Fair. They already had pouring rights at all the venues where the sports were being staged. There was no real incentive for them to pay additional monies to be involved. In addition, because of their strength in the marketplace, I had little leverage in courting their competitor.

As I "shopped" the sports programs, the price I put on the complete sponsorship, naming rights, etc., was at $300,000. Of course, as I got closer to opening day, I lowered it to $150,000. My initial strategy was to cover our (KIEE) share of the cost of the NFL game ($300,000) with the University of Tennessee. As time went by, it was obvious that I had to employ a strategy of selling individual sponsorships for each event and that every event had to cover their own costs.

The original staff of the 1982 World's Fair numbered six. I was the 102 employee hired. The entire staff would total over 500 with over 18,000 employed at the fair.

There were new highway improvements, redevelopment projects, hotels built, and a new convention center.

In addition to the executive and management committees, there were over forty-two local committees that worked collectively with the fair and its organizers. Internal departments included administration, finance, site development, operations, marketing, personnel, security, and world festival. Sports fell under the domain of the World Festival, the entertainment division of the World's Fair which included performing arts as well as sports.

The fair received a variety of proposals for events to be staged at the fair. Some included mud wrestling, a reenactment of the defeat of the Spanish Armada on the Waters of the World, the reflective pool throughout the fair site, and a tight rope artist walking from the roof of the then Hyatt Hotel to the Sunsphere.

The tight rope artist was Jay Cochrane who was known as the "Prince of the Air." He, in fact, visited Knoxville, and I did a logistical tour from the Hyatt to the Sunsphere, surveying the necessary rooftops and where to attach guide lines to support the main cable. His proposal was to walk the tightrope from the Hyatt to the Sunsphere on opening day and then walk back on closing day.

He said he would do it for $86,000. I said, "Is that both ways?"

He responded, "Each way ($172,000)."

I said, "That's a lot of money."

He quickly replied, "Would you do it for that?"

I responded, "Hell no!"

His quotes didn't include insurance or fees to tie off guide lines to homeowners or business rooftops. I also thought, even if I could pay for it, what if he fell?

We parted ways as friends, but a year later, he sold the organizers of the 1984 World's Fair in New Orleans on the idea to walk on a tight rope across the Mississippi River as part of a "One Year to Go" celebration. I attended the event on May 13, 1983. It was amazing. There were fireworks, church bells, balloons, F-4C Phantom jets buzzing the riverfront, and a countdown clock.

My first thought was, *What did they pay him?* My second thought or observation, given my previous logistical tour with him in Knoxville, was *Where will he tie down the guide lines that will support the tightrope itself?*

I got there really early on a windy day. The walk kept getting delayed. In addition, the river had to be closed to all commercial boat and barge traffic. On the previous day, the cranes on either side of the river couldn't hoist the cable to the prescribed height. They brought in bulldozers on each side of the river, and the cable reach the required height.

As Jay made his way across the Mississippi River, holding a balance pole that was forty-eight feet long and weighed seventy pounds, I felt proud of what he was doing but also felt how dangerous it was about 200 feet in the air. If he fell, hitting the water at that height could be deadly. He almost got to the halfway point when he dropped the pole and hung on to the cable.

Panic set in. Would he fall? Would he be rescued? What next? Completing the walk wasn't in question now. It was how he would get down.

What seemed like an eternity but what was probably like forty-five minutes to an hour, he hung onto the cable. Gradually, we saw the cable being lowered toward the river. Would they lower it enough to enable him to jump? What about the river current? As the cable was lowered, a Coast Guard vessel settled under him and took him away to safety.

I happened to be on the side of the river where the boat let him ashore. He recognized me, so I asked him a question. "Was the tightrope moving a lot from right to left?"

He replied, "Not only was it moving from right to left, but it was like a snake going up and down." You could tell he was extremely disappointed.

For a moment, I wondered if he'd get paid. Then I thought, *With this kind of job, you get your money up front.*

CHAPTER 14

WORLD'S FAIR
KNOXVILLE? WHERE?

Knoxville, Tennessee, was known for the home of the University of Tennessee, headquarters for the Tennessee Valley Authority and home of the Dempster Dumpster. So when it was announced that Knoxville was going to host the 1982 World's Fair, surprise is an understatement. Shock is more like it. The first thought of most people was, "Like the New York World's Fair of 1964?" Of course everyone wondered, "How? Where? When? And how can you be involved?"

One afternoon in Stan Huntsman's office, the head men's track and field coach handed me a sheet of paper that outlined a position of Director of Sports at the World's Fair. It also stated that there would be a variety of sports and entertainers appearing over the six-month run of the fair, starting May 1, 1982, and running through October 31, 1982. This was the first time I had any details on the fair or its programs. The article also stated that this would be the first time that sports would be included within the "World Festival of Entertainment" in a World's Fair. It also named Tom Siler, former sports editor of the *Knoxville News-Sentinel*, as the sports consultant for the fair.

The main objective of the World's Fair Sports Program was to host the best international athletic events as possible and provide individuals the opportunity to view events and athletes that they may have read about but haven't seen. Where it may not be possible to host an international event, we would try to procure a national championship event in that sports discipline.

We received many detailed sporting event proposals from a variety of sporting groups that wanted to appear at the World's Fair. Those included a National Powerboat Association sanctioned event on a one-and-a-quarter-mile oval course on the Tennessee River adjacent to Neyland Stadium; a reenactment of the defeat of the Spanish Armada inside the fairgrounds on the "Waters of the World" reflection pool; the Catalina World Cup of racquetball; the World Championship of Karate; a world-class field of runners for a marathon run, finishing inside Neyland Stadium; a women's volleyball match between USA and Japan; a "record makers" exhibition weightlifting competition; a United States Tennis Association Senior event; and an international arm wrestling event involving 24 countries, just to name a few.

We finalized our "official program" with about 20 sporting events in 26 weeks. I "cut my teeth" on selling these non-sponsored events in a package program to Miller Brewing Company, Anheuser-Busch Inc., Stroh's Brewing Company, and Pabst Brewing Company as "The Official Sponsor of Sports at the 1982 World's Fair." Bottom line, there was no additional corporate sponsorship outside of the events named and sponsored individually. There was no television-packaged programming sold, but several sponsored events included television.

With no funding or sponsorship revenue, the World Festival of Sports returned a net profit of $300,000. This revenue was directed to help subsidize the nightly fireworks shows.

CHAPTER 15

SPORTS FESTIVAL AT THE 1982 WORLD'S FAIR

For the first time in the history of World Fairs, sports would be included in the festival programs. It would be branded as "World Festival of Sports at the 1982 World's Fair." The events would be scheduled May 1 through October 31, 1982.

I was a graduate assistant in the track and field program at the University of Tennessee in Knoxville, and Stan Hunstman, the head track and field coach, shared with me an article regarding a sports program within the World's Fair scheduled to be in Knoxville in 1982. Earlier in the year, Stan promoted Dan Stimson to the vacant position of assistant coach. My future in coaching at the University of Tennessee had been determined. There was *no future.*

I reviewed the outline of the job description for Director of Sports and decided to apply. I mailed a resume—yes, mailed, as this was before the internet had been invented. I was anxious in receiving a response and hopefully an interview. My options were limited.

I could teach in high school or seek another university where I could coach.

When I finished my graduate degree at UT, I utilized the job placement services offices and scheduled twenty-one appointments with a variety of companies interviewing on campus. Most, if not all the interviewers, were divided between "You need more work experience" or "How could you be challenged with this job given your Olympic success?" Years later, I realized that most companies sent their junior management personnel to conduct these interviews, of which few had little or no hiring experience.

In the weeks following the interviews, I received twenty-one letters stating that I had neither the skill set nor job experience to qualify for an entry level position. How was I going to gain any job experience unless someone hired me? All that registered in my mind was that twenty-one companies said I wasn't good enough or qualified and rejected me. This was similar to my experience when I was seeking a college scholarship in track and field. They all said I wasn't good enough, and I used this to fuel my ambition to prove them all wrong.

A few weeks went by, and I received a response in the mail with an envelope that had the World's Fair logo on it. I opened the envelope with cautious optimism. I was to contact Julian Forrester at the telephone number provided to schedule an interview. I took note of the two individuals copied on the letter, David Haber and Tom Siler.

In my research for the scheduled interview, I read all the World's Fair articles that had appeared in both local newspapers, the *Knoxville Journal* and the *Knoxville News-Sentinel*. I learned that Tom Siler, former sports editor of the *Knoxville News-Sentinel*, was a sports consultant to the World's Fair. I also learned that David Haber was the producer/director of the Festival of Performing Arts which included sports. In addition, I became aware of the fact that Mr. Forrester had been an employee of the University of Tennessee in the theater department. My confirmation of my interview stated that I would be meeting with all three.

I quickly read the background on each of these individuals. Tom Siler was the only individual with apparent sports knowledge or a sports background. Both Julian Forrester and David Haber had performing arts backgrounds. Mr. Haber had served as the artistic director of the National Ballet of Canada, and Mr. Forrester, who worked in the theater department at the University of Tennessee, would be familiar with their football program if nothing else.

I showed up for the appointment at the World's Fair headquarters at the former House-Hasson Hardware Company building at the corner of Henley Street and Summit Hill Drive, thirty minutes early.

I sat in the lobby, noticed all the activity, and thought, *This place is happening, and I want to be part of it.*

There was a wealth of activity and positive energy, a feeling that wasn't captured in the local newspapers, mostly only negative press stories.

I first met with Julian Forrester. He was a young good-looking individual with a British accent that the women *loved*—a Cary Grant style of guy. After discussing my background and my athletic career, Mr. Forrester stated, "You don't have the necessary experience to be the Director of Sports at the World's Fair. However, there are two sports coordinator positions that you might qualify for."

No experience. Where had I heard that before?

I then interviewed with David Haber who, in addition to being the producer of the Festival of Arts at the World's Fair, was also Mr. Forrester's boss. After visiting with Mr. Haber for about forty-five minutes and a lot of questions about my relationship with the University of Tennessee and my contacts in the world of sports, he paused for what seemed liked minutes but was probably seconds.

He then said, "I have some good news and I have some bad news for you." I held my breath. He continued, "The good news is you have the job as Director of Sports for the 1982 World's Fair."

I thought, *What could be the bad news?*

He stated, "The bad news is that you don't have a budget or any funding. We expect sporting events throughout the entire six-month length of the fair, and they need to be self-funding." With that news, he also stated, "Tom Siler, the fair's sports consultant, is already working on several events, and he'll be reporting to you."

Great interview, great day, and one great challenge. I later learned that the events Tom Siler was working on, he committed $400,000. *I was already underwater.*

The theme of the fair was "Energy Turns the World." It seemed obvious that human energy be included. My strategy was to seek out the highest caliber of national and international sporting events and then sell sponsorships of them to cover the cost. I wanted to give the public the opportunity to see the best and also leverage these events to promote the fair. We also wanted to incorporate other events scheduled locally during the fair into our calendar. With the rich tradition of sports at the university, we wanted to capitalize and leverage their fan base and facilities.

Bottom line, we were charged with providing entertainment and seeking to break even financially.

One of the reasons the sporting events were so successful was because of Tom Siler. His background as a sports writer and the respect he had within the sports media and community was exceptional. His professional contacts were the sole reason some events happened. We made quite a team. I would fill out the calendar of events, sell, and market them. My career in sports marketing had begun. Historically, sports marketing as we today know it started in the early 1980s. Little did I know that I'd be viewed as a pioneer in the industry.

Calendar of Events

Avon Women's 10K

The Avon Women's 10K was held on Saturday, May 8, 1982. A prerace clinic was conducted on Friday, May 7, 1982, in the University of Tennessees' University Center. Runners gathered to pick up their race packets, enjoy refreshments, and listen to speakers. Featured speakers were Nancy Conz, Avon International Champion; Ruth Rothfarb, octogenerian marathoner; and Beryl Bender, yoga expert.

A basketball clinic featuring Nancy Lieberman, nationally known pro-basketball player, and a tennis clinic with Martina Navratilova, Wimbledon, and US Open Champion, and number one ranked women's tennis player in the world, was held at the University of Tennessee Tennis Courts Saturday after the race. The clinics were well-attended, and individuals from the stands were able to volley with the pros.

The prerace activity on Saturday morning began very early with the World's Fair sports staff, high school volunteers, Knoxville Track Club, and University of Tennessee Army ROTC busy preparing for the race. The prerace atmosphere was influenced by the playing of the Olympia Brass Band from New Orleans, a live remote from WIVK, and hundreds of red and white balloons.

The race began at 8:00 a.m. with Mary Pat Tyree, wife of Knoxville's Mayor Randy Tyree, firing the starting gun. At the gun, over six hundred runners converged onto the streets of downtown Knoxville.

The course measured ten thousand meters (6.2 miles) and was through the downtown area, passing the 1982 World's Fair. The route was well-marked and manned with individuals at each mile mark reading splits. An aide station was set up at the halfway mark with Gatorade and water available to all runners.

The race was won by Nancy Conz with a time of 33:14.8 with Karen Cosgrove, second, and Knoxville's Missy Alston Kane, third.

All other runners enjoyed the race and were very pleased at the food available after the race and the medals given to all finishers.

Scottish Games Exhibition

A Scottish Games Exhibition was held at the Court of Flags. Eight of the best Scottish Games competitors from the United States gave exhibitions in three events. The events were the caber toss, tossing the sheaf, and the stone throw. The men that performed here were all well over six feet tall and weighed over 250 pounds.

There were also bagpipes and dancers from Grandfather Mountain, North Carolina, who led a parade through the fair until they arrived at the Court of Flags where they played and danced. An estimated crowd of twelve thousand people watched the hour-long exhibition.

Gymnastics

The daily gymnastics exhibitions at the United States Pavilion proved to be a success. The exhibitors started June 1 and continued through October 30. The forty-four clubs were members of the United States Association of Independent Gymnastic Clubs with Ed

Knepper as the executive director. The equipment, which included tumbling mats, landing mats, one balance beam, one set of uneven parallel bars, one set of parallel bars, one vaulting horse, one pommel horse, and two spring boards, were supplied by Nissen.

The gymnastic clubs during their stay at the World's Fair, which was either three days or four days, were scheduled to perform twice daily. The area for spectators, which seated approximately five hundred with standing room for another five hundred, was always filled. The clubs were well received by the spectators.

The clubs were mainly from the eastern and southern parts of the United States; however, some groups were from Iowa and Texas and as far north as Vermont. The gymnasts ranged from four to twenty years of age. The performances ranged from beginner to national and international caliber.

In hindsight, we could have used more seating and dressing facilities for the performers. Another improvement would be to possibly have a spring floor and better lighting for night performances.

The people at the United States Pavilion were very cooperative and a pleasure to work with. They were responsible for the sound system, storage of equipment, security, and parking for the gymnastic clubs.

DuPont-Stren Casting Exhibition

The DuPont-Stren Casting Exhibition was held in the Waters of the World at the Court of Flags. Two of the top fishermen in the United States, Bill Dance of Tennessee and Roland Martin of Florida, gave the casting demonstration.

Targets were placed in the water, and Bill and Roland each took casts at the target and gave a very good clinic. Bill and Roland stayed later to sign autographs and talked with the fishermen who attended the exhibition.

In conjunction with the casting exhibition, the culmination of DuPont's "Great Knot Search" took place. Hundreds of new knots were submitted from the United States, South America, Canada, and Mexico. After each knot had gone through stress tests, usefullness of the knot, and simplicity, Gary Martin of Indiana was determined the winner of the $2,500.00 prize.

World's Fair Youth Softball Invitational

The 1982 World's Fair Youth Softball Invitational was held in north Knoxville on June 4, 5, and 6, 1982. The tournament featured thirty-six female youth teams, competing in age groups 9–12, 13–15, and 16–18. The hosts were the Knoxville Bluebirds and their coach, Mable Harrel.

The tournament was a great success with all teams enjoying the play and the hospitality of the Bluebirds. Trophies were awarded in all age groups for the top three teams. Adidas supplied travel bags for all the first place teams in each division.

Team Murray World Cup of BMX

The Team Murray World Cup of BMX was held on June 11, 12, and 13, at Bearden High School. Bearden's football field was converted to a bicycle motor cross track, with banked curves and a water jump.

The event drew up to one thousand participants with racers divided by age and ability. Trophies were awarded for each group with the pro's competing for an $18,000.00 purse. Murray was well-prepared and ran an excellent event. The pro finals on Sunday were marred by rain, but the well-constructed track made racing possible.

The event drew many spectators and was a hit with the local media. *PM Magazine*, a nationwide syndicated television show, aired a segment on the event. In addition, Murray brought the BMX Trick Riders to perform during the breaks on the races. The Trick Riders also performed at the Court of Flags at the 1982 World's Fair.

This was the largest and richest event in the history of BMX. As a residual for Bearden High School and in lieu of facility rental, the football field was completely redone with an underground sprinkling system.

TAC Track and Field Championships

The Athletic Congress USA/Mobil Outdoor Track and Field Championships were held at the University of Tennessee's Tom Black Track on June 18, 19, and 20, 1982. The meet attracted the United States's premiere track and field athletes to compete for Mobil Grand Prix monies and to vie for spots on various US teams.

The Mobil Grand Prix consists of fifteen events, eight for women. The Grand Prix is based on three-meet scoring, two meets prior to the Championship plus the USA/Mobil Outdoor Track and Field Championships. The prize money in each of the fifteen events will be $2,500.00 for first place, $1,000.00 for second place, and $500.00 for third place.

The championships were very well run. The athletes were pleased with the facilities but felt the crowd was small.

International Baseball

The 1982 World's Fair International Baseball Tournament was held at Bill Meyer Stadium on June 23–25. The event was sanctioned by the United States Baseball Federation. Four out of the top five teams in the world competed in this double round-robin tournament. The teams consisted of players nineteen years of age and under from Mexico, Australia, Japan, and the United States.

As the tournament progressed, one could see the teams from the United States and Japan were the teams to beat. At the end of the tournament, the United States had to beat Japan in a tiebreaker. The final standings in the tournament were the United States first, Japan second, Australia and Mexico finishing third and fourth, respectively. The people that attended the games saw some very exciting and well-played baseball.

Bowie Kuhn, the Commissioner of Major League Baseball, attended the opening game and threw out the first pitch. Baseball was an exhibition sport at the 1984 Olympics, and this tournament did a lot in helping establish baseball as an Olympic event.

1982 World's Fair Boxing

The 1982 World's Fair Boxing program was held at the Knoxville Civic Coliseum on July 8, 1982. On the card were six bouts including former World Heavyweight Champion John Tate of Knoxville and highly ranked featherweight Bernard Taylor. Both Tate and Taylor won their fights.

This was one of two events where we sublet the Coliseum, received a guarantee, and held the promoter responsible for the event.

Gymnasticade '82'

Gymnasticade '82, "Greatest American Heroes," was held at the Civic Coliseum on Friday, July 9, at 7:30 p.m.

The event featured gymnastics greatest American Heroes—Bart Conner, the top-ranked male gymnast in the United States; Tracee Talavera, 1980 US Olympic Team member; and Tifney Quences, US Junior Champion. The format was similar to ice skating's Ice Capades and is a noncompetitive production put under lights and accompanied by music.

While Gymnasticade '82 gave each gymnasts an opportunity to show off their skills in individual routines, it also gave the audience a chance to see a fantastic dance troupe. The TNT's from Omaha filled the show with dance numbers and Gymnastics. The TNT's did several numbers which won the hearts of all who were in attendance. A trampoline group from the Stained Glass Gym in New Jersey also performed.

The event was well done and received good support from the local media. McDonald's of Knoxville lent their support as did Cherokee Distributors. McDonald's ran ticket discounts in their local restaurants while Cherokee gave away tickets on a local radio station. Local media coverage was good with Bart, Tracee, and Tiffiney appearing on *"Live from the Sunsphere"* and a performance for the local cameras with two short exhibitions from the US Pavilion.

The 1982 World's Fair Invitational Rugby Tournament

The 1982 World's Fair Invitational Rugby Tournament was held on July 17–18, 1982. The event featured 40 of the best teams from around the United States.

The tournament began at 8:00 a.m. at Forks-of-the-River Industrial Park with the teams playing in round-robin competition. The day's play ended at 6:30 p.m. with a total of 80 games having been played. The teams record of play determined the seeding for Sunday's play.

The eight teams with the best records were organized into Division I, the next eight teams, two and so on, until all divisions were filled. Playoffs in Division II, III, IV, and V, and all play in Division I were held at Evans Collins Field on Sunday afternoon.

The International Rugby Tournament proved to be very rough and exciting with spectators and participants pleased with the outcome.

Canoe and Kayak Invitational

The Marathon Canoe and Kayak Invitational was held on the Clinch River at the Oak Ridge Marina July 17 and 18. The event was sanctioned by the United States Canoe Association and co-sponsored by the Oak Ridge Rowing Association.

Over 200 entries were received for the fourteen event invitational. The longest race was 24.5 miles with the shortest being three miles. Also, the Voyageur Brigades set up a primitive camp at the Marina. In addition to the authentic costumes, they had skits and crafts demonstrations. The Voyageurs also had a race using their war canoes. These canoes were twenty-six feet long, and eight people were in each canoe during their three-mile race.

Medals were given to the first four places in each event. Participant patches were given to each entrant.

International Basketball

The 1982 World's Fair International Basketball Tournament was played at the Knoxville Civic Coliseum August 5–7. The tournament was a round-robin tournament consisting of four teams. The teams were Canada, PROC (China), Yugoslavia, and the United States. The team from Yugoslavia had won the gold medal in the 1980 Olympics while the United States team was made up mostly of 1982 college players. The Canadian team consisted of Canadians who played at universities in the United States.

The Chinese team played good basketball but did get beat physically.

The final results were Canada (first), United States (second), Yugoslavia (third), and China (fourth).

This tournament was a preview of the '82 World Championships which were to take place August 20–22 in Cali, Columbia.

NFL World's Fair Pro Football

The fourth largest crowd ever to view an NFL football game highlighted the 1982 World's Fair Sports Schedule. The Pittsburgh Steelers, four-time Super Bowl Champions, met the New England Patriots in an NFL exhibition game.

The community supports the University of Tennessee Football program, and we tied this game to their season ticket sales to insure its financial success. This particular event was brought to Knoxville by Tom Siler and his contact with Bill Sullivan, owner of the New England Patriots.

The Pittsburgh Steelers won an exciting game, 24–20.

US-USSR Swim Meet

The best swimmers in the world were in Knoxville, August 26–28, 1982. The United States has long been recognized as the world leader in swimming, and the Soviets boasted Olympic champions Vladimir Salnikov, Sergey Fesenko, and Aleksandr Sidorenko.

It was a classic confrontation between the team that hosted the last Olympics and the team that didn't get to compete there but is hosting the next Olympic Games. The US prevailed.

The meet was sponsored by McDonald's and was televised nationally by ESPN.

The National Slo-Pitch Conference Championships

The 1982 World's Fair and the National Slo-Pitch Conference presented the National Slo-Pitch Conference Championships at Bill Meyers Stadium, August 27–29.

The National Slo-Pitch Conference (NSPC) is made up of twenty-seven of the nation's top amateur Slo-Pitch Softball teams. They compete against one another on a regular basis. The NSPC Championships brings together the top ten teams of the conference via qualifying tournaments for the championships.

The ten teams participating in the 1982 NSPC Championships were: Howards/Western Steer, Denver, North Carolina; Jerry's Caterers, Miami, Florida; York Baseball/Ken Sanoers, York, Pennsylvania; Fab Masters, Lexington, North Carolina; Pace Electronics, Rochester, New York; Tnemec, Indianapolis, Indiana; Elite Coating, Gordon, Georgia; Rule and Lee, Maryville, Tennessee; Southside Sports, Lexington, Kentucky; and Houk Drilling, Tulsa, Oklahoma.

Ten teams competed in the three-day event. Ken Sanders of York, Pennsylvania, coming from the losers bracket to take the crown; Jerry's Caterers of Miami, Florida, captured second place; with Elite Coating of Gordon, Georgia, in third. Fourth place went to Maryville's Rule and Lee.

Cherokee Distributor, the local Miller distributor, helped sponsor the event and was responsible for the trophies.

PGA Cup matches

The 1982 PGA Cup Matches were played at Holston Hills Country Club. This golf match put nine club professionals from the

United States against nine club professionals from Great Britain and Ireland. The format featured three four-ball matches and three foursome matches, then finished with nine singles matches.

The Holston Hills Country Club golf course was in excellent condition for the Cup Matches. Also during the week, a Pro-Am tournament was held as the professionals teamed with some local amateurs and had a good time. As the professionals played in the Pro-Am, they also gave the amateurs a few tips on their game, which was appreciated.

The United States did win and retain the Llandudno International Golf Trophy. Since the first of the PGA Cup Matches, the United States has won seven, lost two, and tied one.

Hungry Fisherman, Lowrance, World's Fair Bass Tournament

The Hungry Fisherman, Lowrance, World's Fair Bass Tournament was held September 23–25, on Loudon and Tellico Lakes, with headquarters at the Fort Loudon Dam Marina. This tournament was one of the richest events in bass fishing history with $100,000 in prize money, plus a $15,000 Ranger fishing boat with the World's Fair logo embedded in the fiberglass body. The boat would be one of a kind, making it a collector's item and worth much more than $15,000. The boat went to the fisherman who caught the largest fish during the three days.

The field was limited to 126 entrants, and that was filled rather quickly since first prize was $50,000 in cash. Some of the best fishermen in the United States entered the tournament.

The spectator turnout was about 1,500 each day to witness the daily weigh-in. On the final day when the winners were announced, the first prize of $50,000 was brought in cash by armed policemen in a fishing net. Later, it was taken back to the bank and converted into a check.

The event was well-run, and the town of Lenoir City did a great job in assisting in the tournament. The fishermen liked the waters of Loudon and Tellico Lake.

Indoor Soccer League

The Major Indoor Soccer League sponsored an exhibition between the Cleveland Force and the Memphis Americans on October 8 and 9, 1982, in the Knoxville Civic Coliseum.

Indoor soccer is similar to hockey with both using dasher boards to surround the playing area. Soccer uses a large carpet as their playing surface which promotes fast play.

Friday's game drew 2,000 spectators who saw the Memphis Americans beat the Cleveland Force, 8 to 4. The match was tied at 4 with two minutes left in the fourth period.

Saturday's game was won by Cleveland, 10 to 4, and was not as exciting as Friday's contest. Spectators were made up of many young soccer players and their families. They were treated to two fast and furious games.

The member of the Memphis Americans conducted several clinics on Saturday for the young players in the area.

The introduction of indoor soccer to Knoxville was a success with everyone enjoying the fast-paced action.

NBA Basketball Game

The two best teams in NBA history were selected as the teams to compete in the World Festival Sports Departments final event. The Boston Celtics played the Philadelphia 76ers in an exhibition game at a sold-out William B. Stokely Athletic Center. We again partnered with the UT athletic department and made a sizable profit. These two teams brought some of the greatest names in basketball: Larry Bird, Julius "Dr. J" Erving, M. L. Carr, Cedric Maxwell, Moses Malone, and Bobby Jones.

CHAPTER 16

YOU WANT MOONSHINE WITH THAT?

At the 1982 World's Fair, there were a number of companies and corporations that became sponsors in a variety of ways. Some had "official" status, others were "suppliers," and some provided services. All utilized the logo and were legally bound to promote the fair.

One company, Stokely-Van Camp, had local ties, although their headquarters were in Indianapolis, Indiana. The Stokely brothers built a cannery in 1898 near the family farm in Newport, Tennessee. Their family attended and supported the University of Tennessee for decades. The Stokely name adorned many buildings and facilities on university campus over the years. William B. Stokely Athletic Center hosted the volunteer basketball, track, and volleyball teams and concerts for many years before it's demolition in 2014.

Many members of the Stokely family attended the University of Tennessee, served on a variety of UT boards, trustees, and councils. Currently, there is Stokely Hall, a residency hall for students and athletes, located near the old site of William B. Stokely Athletic Center.

Stokely-Van Camp had many products in their portfolio. They included Van Camp's pork and beans, tomato catsup, applesauce, sliced peaches, various canned and frozen fruits and vegetables, and, yes, Gatorade. The Company's Purity Mills Division distributed Popeye Popcorn as well as Popeye branded cereals.

My first introduction to the Stokely-Van Camp World's Fair sponsorship was through the communications department. The announcement had been made publicly. It listed two specific elements that Stokely-Van Camp would be sponsoring—the Stokely-Van Camp Folklife Festival, an area that would have daily performing arts and the Gatorade Sports Hall of Fame. The Gatorade Sports Hall of Fame would include a variety of sports memorabilia from the world of sports. The details of each had yet to be determined.

Somewhere in its development and design process, someone decided that "if it involved sports, Schmidt needs to be in the loop." In the loop meant that in addition to my sports department responsibilities, I now would be charged with procuring sports memorabilia for the exhibit. I was later included in the selection process for the design firm that was to build the exhibit.

My contact from Stokely-Van Camp in the process was Andrea White Randall, a recent hire for Stokely and a graduate from the University of Tennessee, Knoxville. She was from the south, well-educated, extremely intelligent, and with a great sense of humor. She never called me Bill. It was always "Schmidt." She was a true professional and the point person in the Stokely-Van Camp World's Fair Project, a great leader with a strong personal and communication skill set.

The initial line item for the Stokely-Van Camp Folklife Festival was $846,000 budgeted in the World Festival Elements Budget, December 22, 1981. This included performers, staff, and entertainment. There were three stages where there was daily entertainment. It was an area where crafts, foods, and lifestyle of the south-central Appalachian region was celebrated. Among the entertainment were banjo-pickers, singers, cloggers, cooks, copper and tinsmiths, storytellers, quiltmakers, as well as a working moonshine still. This line item didn't include the Gatorade Sports Hall of Fame. Staffing, etc., were lumped in the "overhead items" of this budget.

The Stokely-Van Camp Folklife Festival was a very popular and well-attended entertainment area. It was entertainment all day and crowded. The crafts and professionals showcasing their skills were of interest to everyone. The "working still" was built on-site and was functional. About three months into the fair, I was asked to sign a purchase order for corn. My first question, "Corn for what?"

They said, "For the still, to make moonshine."

Now I know that none of the sports on our calendar included "shine tasting."

I asked the question, "What happens to the shine after it's made?"

The response I received was that it was continually run back through the still, over and over.

"Why again do we need more corn?" I signed the purchase order. I wasn't certain I had the authority, but the fair was up and running and successful. They weren't giving out samples, but for some reason, we needed "more corn for more shine."

Years after the fair, I found that they were, in fact, distributing pint-sized Mason jars with a label from Second Creek Distillery. Collector's Edition, I'm sure. I also heard many stories about Folklife staff and workers enjoying "tastings" on numerous occasions. It didn't bother me. I just felt left out, but I did have a sports program to run, and I had to find a way to pay for it.

CHAPTER 17

THE GATORADE SPORTS HALL OF FAME

Stokely-Van Camp's sponsorship agreement with the 1982 World's Fair included three elements: The Stokely-Van Camp Folklife Festival, the Gatorade Sports Hall of Fame, and renovation of the L&N Hotel (located on the Folklife site).

Stokely-Van Camp also had "Official Popcorn Status" for their Popeye popcorn brand that was sold in mobile fleets of red, white, and blue kiosks throughout the fair site. Gatorade was also sold through concessionaires on site.

Stokely-Van Camp proved to be one of the most active and leveraged sponsors of the World's Fair. At the Stokely-Van Camp Folklife Festival, it linked the history of the local Stokely family farm and processing plant east of Knoxville and the arts and crafts of the Southern Appalachian region of the United States. A 250-seat amphitheater along with three additional stages showcased performers, artisans, and craftsmen of the region.

Stokely-Van Camp leveraged the fair to promote a variety of their products nationwide through consumer-driven contests with the World's Fair activities. Their "Down-Home Cookin' Contest" involved entrants submitting an original recipe utilizing at least one of Stokely's finest products or Van Camp's pork and beans. Categories included desserts, entrees, side dishes, and bakery items. The entries were judged on the basis of originality, ease of preparation, and thoroughness of instruction.

The Grand prize winner received $10,000 and an all-expense paid trip for four to the 1982 World's Fair. There were four first prize winners receiving $2,000 each and a hundred runner up prize winners receiving a Smoky Mountain basket and a case of various Stokely-Van Camp products.

Another consumer contest involved country singer Tom T. Hall promoting entering the Van Camp's Beanee Weenee "Grub-Steaks." Contestants competed for a fully-equipped 1982 Dodge crew cab pickup truck, expense paid trips to the World's Fair, a freezer filled with 250 pounds of beef, cases of VanCamp's Specialties, and other prizes. Stokely-Van Camp utilized radio and television commercials, billboards, and special product labels to build and drive consumer awareness and its association with the World's Fair.

Stokely-Van Camp signed the official contract with the Knoxville International Energy Exposition (KIEE) on August 17, 1981, after seven months of negotiations. The Stokely negotiating team consisted of Andrea White-Randall, Jack Mooney, and Craig Devine with oversight from William B. Stokely III, Chairman of the Board. These individuals were also responsible for the development of concepts and content for all elements with regard to Stokely Van-Camp's involvement with the World's Fair.

The Gatorade Sports Hall of Fame display was located in the Lifestyle and Technology Pavilion, a large structure that became Knoxville's Convention Center after the Fair. It was a 3,100-square-foot area showcasing nine sports, a University of Tennessee exhibit, sports sculptures, mural sports art, Leroy Neiman works, a theater, a speaker's stage with the Gatorade 88 stock car named "Bertha" driven to nineteen victories by Darrell Waltrip on NASCAR racing circuit as *the* focal point of the exhibit.

The ten Plexiglas display modules and presentation area were manufactured by Dimensional Designs Inc., a firm chosen by the Stokely team of Craig Devine, Andrea White-Randall, and Jack Mooney. Jack, Andrea, and Craig selected and procured all the items of memorabilia as well. I was involved in a limited way mainly for my point of view, specific items of memorabilia, and insurance of certain items.

The Modules

Football

Uniform worn by LA Rams great, Merlin Olsen; autographed football from the 1929 Green Bay Packers championship team; early shoulder pad, helmet, and nose guard, early football shoes, football autographed by Notre Dame's famous "Four Horsemen;" "Holding the Ball" sculpture by Joe Brown; Pat Sullivan's (Auburn University) Heisman Trophy, 1971; NFL Super Bowl Championships rings by Balfour.

Swimming

John Naber's four Olympic gold medals and one silver medal won at the Montreal Olympics 1976; the starting platform Lane #4 from 1972 Munich Olympics used by Mark Spitz; Johnny Weissmuller's two Olympic medals from the 1924 Olympic Games in Paris, his three National Championship medals, and his Exposition of Progress Medal from 1922; the Sullivan Award given to Tracie Caukins; Olympic gold medal of University of Tennessee star Dave Edgar won at Munich Olympics 1972; warm-up uniform used by Mark Spitz during the 1972 Munich Olympics; pictures of Mark Spitz and John Naber.

Track and Field

Jesse Owens' running singlet from the 1936 Berlin Olympics and the baton used by the winning United States 4 X 100 relay team of Foy Draper, Frank Wykoff, Ralph Metcalfe, and Jesse Owens in world record time of 39.8; antique starting blocks with the first medal ever won by Jim Thorpe in the 220-yard hurdles; an early leather-bound shotput; Steve Prefontaine's running uniform and shoes; sculpture of "Jesse Owens" by Joe Brown; ten-time USA Olympic gold medalist Ray Ewry's track shorts; three-time Olympic gold medalist in 1960 Rome Olympics Wilma Rudolph's hat; Olympic medals from Ralph Boston—gold, Rome, 1960, silver, Tokyo, 1964, and bronze, Mexico, 1968; and his Olympic warm-up suit and a displayed Olympic flag.

Basketball

Bob Lanier's size 22 shoes; Bob Cousy's Boston Celtics uniform; Oscar Robertson's Cincinnati Royals uniform, an early basketball; 1890s uniform-long pants, turtleneck; sculpture "Break" by Joe Brown.

Boxing

Life-sized casts of the fists of Primo Camera, Jack Dempsey, and Muhammad Ali; Loving Cup given to Jack Johnson by Jess Willard; Jim Corbett's walking stick; gloves used by Joe Louis; the New American Belt given to James "Jem" Mace in 1870; sculpture "Sugar Ray" by Joe Brown; ringside bell used during the famous John L. Sullivan-Gentleman Jim Corbett fight in 1892 and Corbett's gloves; numerous tickets from classic fights; Joe Louis-Max Schmeling fight poster; a glove from the Muhammad Ali-Joe Frazier fight; an advertisement featuring Jack Dempsey.

Baseball

Babe Ruth's locker from Yankee Stadium, his glove, bat, and a signed baseball, his jersey, and hat; Casey Stengel's jersey and hat; Carl Yastrzemski's jersey and hat; Frank Robinson's uniform; Pete Rose's uniform; Commissioner's Trophy (World Series Trophy); World Series Championship rings.

Golf

President Gerald Ford's clubs and bag; the Walter Hagen Trophy; Tom Morris driver; Edinburgh Maker driver; R. Forgan smooth face mashie; Arthur Andrews mashie niblick with deep grooved face; James Morris putter; Track iron; Tug Tyler brassie with copper-coated shaft; Spaulding Kro-Flite No. 1 wood; Feather ball; Gutta Percha Ball; Rubber Core Ball; sculpture "Young Golfer" by Joe Brown; and a variety of early golf clubs (1700–1800) believed to be brought from Scotland by early settlers in North Carolina.

Tennis

The racquet used by Arthur Ashe in his Wimbledon Championship in 1975; spiked tennis shoes worn by Alphonso Smith, winner of over fifty national titles; court tennis racquet used in ancient game of court tennis, the game from which lawn tennis spawned; the Championship trophy of the Virginia Slims Circuit; antique tennis ball signed by Bill T. Tilden; sculpture "Arthur Ashe" by Joe Brown; an art print depicting the US Open.

Hockey

Mike Eruzione's 1980 USA Olympic Jersey and skates; the USA flag that US Olympic Hockey Goaltender Jim Craig had draped around him at the 1980 Olympics; early hockey stick, puck, and skates; sculpture "Hockey Player" by Joe Brown; and Stanley Cup Championship rings.

University of Tennessee

1972 Men's NCAA National Cross Country Championship Trophy.

1974 Men's NCAA National Track and Field Championship Trophy.

1978 Men's NCAA National Swimming and Diving Championship Trophy; A Tribute to Johnny Majors All-American; Photos of National Championship Footballs Teams 1950, 1951, SEC Championship Football Trophy; 1951 Cotton Bowl Championship Trophy; and photo of Ray Mears SEC Champion Men's Basketball.

Gatorade Racing Team Exhibit

This was a larger exhibit case that featured and showcased the success of the Gatorade Racing Team in NASCAR Racing. In the exhibit were trophies won at 1982 Daytona 500 by Bobby Allison, Most Popular Driver Award 1981; Bobby Allison, 1982 Harley Earl Award; Bobby Allison, "Clash of '82" Trophy; photo of Bobby Allison drinking Gatorade in Victory Lane, Daytona 500, 1982; and photo of William B Stokely III with Bobby Allison in Victory Lane in 1982 at the Daytona 500.

Other elements

The Gatorade Sports Hall of Fame had a video theater that ran sports clips of the Gatorade 88 Racing Team, Olympic Films by Bud Greenspan and numerous highlight films from a variety of sources, including ABC Wide World of Sports. There was an area where guests speakers could address the public. Speakers included Bobby Allison and Heisman Trophy winner Pat Sullivan.

Make no mistake about it, The Gatorade Race Car (Bertha) was not only the focal point of the Hall of Fame but the draw for the fair-goers. After all, this World's Fair was in the heart of stock car racing country and its rich history in tobacco moonshine runners.

After the Gatorade Hall of Fame opened, the exhibit was the most popular attraction after the China Exhibit. Crowds became so active taking photos of the car and trying to climb inside we had to post additional security as well as a "velvet rope" with stanchions for crowd control. This was in addition to the Gatorade-themed outfitted hosts and hostesses who presided over the daily operation of the hall who were also University of Tennessee students.

One of the hostesses that I also coached in high school track and field, Tina McClain, would go to be Tina Wesson who won the second season of the television series *Survivor: The Australian Outback* in 2001.

CHAPTER 18

941 NORTH MERIDIAN STREET

The 1982 World's Fair in Knoxville, Tennessee, proved to be a success on many levels. We in the Sports Department had produced twenty-one events in six months and created a surplus of $300,000. The entire program paid for itself.

The goal of the program was to secure national as well as international sporting events highlighting "human energy." The marquee events were: Avon Women's 10K Road Race, USA National Track and Field Championships, USA versus USSR Swimming Meet, PGA Cup Matches of International Golf, an NFL Exhibition Game, and an NBA Exhibition Game.

For Stokely-Van Camp, the company that produced canned beans, vegetables, vegetable oils, popcorn, and Gatorade—it was extremely successful. The Stokely Company was founded by five brothers and their mother in nearby Newport, Tennessee. The company, Stokely Brothers, was founded in 1898. Stokely-Van Camp was able to leverage the 1982 World's Fair to showcase their products as well as their deep heritage in East Tennessee.

The Stokely-Van Camp Folklife Festival area included stages and amphitheaters that displayed and presented traditional Appalachian cultural events, music, and arts and crafts. There were designated "Special Theme Weeks" devoted to folk medicine, Native Americans, women's culture, and other topics. One of the featured exhibits was the Smithsonian's acclaimed "Portraits and Dreams," photographs of

Appalachia by Appalachian children. There was also an operational moonshine still on the property.

The Gatorade Sports Hall of Fame was located in the Lifestyle and Technology Center on the seventy-two-acre fair site. It was 3,000 square feet, showcasing some of greatest items of sports memorabilia and sports art. This included Pat Sullivan's Heisman Trophy; Babe Ruth's 1927 foot locker, bat, and glove; Mark Spitz's starting block from the 1972 Munich Olympics; John Naber's Olympic swimming medals; Ralph Boston's long jump collection of gold, silver, and bronze Olympic medals from Rome, Tokyo, and Mexico City; Steve Prefontaine's Oregon track uniform; Major League Baseball collection of World Series Championship rings; NFL collection of Super Bowl rings; USA flag from 1980 gold medal "Miracle on Ice" hockey team; and the art of renown sculptor, Joe Brown, with the sports art of Peter Max and Leroy Neiman.

When the World's Fair ended on October 31, 1982, I stayed employed for about another month and a half. I took the opportunity to return John Naber's Olympic medals personally to him in Pasadena, California. This also provided me the opportunity to meet with the organizers of the Los Angeles Olympics, scheduled for the summer of 1984.

Several former employees of the World's Fair had already relocated to Los Angeles to work with the Los Angeles Olympic Organizing Committee (LAOOC) as consultants or in full-time roles.

One of them was Ed Litrenta. I contacted Ed and asked him to arrange an interview for me with the LAOOC. While he was working on scheduling an interview with the appropriate human resource person, I drove to Los Angeles with John Naber's medals with the goal of interviewing for a position or at least an introduction to someone in human resources. Ed Litrenta confirmed that he had spoken to an individual in human resources, and they would meet with me at the LAOOC headquarters office building on the UCLA campus.

I arrived in Los Angeles and traveled to Pasadena to deliver John Naber his Olympic medals. When John Naber lent us his medals, he had a request that they'd be insured individually and as a group.

We settled on insurance that covered them individually. What John didn't know was that when the Gatorade Sports Hall of Fame was dismantled and items returned, I couldn't locate any of his medals. After a few days of panic, I located them on the floor in the back of a walk-in safe at the headquarters building that everyone had access to and was never locked. It was then that I decided to return the medals personally, taking no chances of them being misplaced or lost in shipping.

After a cordial meeting with John, I departed for Westwood, California, and my meeting with the LAOOC representative. I arrived at the prescheduled time before noon at their headquarters. It was a newly constructed building with a small sign outside, stating "Los Angeles Olympic Organizing Committee." I entered the lobby and notified the attendant that I had an appointment with Human Services. After numerous calls to the HR department, it was determined that no one in the department was there and obviously no appointment or interview was scheduled.

I called Ed Litrenta. He said the LAOOC was a mess. They were poorly organized, and he confirmed a meeting had been scheduled. This was a Friday, and I decided to enjoy lunch in Westwood before departing on my return drive to Knoxville.

After the World's Fair, I determined there were limited opportunities in Knoxville and that I would have to search for employment elsewhere. I started with a plan to contact all the World's Fair sponsors as well as the sports organizations I'd come to have relationships with throughout the fair. One of these was Stokely-Van Camp whom I had helped with the coordination of their Gatorade Sports Hall of Fame.

After numerous "rejection" and "no positions available" letters, I was contacted by a human resources from Stokely-Van Camp. Now, initially, I thought it was a "courtesy interview" for the assistance I had provided on their Gatorade Sports Hall of Fame. Either way, I was excited and was going to be well prepared for the interview and possible employment with Stokely-Van Camp at their headquarters in Indianapolis, Indiana, at 941 North Meridian Street.

It was a cold day in February of 1983 when I visited Stokely-Van Camp in Indianapolis. It was snowing when I arrived at 941 North Meridian Street. I entered the lobby and was greeted by a receptionist who confirmed my meeting with Robert Calvin, Vice President of US Grocery Products Group. As I waited in the lobby, I noticed the various NASCAR trophies showcased along with photos of driver Bobby Allison and CEO William B. Stokely in Victory Lane at Daytona in 1982. The Gatorade 88 race car was the center of the Gatorade Sports Hall of Fame exhibit in Knoxville at the 1982 World's Fair.

Robert Calvin was a very personable and charming individual who had a deep history in sales at Stokely-Van Camp within their broker organization. We met for an hour, and he outlined my schedule of interviews for the day.

The list of interviews included individuals from both marketing and sales in addition to institutional sales, all within the US Grocery Products Group. They included Scott Dissinger, Mike Yetter, Kent Miller, and Doug Stein—who were really great people that laid the groundwork and relationships that I would later cultivate in my time at Stokely-Van Camp and at the Quaker Oats Company.

Robert Calvin met with me again at the end of the meetings. He explained the challenges with Gatorade and the variety of proposals they'd receive daily and the limited funding available. It sounded familiar and in common with my experience at the World's Fair. He said, "Honestly, we have no idea the cost, worth, or value of these proposals. You've had the experience in evaluating proposals as well as the cost in producing events. You'd be an asset to this organization."

I was flattered and excited that this could lead to a new job.

In March, I was extended an offer and an opportunity to work at Stokely-Van Camp. I accepted the offer and relocated to Indianapolis, Indiana, with the title of Director of Promotional Development—Gatorade. My housing costs were covered in my offer, and I took up residency at the Hyatt Regency while I searched for permanent housing. After one month at the Hyatt Regency, I notified Human Resources that I could lower their cost of my housing by moving into the Indianapolis Athletic Club, which I did. It was about one-third of the monthly rate of the Hyatt Regency. The only caveat was that I had to vacate my room over the Memorial Day weekend. All of the rooms were reserved for the Indianapolis 500 Race weekend.

Working at Stokely-Van Camp was great! I loved the people, the challenges, and it was my first introduction to corporate America. Sure, there were the politics, budgets, egos, but everyone on the Gatorade brand worked as a team. I found out later that many people thought I got the job because I graduated from the University of Tennessee of which William B. Stokely was an alumnus and that I knew William B. Stokely. I did graduate with my master's degree from the University of Tennessee, but I had only met Mr. Stokely once during the World's Fair.

I was a valued resource and loved going to work each day. I was asked my opinion on a variety of proposals, contracts, and promotions. I was eager to learn the current involvement of Gatorade and its relationships within the sports community. I studied and reviewed all their contracts and their public relations campaigns. I became familiar with their marketing budgets and the extent of their spending.

In February of 1982, Bobby Allison won the Daytona 500 behind the wheel of the Gatorade 88 Race Car, establishing a strong presence in NASCAR, and in June of 1982, Gatorade had signed a three-year contract with the PGA Tour.

Gatorade had a licensing agreement with the NFL, provided cups, coolers, and powdered product to numerous running events and, along with the Indianapolis Sports Corporation, sponsored the National Sports Festival in Indianapolis. They were also exploring relationships within the athletic training profession and Major League Baseball with Gene Gieselmann, Head Athletic Trainer with the St. Louis Cardinals. Stokely-Van Camp also manufactured Gatorlode 280, a carbo-loading drink with 280 calories targeting distance runners. Stu Mittleman, the ultradistance running champion, had a relationship with the brand. I was arriving at Stokely-Van Camp at 941 North Meridian at a time the Gatorade brand was experiencing growth in the marketplace and presence in the sports community.

The nightmare of Stokely's consumer launch in forty-six-ounce cans is widely known. The salt content was so high that it ate through the cans on the shelves. Then they switched to a thirty-two-ounce glass bottle, but this prohibited sports team usage because of the likelihood of breakage. A powdered product was developed for sports team use with the knowledge of water to powder mixing and to taste. It would be a challenge.

After the launch of the orange flavor, fruit punch eventually found its way to the powdered form and in liquid to the consumer. Initially, the fruit punch flavor contained red dye #9, a dye that stained players uniforms as well as synthetic playing surfaces. The trainers as well as the equipment managers said they couldn't get the red stain out from the uniforms when they were laundered. The fruit punch flavor when spilled on a synthetic surface turned black and couldn't be removed.

I arrived twenty-six years after the group from the University of Florida, who developed Gatorade, came through those same doors and created the Gatorade Trust that paid them five cents a gallon royalty on all product sold. There was only one flavor, the original lemon-lime. Stokely later launched an orange flavor. My career with Gatorade had been initiated through my association with the Gatorade Sports Hall of Fame at the 1982 World's Fair, and now my career with Gatorade had begun as I arrived at 941 North Meridian Street.

CHAPTER 19

GUARDIANS AND GATEKEEPERS

There were numerous times and occasions when situations in my life proved to be valuable learning experiences. Experiences that would outline not only how I handled my approach in relationships but also how I would negotiate deals, concepts that they don't teach you in business school, situations that involve intuition and "street smarts."

I was smart enough to know that "I wasn't the smartest guy in the room." I could learn from anyone and everyone who had different areas of expertise as well as different experiences in life. I became a good listener, initially because I was shy and didn't want to draw attention to myself but honestly because I lacked self-confidence. That would change.

I was introduced to the athletic training community organizations by John LeGear, a communications professional who had already been working with Stokely-Van Camp. The first athletic trainer employed as a consultant by SVC was Gene Geiselmann. He was the athletic trainer for the World Champion St. Louis Cardinals baseball team. He was providing insight as well as expertise regarding, PBATS., the Professional Baseball Athletic Trainers Society.

Gene Geiselmann was absolutely the best. His introduction to PBATS enabled Gatorade to acquire exposure in the dugouts of Major League Baseball. It was no coincidence that our Gatorade coolers were very prominent in the playoffs and World Series games of the St. Louis Cardinals. Gene would strategically place coolers where he knew the television cameras would be sure to focus on them. He would say, "I knew Whitey would be in the top corner of the dugout, so I placed a Gatorade cooler there where he could lean on it." Whitey was Whitey Herzog, the manager of the St. Louis Cardinals from 1980–1990.

Gene also introduced me to the marketing department of the St. Louis Cardinals, and I executed a marketing plan that included signage, tickets, a game day promotion, and most importantly, placement of Gatorade cups and coolers in the dugouts. This also helped Gene and his relationship with his front office, a win-win situation.

As I was baptized into the organization, I listened to what their goals were as a group, and with John LeGear, we developed programs to implement their strategies as an organization. I asked the obvious questions, John LeGear would develop and execute the programs, and Gatorade would provide the funding. Some of the programs included a PBATS newsletter, personal directory, a PBATS advisory board, and educational programs for the minor league trainers. I later did an overall sponsorship with Major League Baseball that satisfied their need for funding the exposure the teams were giving us. It also kept the league in the Gatorade/PBATS relationship.

MLB was always fearful that the baseball trainers were going to unionize. These relationships kept the communication highways open and without any surprises. The MLB trainers, i.e., PBATS, would also be our eyes and ears regarding any new or competing products entering the marketplace as well as a resource for when Gatorade wanted to expand our product offerings.

In the NFL, the National Football League, Gatorade had a promotional rights agreement negotiated in September of 1984 that was for five years. The term of the NFL contract was from April 1, 1985, through March 31, 1990. This contract was negotiated prior to me joining the Quaker Oats Company. I had no input in the negotiations, and the contract was negotiated by Robert E. Calvin, former VP of Sales at Stokely-Van Camp. Bob was a holdover from SVC and was my direct supervisor when I joined Gatorade in Chicago in 1984.

Bob was director of sports marketing, and I was director of sports development. In the hierarchy of the Quaker Oats Company guidelines, directors didn't report to directors. When I negotiated the terms of my employment before joining the Quaker Oats Company, we agreed on the title of "director," a base salary of $55,000, a golf club membership in my name, four weeks of vacation, moving expenses, a housing allowance for three months, and closing costs on the purchase of a home. The only item on my request list that Quaker didn't grant me was a company car.

I was so excited to join the Quaker Oats Company to leverage and develop my skillset as a negotiator and engage in marketing, advertising, and public relations with one of the largest food companies in the United States with products and offices around the world. The "jewel" of the portfolio of the Quaker Oats Company was Gatorade. At this point in history, that had not been defined. I also learned that a corporation can elect to change or modify its rules when necessary. The first one was "a director could report to another director." I would later become acquainted with changes with my golf club membership and the championship rings gifted to me by Michael Jordan.

The NFL agreement made no mention of the athletic trainers that were employed by each team. The contract did mention supplying cups, coolers, and product to the member teams and that the NFL would use "best efforts" to insure that NFL Member Clubs would continue to use the cups, coolers, and product. Sounded good, but there was no guarantee that they had to use our product or the cups and coolers. The agreement was more an advertising and media package that gave Gatorade the designation of "supplier to the NFL."

The National Football League granted the Quaker Oats Company a promotional rights agreement for Gatorade but had no idea how or who would execute getting the product on the field. When asked, their response was, "We assume you'll use the trainers as we don't have a designated employee to execute that." Hard to believe that I knew the NFL trainers were the "gatekeepers and guardians of kingdom" and the NFL didn't. Advantage Bill Schmidt.

The NFL trainers were loosely organized as the National Football League Athletic Trainers Society (NFLATS) in the mid and late 1960s. A limited number of them attended the National Athletic Trainers Association (NATA) Conventions each year. The NATA was the overall governing body for all athletic trainers regardless of their sports affiliation or organization. Its primary goal was to provide certification for membership as well as continual education programs and symposiums.

In 1982, this NFLATS group reorganized from under the NFL and renamed themselves the Professional Football Athletic Trainers Society (PFATS). They elected Jerry Rhea, the Atlanta Falcon Head athletic trainer, as its first president and held their own meetings in concert with the NATA National Conventions. It was also mandatory that all PFATS members attended. They now were organized and set out to establish their mission and purpose in the profession of athletic training.

My first meeting with a few of the PFATS members was in Los Angeles at the Rams facility. John LeGear introduced me, and I outlined the new Gatorade NFL agreement and how excited I was to be working not only with the NFL but also with PFATS. We had no formal agreement or sponsorship of PFATS at that time. John LeGear was my conduit to the professional training profession, and I hired the agency that employed him to help establish and manage these relationships.

In 1991, he started his own communications company, Timothy Communications, and we employed him directly to manage our account. We pulled resources to first sponsor PFATS, then provide elements like PBATS with a newsletter, personal directory, and an advisory board. The first initial sponsorship was less than $40,000. A small price to insure that Gatorade got to the NFL sidelines and displayed in the appropriate manner.

PFATS proved to be our most valued partnership alongside the NFL who was delivering exceptional television ratings, and our in-game exposure continued to grow. The NFL season schedule was out of our seasonal television advertising campaign, but we expanded our NFL team marketing sponsorships and increased our PFATS funding. I later negotiated a $1,000,000 contract with PFATS over a seven-year period with their president at the time, Dean Kleinschmidt, head athletic trainer of the New Orleans Saints. I liked the sound of a "million-dollar deal," and so did the PFATS membership.

When coaches get fired in the NFL, usually, the entire training staff is also let go. The new coaches hire a new training staff, and the old staff is sent packing, no severance package or exit monies.

PFATS decided to use the Gatorade money to fund their own severance program. They developed a formula where each athletic trainer had a certain share of these funds, and upon being fired or retiring, they would be "paid out" with a check in hand based on years in the NFL and as a member of PFATS. Those trainers that were fired or retired were so gracious and thankful for our support during their transitional period.

The National Basketball Trainers Association was probably the first professional sports association of trainers organized in 1971 at the NATA Convention. Joe O'Toole, head athletic trainer for the Atlanta Hawks, was elected Chairman in 1974. There were seventeen NBA teams, and all of them had athletic trainers present at their meetings during the National Athletic Trainers Association Conventions. Today, there are thirty NBA teams, and the NBTA is now known as the National Basketball Athletic Trainers Association (NBATA).

When I first met with NBATA, the NBA had just survived a widely known period of drug use by their players, and they had little or no television ratings. They had just hired a new NBA Commissioner, David Stern, an attorney who had been the NBA's general counsel.

I had little knowledge of the NBA and honestly had never watched a game in person or on television. In fact, it was difficult to find a television broadcast of NBA games. Many of the broadcasts were tape delayed, and very few were live.

When I first met with NBA Commissioner David Stern in 1985, there were only four NBA sponsors, American Airlines, Schick Razors, Spalding, and Gatorade. In that initial meeting, David Stern said he was going to grow the NBA, and he could only do it with our help.

The NBA did grow from seventeen to thirty teams. Sponsors grew to over a hundred, and where that first meeting was in one room, the Annual NBA League and Marketing meetings would require a resort with over 1,200 hotel rooms with additional meeting and breakout rooms to accommodate all NBA team front office staff and marketing partners who attended.

David Stern did usher in real growth, and he was also helped by the renewal of the Boston Celtics-Los Angeles Lakers rivalry with Larry Bird and Magic Johnson. They were later joined by a young junior from the University of North Carolina, Michael Jordan, who had just led the US Men's Olympic Basketball Team to a gold medal at the 1984 Olympics in Los Angeles. Stern also had CBS as a broadcast partner and parlayed media broadcast rights to sponsors delivering exclusivity in a variety of categories.

Joe O'Toole along with fellow founding members of NBATA, Ron Culp, head athletic trainer of the Portland Trailblazers, and David Craig of the Indiana Pacers helped shepherd me along with John LeGear through those early challenging times. The "field of play," the basketball court, proved to be crowded, and the ideas that NBATA provided us gave us additional exposure as television broadcasts and audiences grew. In return, like PBATS and PFATS, we provided NBATA with funding, personal directories, newsletters, advisory boards, and symposiums.

There were a few competitors in our category that had arrangements with a few team trainers that did provide courtside exposure. "Sqwincher" and Pripps Plus were two of them. These "arrangements" went away for the betterment of NBATA Gatorade relationship.

Like the NFL, the NBA had no idea of how important the trainers were and how they controlled the "field of play," the courtside area.

There were several instances where the trainers provided us an exposure opportunity, and later, the team would sell it back to us as a sponsorship element or the league would prohibit us from doing it.

The trainers had a need for ice packs near the court if a player had a cramp, sprain, or minor injury. We procured a soft crushable cooler about gallon size that was orange with the Gatorade logo prominently displayed. The cooler had to be soft as not to create an injury if a player ran into it. In addition, the trainer would carry the cooler on to the court and position it beneath their seat, easily noticeable during the television broadcast.

Gatorade coolers, cups, and squeeze bottles gained NBA presence at courtside through a sponsorship agreement with the individual teams. As we renegotiated team deals, some teams packaged the Gatorade soft crushable coolers that were the trainers' idea and provided free back to us as a line item element for $10,000.

As the NBA grew in popularity, NBA Properties, the marketing department of the NBA, took over all courtside rights for playoff and championship games. Our NBA contract would provide us with visibility for coolers, cups, and squeeze bottles, but the NBA would use some of the elements we developed for their own advertising and visibility. This would include towels and seat back covers.

The National Hockey League had their athletic trainers as well. We had a growing Gatorade business in Canada, and our Canadian sports marketing group there had to have visibility at their national sport, hockey. I took the lead role, along with John LeGear, to establish a relationship as well as a formal agreement similar to those we created with the other professional sports athletic trainers.

The NHL trainers had a unique relationship with their equipment managers. Gatorade hosted a meet and greet hospitality function with an open bar and heavy hors d'oeuvres. Yves Lafortune, the Gatorade Business Manager for Canada, said, "No one has paid any attention to these groups and be prepared for a big bar and food bill." He was right, but we gained their trust, and they organized as the Professional Hockey Athletic Trainers Society, PHATS, and the Society of Professional Hockey Equipment Managers, SPHEM.

The National Athletic Trainers Association (NATA), headquartered in Dallas, Texas, is an association that provides certification and support to the athletic training profession. Its membership includes all the professional sports athletic trainers, college athletic trainers, high school athletic trainers, health rehabilitation service providers, and physical therapists.

My first introduction to the NATA was through John LeGear. I, along with John, met with their board of directors at a NATA National Convention. The NATA President at that time was Otho Davis. He was also the Head Athletic Trainer for the NFL Philadelphia Eagles. Otho was very familiar with the Gatorade sponsorship of the Professional Football Athletic Trainers Society (PFATS), and I was looking for synergies with the entire athletic training profession. Their association numbered about 8,000 members.

With the strategy I developed, "Own the Field of Play," I knew who the gatekeepers were, the athletic trainers. They were the guardians of the sidelines, dugouts, courtsides, and every site of all sports that were contested. As an athlete myself, I knew how important their role was in managing the health care of these sport athletes and sports enthusiasts.

Having secured visibility in the professional sports stadiums and arenas in the United States, I turned my focus on the college and university segment. I knew that the NATA couldn't dictate what products their members should use, but I did know that building a relationship would build a bridge, and building a bridge would ultimately lead to contracted agreement. The majority of the NATA members were college and university athletic trainers, and they all purchased products for their profession. I just needed to get an audience and educate them on the health benefits of Gatorade and the financial benefits of being associated with the brand.

I later negotiated a contract to be the "First Corporate Sponsor of the NATA." We supplied them with funding, and they provided us a forum to exhibit, educate, influence, and sell Gatorade and products developed by Gatorade. These gatekeepers were "key influences" in their profession, and our relationship with them was expanding at all levels.

We leveraged the NATA relationship and my personal one with Otho Davis to host a luncheon for over 200 trainers from a hundred colleges and universities. This was the forum I needed and the endorsement I needed from the NATA moving forward.

I knew that the college and university sponsorships would have to be implemented over time because of budgetary constraints. I'd target the high-profile colleges and universities that were the most successful and had a history of championships and television exposure. This was clearly the sports of football and basketball as was defined in my "targeted sports" strategy.

I would use the National Coaches poll as well as the Associated Press polls of the top twenty-five teams in each football and basketball and then contact them directly to first establish a relationship, visit the campus and reach a contracted agreement. I also wanted the athletic trainers of each institution to be our conduit to initiate the communication.

At this hosted luncheon, I addressed the group and explained to them in brief detail my goal for Gatorade to sponsor college and athletic programs around the country. I also explained this would be for strategically targeted programs. I also explained the relationships and commitment we'd made to the athletic training profession. I mentioned that Gatorade was going to be around for a long time, "and although coaches and athletes move on, our commitment to you and your profession will be strong and continue to grow."

I left time to have a question and answer period after my comments. After a few logistical questions regarding coolers, cups, and product, without mentioning the financials, I noticed the hand raised by a gentleman of whom his reputation I was aware. It was Spanky Stephens, head athletic trainer for the University of Texas Longhorns. Spanky, known for not mixing words, asked, "What's in it for us?" He was spot on, but I wasn't about to pay any athletic trainer to endorse Gatorade. There were a few trainers who received funding by representing a brand or product. I didn't want to go down that road. I focused on how Gatorade could help them with their athletic programs and individually with community and personal causes.

I met with Spanky Stephens after the meeting. It didn't hurt that he viewed as me as an adopted Texan, having competed at the University of North Texas. The University of Texas was high on my list of "must have" football programs. They also hosted many high school camps and events on their campus in Austin, Texas, another reason for having them in our program. I reached a contract with DeLoss Dodds, the athletic director at the University of Texas, and positioned Spanky Stephens as a key reason for our sponsorship. I'm sure to DeLoss it was all about the money. DeLoss was the former head track and field coach at Kansas State University, and we had an relationship when I competed, and now we had one of a business nature.

DeLoss Dodds went on to be one of the most successful athletic directors in collegiate history winning nineteen National Championships and 287 conference titles. Spanky Stephens continues to be one of the most respected athletic trainers in the United States and serves as the executive director of the Texas State Athletic Trainers Association. He's a valued friend, and we've shared many memories, laughs, and a few rounds of golf. I love the man! He's like my brother.

Another athletic trainer, Tim Kerin, the program and convention committee head for the NATA, helped integrate Gatorade into all the facets of their organization. Overnight, we had great exhibit locations and presence at their national convention and their district meetings. Tim was also a fellow Western Pennsylvania guy and the head athletic trainer at the University of Tennessee, Knoxville, Tennessee.

I was completing my graduate degree and still competing when I met Tim Kerin. He opened his training room for any needs or injuries I had or treatment I needed. He was also an athletic trainer for the 1980 US Olympic Team. A great athletic trainer, an exceptional guy, and a dear friend. After his sudden death in 1992, I initiated the Tim Kerin Award for Excellence in 1994. The award is presented annually at the NATA Convention to the athletic trainer who bests embodies Tim's finest qualities of service, dedication, and integrity. Gatorade also made a donation to have the University of Tennessee's Athletic Training Room to be named the Tim Kerin Training Room.

With the many opportunities and events that Gatorade sponsored, I was able to invite numerous athletic trainers as our guests to: Super Bowls, Indianapolis 500 Races, MLB World Series, the

Daytona 500, and golf outings. These invitations were a "thank you" for their support.

The athletic training profession and the individuals I have met and have relationships with are the most caring individuals on the planet. They are health care professionals, and I'm fortunate to have been able to helped further their mission and grow their organization while I was at Gatorade. The National Trainers Association (NATA) membership is now over 43,000 members.

I was honored by being elected as an honorary member of the NATA, the Professional Football Athletic Trainers Society (PFATS), the National Basketball Athletic Trainers Association (NBATA), and the Professional Baseball Athletic Trainers Society (PBATS). It was truly a labor of love providing them with resources through Gatorade while personally building lifelong relationships.

From the time the first athletic trainer touched Gatorade—Brady Greathouse at the University of Florida in its development in the mid-1960s through the 1990s—it wouldn't be what it is today without the athletic training profession. I'm extremely proud of what I built and the relationships I established.

After all, it's all about relationships and understanding who are the guardians and gatekeepers.

CHAPTER 20

LOS ANGELES
"RINGS" SUCCESS

In the history of staging an Olympic Games, financial costs have escalated. The kidnapping and murder of the Israeli athletes during the Munich Olympics in 1972 dramatically changed the Olympic Games forever. Aside from venue construction, security planning and implementation of security protocol is the number one concern of any city and country who bids on hosting an Olympic Games.

Moreover, those countries and cities that have hosted an Olympic Games have seen huge losses and debt. This debt was guaranteed to be paid by the host nation and/or the local government as set out in the contract with the International Olympic Committee (IOC) by the host nation. In addition, the planned use of the facilities and venues constructed for staging the Olympics normally don't materialize and lay vacant and unused in most cases after the Olympics are over.

The Olympics Games have not been staged without controversy, involving politics, financial debt, terrorism, world wars, boycotts, and more recently, a worldwide pandemic. The modern-day Olympics and the International Olympic Committee (IOC) were founded by Baron de Coubertin in Paris in 1894. The first modern Olympics were held in Athens, Greece, in 1896. Fourteen nations and 242 athletes participated, all male. The ancient Olympic Games can be traced back to 776 BCE and were staged as competitions between soldiers, armies, cities, and nation states. Today's modern

Olympics have hosted over 200 countries in as many as thirty-three sports for both men and women.

The Los Angeles Olympics would be no exception in a variety of ways. The bidding process for Los Angeles started in 1977. The Southern California Committee for the Olympic Games (SCCOG) was formed in 1939 for the purpose of returning the games to Los Angeles. The city of Los Angeles had previously unsuccessfully bid to host the 1976 and 1980 Summer Olympics. They were beat out by Montreal for 1976 and Moscow for 1980. The bidding process is accompanied by the endorsement of the National Olympic Committee. In this case, it was the United States Olympic Committee (USOC).

Before the final selection process was complete, the only other bidder to host the 1984 Summer Olympics, Tehran, Iran, withdrew. They cited civil unrest as their reason for withdrawing. It then fell to the United States as the *only* country bidding to host the Games. The USOC had to decide between New York and Los Angeles as the host city. The IOC had no other options or bidders.

The USOC decided on Los Angeles. The only caveat was that the US Government and the USOC would not sign the agreement to guarantee any and all liabilities for the organization, presentation, and conduct of the games. Based on the IOC and the Olympic Charter, someone had to be held liable for debt, expenses, and all aspects of hosting and staging an Olympic Games. It fell to the City of Los Angeles to accept that responsibility. They declined.

So for the first time in Olympic history, the Olympic Games were awarded to a completely privately financed organization. A group of southern California businessmen organized as the Los Angeles Olympic Organizing Committee (LAOOC) that prepared to take on this monumental endeavor. They did negotiate terms where if the LAOOC were to realize a profit, 40 percent would go to the USOC, 40 percent would stay in Los Angeles, Southern California, and 20 percent going to the National Sports governing bodies in the United States. The IOC agreed on their assumption that the LAOOC would lose money like each previous Olympic Games Host

Committee. Wow, were they every wrong and to the benefit of youth sports in the Los Angeles community.

My trip to Pasadena, California, at the end of the 1982 World's Fair was twofold. I wanted to personally return the Olympic medals that John Naber loaned to Gatorade for display at the Gatorade Sports Hall of Fame and interview for a position with the LAOOC at their headquarters in Westwood, California. Ed Litrenta, my former roommate and good friend from the World's Fair, had already secured a job in human resources at the LAOOC. He said the interview had been scheduled, but when I showed up on that Friday afternoon, there was no one in human services scheduled to interview me. Friday afternoon, the week before Thanksgiving, and everyone was gone for the weekend. I left and began my long drive back to Knoxville, Tennessee.

When I returned to Knoxville, I began my job search. I knew the University Athletic Department was probably the only obvious employer for me in Knoxville. The reality sunk in that if I wanted to continue my career in sports marketing, I'd have to relocate. My relationship that I built with Stokely-Van Camp via the Gatorade Sports Hall of Fame at the 1982 World's Fair seemed the obvious place to start. I had established a relationship with some of their executives and proceeded to contact them. My inquiries resulted in an interview in Indianapolis, Indiana, at their corporate headquarters. Two weeks later, in March, I was relocating to Indianapolis as Manager of Sports Development for Gatorade.

About the second week in June of 1983, I received a telephone call from a person in human services from the LAOOC. They said that they wanted to hire me, but they couldn't define the position. They did say that likely, it would be in the sports department. I listened to what they had to say. They didn't discuss salary but vaguely described that the LAOOC was implementing the operational phase of the Olympics and needed experienced candidates like me.

The conversation concluded with me thanking them for their interest in me as well as the opportunity. I also expressed to them that I was flattered but was extremely excited with my current position at Gatorade and the challenges before me.

During the July Fourth weekend, Indianapolis is truly the "All-American City," and it had the greatest of celebrations—a great parade and an incredible fireworks display fired from atop of one of the bank buildings downtown. I was excited about being there and was looking for a home north of the city. I had decided on a town-house that was the model for the development. It, of course, had all the upgrades, and I was working with a realtor to finalize my offer and submit it to the developer.

The second week of July, I received another call from the LAOOC. This time, it was an individual by the name of John Svenson who identified himself as Vice President of Sports at the Los Angeles Olympic Organizing Committee. He had my undivided attention. He proceeded to say that they had evolved to the operational phase and needed my expertise moving forward. He said the position would be that of an associate vice president of sports in the Sports Department. He said that there were twenty-three sports that were on the Olympic calendar for Los Angeles, but he couldn't specify what sports would be assigned to me.

My excitement and interest were there, but I would be cautious with my response and my questions. He elaborated on the current structure but still couldn't define my role or the sports I would be managing. In my current position at Gatorade, I was building a brand and operating in a position that would last beyond the time frame of the 1984 Olympics and well into the future. I explained to him that I was extremely happy at Stokely-Van Camp and couldn't leave for Los Angeles without some clarification on my role and responsibilities. He said, "I'll call you back in a couple of days." I thanked him for the call.

Three days later, he called me back. He said, "I can definitely assign you management over track and field (athletics) and boxing." Now these two sports made up the "Big Five." Also in the top five for television viewership and popularity were gymnastics, swimming, and basketball.

I thought, *Holy shit, where do I sign?* I had to go. It was not a question of loyalty to Gatorade, who just hired me. It was about an opportunity to work at the 1984 Los Angeles Olympics and be responsible for a sport that I had competed in the Munich Olympics in 1972. It was a once-in-a-lifetime opportunity.

I met with the president of Stokely-Van Camp, Robert Rice, and informed him of my decision and to apply for a "leave of absence." My intentions were to return to my position after the conclusion of the games in August 1984. I said I didn't want to leave, but I had to go.

He said, "Then don't go." Also, there was no guarantee that Stokely-Van Camp wouldn't be acquired. Numerous companies were actively bidding to acquire it.

On July 27, 1983, I received the following Western Union Mailgram:

> Dear Mr. Schmidt:
>
> We are pleased that you have accepted our offer of employment for the position of associate vice president in the sports department reporting to Chuck Cale. Your initial salary will be $55,000. The LAOOC will also provide a relocation allowance.
>
> You are scheduled to attend an orientation meeting on Monday, August 15th, 1983, at 900 a.m. in Room 104.
>
> Sincerely,
> Stella Cendejas
> Human Resources Department
> Los Angeles Olympic Organizing Committee

My decision was real, and so was my future for the next year.

I drove to Los Angeles about a week before my scheduled orientation meeting, arriving August 8 in Huntington Beach, California. I would be sharing an apartment with Ed Litrenta. The drive to the LAOOC Headquarters in Westwood, California, would be one to one and a half hours. It would depend on what time you departed.

The drive time of two to three hours each day was too excruciating. After a month, we located an apartment on Venice Boulevard in Venice, California. It was a twenty-minute drive to Westwood and later a ten-minute drive when the LAOOC headquarters relocated to the Marina Center, just four miles away.

I arrived at the orientation meeting early, dressed in a coat and tie, per Ed Litrenta's suggestion. There were about twenty-five people in attendance. Priscilla Florence, personnel director for the LAOOC, was introduced by Stella Cendejas, and she welcomed us to the LAOOC. She stressed the significance of all of us joining the staff and the current change from a planning stage to that of an operational stage. We also knew what "number hire" we were at the LAOOC. The lower the number, the earlier you were hired. I really don't remember what my "hire number" was. It seemed meaningless when, to me, you were working twelve-to-sixteen-hour days.

Priscilla Florence was about twenty minutes into her orientation when Peter V. Uebberoth, President of the LAOOC, entered the room. I had done my research on Peter and had listened to an interview he had done about a year earlier. He was charismatic, and after listening to his interview, he inspired me to want to work at the 1984 Los Angeles Olympics. I was working at the 1982 World's Fair at the time of that interview.

Now I've been blessed with great intuition, and my first impression of individuals has almost never failed me. When Peter Uebberoth entered that room, I sensed a man that was not only in charge but a man that was in control. Many of those reporting on Peter's style called him "ruthless and shy." I found him to have a mystique about him. He acknowledged me in the room as an Olympian and from the Knoxville World's Fair. My relationship with him during my time at the LAOOC was better than most.

Peter would always find a way to test you. He would test your knowledge as well as your loyalty to him and the LAOOC. There were many who would ask, "Have you taken Peter's test yet?" I later learned through Ed Litrenta as well as from current staffers that you would be called into a room with others to take "Peter's test." It was a series of questions about the Olympic movement, the origin of the

Olympic rings, the LAOOC, the IOC, the USOC, and how Los Angles was awarded the Olympic Bid. It was also rumored that if you failed "the test," you'd be let go from the LAOOC.

Firing seemed to be a bit severe, but in the long-term, it was Peter's goal that if you were going to work at an Olympic Games, you should damn sure know something about the Olympic Games and its history, leadership, and organization. I couldn't agree with him more. It seemed asinine to many. My background was different from the average LAOOC employee. After all, I had a little Olympic history myself. By the way, I never heard of anyone failing the test or, for that that matter, being let go.

He would also try to intimidate you, but he also could be very complimentary and gracious. It wasn't uncommon for Peter to call on someone at any function to voice their opinion on any topic that was on top of his mind. That made many people feel uncomfortable. "Oh, I hope he doesn't call on me syndrome." Many felt it was part of Peter's control strategy. I believe it was, and it worked for him. It also challenged individuals. I believe that was also part of his strategy.

Ed Litrenta, who worked in Human Resources at the LAOOC, recommended Ed Keen—who also worked at the 1982 Knoxville World's Fair—be hired for the position of Vice President of Architecture and Construction. I, too, worked with Ed Keen in Knoxville and witnessed his success firsthand.

One day, while walking through the Marina Center, Peter stopped me. He said, "I hear you're high on this Ed Keen guy from Knoxville?"

I replied, "Absolutely. He came in under budget and on time."

He then said, "Would you bet your job on it?" Another intimidation tactic by Peter but also a way for him to measure your commitment.

I said, "Yes, I would." We hired Ed Keen. We also hired three other individuals who had worked at the 1982 World's Fair.

Pete Soukup was hired as Assistant Director of Exposition Park. It was the 133-acre area around the Memorial Coliseum and the Sports Arena. During the actual time of the games, I had overall responsibility for track and field at the coliseum and boxing at the sports arena which were in Exposition Park.

Fred Rankin, former project engineer for Ed Keen in Knoxville, was hired as Construction Manager at the LAOOC and reported to Ed Keen in this new position. John Underwood, former detective sergeant for the Knoxville Police Department and internal control for the World's Fair, was hired as Security Administrator for the LAOOC.

With myself, Ed Litrenta, Ed Keen, Fred Rankin, Pete Soukup, and John Underwood, we were known as the "Knoxville Mafia" inside the LAOOC and as the "Knoxville Connection" outside the walls of the LAOOC. Our experience proved vital to the success of the LA Olympics. Ed Keen had the biggest influence as I believe the construction would never have been completed for the opening of the games by his predecessor.

Another time, about one month before opening ceremonies, Peter stopped me again and asked me for my opinion. He said, "Who do you think should light the Olympic flame?" Historically, each host nation has an iconic athlete from their country to light the flame. It's kept a secret until the day of the event.

I said, without hesitation, "Al Oerter, four-time Olympic gold medalist in the discus throw 1956, 1960, 1964, 1968, and four new Olympic records each time."

Peter replied, "That is a great choice." It made me feel like he or his staff hadn't come up with Al Oerter's name at all.

In the opening ceremonies rehearsals, four athletes rotated in pretending to light the Olympic flame. This was to keep it a secret as to who would actually be lighting it. During one of the rehearsals, Al Oerter pulled his hamstring while ascending the steps to the base of the Olympic Cauldron. I believe up until that happened, Al Oerter was going to light the Olympic flame. He was replaced by Rafer Johnson, Olympic gold medalist in the decathlon in 1960.

At the Olympic Games, there are backup systems to backup systems. For opening ceremonies, the stairs that led to the Olympic Cauldron had a backup hydraulic system to the first hydraulic system. If they both failed, there were twenty-plus weightlifters hidden nearby to perform the task. And if the torch extended to light the trail to circle the Olympic rings and ultimately light the cauldron didn't work, there was a guy with a Bic lighter prepared to make it happen.

As was the case with most officers at the LAOOC, we were sometimes asked to change responsibilities or add some. After the first two months at the LAOOC, I was asked to oversee the Olympic Torch Relay. This was the running of the Olympic Torch through various towns and cities across the United States, culminating in Los Angeles with the opening of the games. The logistical challenge of the event made it challenging, but I was there to manage boxing and track and field.

They later added baseball, Judo, Modern Pentathlon, soccer, weightlifting, and wrestling to my responsibilities. In addition, I had responsibility over all training sites (sixty-one) and procurement of all athletic equipment for all twenty-three Olympic sports. Baseball and tennis were demonstration sports.

My associate vice presidents of sports were John Svenson and Hank Tatarchuk. They each had sports assigned to them, and on occasion, we decided among ourselves how we would divide up the sports as well as the responsibilities. There were commissioners and sometimes co-commissioners assigned to each sport. We managed them through the "Venuization Period," then turned the facility and the management of the sport over to the commissioners and the respective sports managers in May of 1984.

The venue development department was headed by Mike Mitchell, a hired gun who could "get the job done." That was any job. They would assign Mike Mitchell as an attack dog to evaluate a particular department or process. He was exceptionally good at what he did, but he wasn't there to win any popularity contest. I went through all the venue processes as it pertained to the sports I managed. In boxing, Kenneth Shropshire, the sports manager and I got so bored with the process we labeled some rooms at the sports arena with fictitious names to "test the system." We did get one room through the process that had no purpose or real activity scheduled. *We won!*

The venue development review for the memorial coliseum was assisted by the track and field commissioner, H. D. Thoreau. He was a track and field enthusiast and had Olympic experience, having worked at the Squaw Valley Winter Olympics in 1960. He was straightforward in his thoughts and ideas and could be stubborn with his approach and his communication. He had strong convictions about how the track and field competition should be conducted.

On one occasion, as we walked the athletes' route from competition to exiting the field to drug testing, the press interview area, and exiting the stadium, I noticed something that was concerning to me. H. D. had the athletes, after they competed, going into the stands to exit and enter the transition zones. When I asked H. D. about it, he said, "That area of seating will be for Olympic athletes, so it won't be a problem."

I said, "If I were an athlete who just had a poor performance, the last people I'd want to see were other Olympic athletes." Then I said, "The Olympic Games were here in 1932, how did they exit the stadium?"

H. D. said, "Through the tunnel on the field at the end of the stadium, but it's blocked and has television and power cables running through it now and isn't accessible."

I said, "Let's go look at it."

We entered what looked like a cave from inside the bowels of the stadium and walked the tunnel until it abruptly ended. There was a wall and cables were everywhere. The Los Angeles Raiders played their home games at the coliseum, and beyond that wall was an entrance to the field. I knew it was going to cost something to excavate this entry way, but it was the right thing to do, and we did it. I felt this was one moment where my previous Olympic experience had made a difference.

The co-commissioner of track and field and specifically for the men's and women's marathons was Bill Bedford. The marathon would start at the track at Santa Monica College track and finish at the memorial coliseum. This would be the first time the women would be contesting in a marathon in the Olympic Games. For years, it was thought that the distance would be harmful to women. Joan

Benoit, from the USA, won this first women's Olympic Marathon and proved the so-called "experts" wrong.

Santa Monica College was also one of the sixty-one training sites throughout Southern California for the Olympic Games that I was responsible for managing. My first goal was to have adequate amounts of the exact sports equipment necessary at all these facilities. They had been woefully underequipped. I was also responsible for securing the equipment for all twenty-three sports being contested at these Olympic Games, an education in sporting goods manufactures but also a labor of love.

A training site manager for Santa Monica College hadn't been named when I arrived at the LAOOC. I asked, "Who is their track coach?"

The reply, "Tommie Smith."

I said, "Let's don't reinvent the wheel. Tommie Smith is our Santa Monica training site director."

I did get push back. "You can't hire him. Did you know that's the Tommie Smith who raised his gloved fist at the Mexico Olympics and was banned from the Olympic Village in 1968 along with John Carlos?"

"Yes," I said. "He has Olympic experience, and besides, he knows that facility. He's our manager."

Tommie Smith was exceptional. He had a great staff and did an incredible job. This experience at Santa Monica College also made me aware of the fact that everyone at these training sites would never see an Olympic event live and in person. It was at this point I ordered multiple televisions for all the training sites. At the conclusion of the games, I had each site manager gift these television to individuals on their staff whom they deemed to be "outstanding."

On the day of closing ceremonies, I was in the skybox where President Reagan sat when he opened the Games on July 28. It was now August 12, and by all reports, the Games of the XXIII Olympiad had been a success. I was there with my twin brother, Bob, as my guest. Peter had invited a few individuals to join him. It was special and gracious of Peter.

Early in the day, as we sat looking through this bulletproof glass that had been installed for President Reagan's visit, Peter commented to my brother, "You see all that out there? Your brother is responsible for that and the Games' success." An overstatement for sure but most appreciated by me and especially my brother.

My brother knew that Peter Ueberroth was moving on to be Major League Baseball Commissioner after the 1984 Olympics were over. Bob, never having met a "stranger," had conversations all that day with Peter. Years later, Bob said he had one idea that he shared with Peter—Inter League Games. Brother Bob takes credit for that idea, although Peter wasn't commissioner of Major League Baseball when inter-league play was implemented. *Please don't tell Bob!*

The 1984 Los Angeles Olympic Games were the most successful Olympic Games in history, generating a surplus of $225 million. There were over 70,000 staff and volunteers. Peter V. Ueberroth as President and Harry Usher, Executive Vice President and General Manager, led a group that over delivered on an Olympic Games that was privately financed without a dollar of public money and one that no one wanted to host. Quite a legacy.

In my opinion, the 1984 Olympic Games were an overwhelming success due to these four basic reasons:

(1) *The people.*

There were 72,000 staff and volunteers, the largest project in a peace time world. The staff grew from 5 in 1978 to 500 in 1983, 1,500 in the spring of 1984, volunteers added two months before the games to 30,000 and 72,000 one month before the games.

I arrived in August of 1983, and with less than a year before opening ceremonies, all venue contracts and construction hadn't been completed. Ticketing applications and procedures for IOC delegates seating weren't finalized.

What we accomplished in that last year was incredible. It's a tribute to all those who worked at the LAOOC. People decided we are going to make this a success and overcome all the negative media, the Soviet Boycott, and the multitude of problems that everyone was quick to point out. These were dedicated people that gave their time, effort, and overall commitment to its success. In my mind, I viewed that certain factors would contribute to these games being successful. The United States hadn't competed in an Olympic Games in eight years, Montreal 1976. The United States hadn't hosted a Summer Olympics in over fifty years, Los Angeles 1932. Television network broadcasts would plan the longest hours of Olympic coverage in history.

(2) *Corporate America*

ABC Network purchased the television rights for $125 million, a record amount at the time. Major sponsorships in a variety of categories started at $4 million initially and graduated to $7 million and up. Coca-Cola, McDonald's, Anheuser Bush, 7-Eleven—all paid premium dollars for the association with the "Rings of LA." One major US company that was thought to be a "lock" on being a sponsor in the film and photography category was Kodak. They balked at Peter's structured program but later regretted it when Ueberroth sold the rights to Fuji Film of Japan. Companies, also in addition to the sponsorship fees, built venues for the 1984 Olympics. McDonald's built the swimming complex, and 7-Eleven built the velodrome.

(3) *Technology*

There was new hardware never before used as well as new television broadcast techniques. Results and distribution of results were done electronically. Measuring and timing devices were specifically developed to have greater accuracy.

(4) *Luck*

Up until the games, Los Angeles was experiencing the worst smog and cloudy conditions ever. It stayed clear for the entire duration of the games. Bomb scares were a way of daily life, but there were no major incidents. There was a bomb scare on the day of opening ceremonies that delayed the opening by thirty minutes. In practice, never did all the sixty grand pianos roll out from the Peristyle end of the stadium for "Rhapsody in Blue." Day of the opening, they did. One of the "Welcome" balloons on opening ceremonies hit a transformer and blacked out West Los Angeles. It could have ruined opening ceremonies. One of the balloons was found in Maryland. In the practices for the closing ceremonies, the "spaceship," the only time it was lifted off the ground, "folded like a silver taco." At closing ceremonies, it worked.

Peter V Ueberroth was the right man for the job! He was named *Time Magazine's* "Man of Year" in 1984. The LAOOC left a legacy that will forever positively impact youth sports in Southern California and all the individuals who worked with the LAOOC, and the 1984 Los Angeles Olympic Games will be forever changed by what we experienced.

CHAPTER 21

HOW DO YOU CROWN
A CHAMPION?

Gatorade has a long history of being there, and now with a strategy to "own the sidelines," I proactively set out to accomplish just that. It certainly wasn't done by writing checks but through building personal relationships with key influencers and decision-makers. One other key tenet that would be built into our foundation of service, "Overdeliver on what you promise."

Gatorade was invented by a group of scientists at the University of Florida in the mid-1960s and acquired by Stokely-Van Camp in 1967. The product was originally sold only to athletic teams but later was sold through food brokers to grocery stores. The Florida "Gators" football teams had improved their season record year over year while consuming Gatorade in the early trials monitored by the scientists.

Product was sold regionally, and early sales to athletic teams were determined more by who you knew, rather than calling a sales associate to place an order. As popularity grew and the story of the athletic performance of Gatorade grew, various sports teams, athletes, musicians, performers and artists were using the product and confirming the benefits of consuming it.

Hank Stram, the legendary coach of the Kansas City Chiefs, heard about Gatorade from his good friend, Ray Graves, the football coach at the University of Florida. Graves shared with Stram the importance and impact the product had on his team and their performance.

Stram was not a stranger to winning. As a coach, his 1966 Chiefs (11 wins, 2 losses, and 1 tie) played in the First AFL-NFL World Championship Game (today known as Super Bowl I) but lost to the Green Bay Packers 35–10 on January 15, 1967.

The Kansas City Chiefs also appeared in the Fourth AFL-NFL World Championship Game, (later designated as Super Bowl IV), on January 11, 1970. The Chiefs (11–3) defeated the Minnesota Vikings (12–2), 23–7. As the story goes, Coach Stram, unable to procure Gatorade, reached out to one of the food brokers and was able to acquire product by having it diverted from Jacksonville, Florida, which was a retail test market in January of 1970 to his training facility. Hank Stram cited Gatorade as the reason for their win. "We had Gatorade, they didn't."

Years later, Stokely-Van Camp would employ Hank Stram as a Gatorade spokesperson and sponsor numerous events and utilize him for appearances and entertainment purposes. Hank went on to a broadcast career in radio and television after his coaching career ended. He was widely known and respected.

There were two specific events where Stokely-Van Camp utilized Coach Stram. He would be the master of ceremonies at a black-tie social event hosted by SVC in Indianapolis, Indiana, on the evening before the Indianapolis 500. Stokely-Van Camp would have 250 rooms at the Hyatt Regency Hotel and host 500 guests for the evening and the next day's 500 race. Two great events for entertaining key accounts, food brokers, city officials, dignitaries, and special guests.

Another event where Hank Stram's name and appearance was utilized was for a charity golf tournament in the key Gatorade market of Jacksonville, Florida. It was "The Hank Stram/Gatorade Celebrity Golf Classic." It was one of the first events I attended as a Stokely-Van Camp employee. I was there to review the organization, the signage elements, entertainment value, alignment with local authorities and retail leverage of the event. Bottom line, "What were we getting out of the sponsorship and how would I improve it?"

I was extremely impressed with the event, the entertainers who not only played golf but who also performed, the prizes, the signage, and the "goodwill" to the Jacksonville, Florida, community. It was well attended and the community volunteers were extremely active in the organization and the presentation of the tournament. The beneficiary or charity of the event was the Women's Center for Battered Women of Jacksonville, Florida.

In my final analysis, our tournament costs and expenses were too high, and we gave very little, next to nothing to the charity. We'd receive greater exposure if we tied in with a local supermarket chain for a promotion and just wrote a check to a charity of our choice. Great entertainment event? Yes. Did it meet our strategy in the marketplace efficiently and drive sales? Definitely not.

In the irony of all ironies, six months later, I was directed to meet with Coach Hank Stram and let him know that he would no longer be employed as a spokesperson for Stokely-Van Camp. Yes, one of my first official duties at Stokely-Van Camp was to fire Hank Stram.

I liked Hank Stram. He put Gatorade on the sidelines of its first Super Bowl. He was from Gary, Indiana, a town similar to Pittsburgh, a steel town, like where I grew up. As likable as Hank was, he was sometimes his own worst enemy. Stokely-Van Camp executives scrutinized his expense reports, and some of his behavior at the Indianapolis 500 social events were, even at that time, deemed to be "socially offensive."

I met with Hank on numerous occasions before I had to let him go. I explained to him all the examples given to me by both the executives and the accounting department of Stokely-Van Camp. He said, "I was great at the black-tie event. Everyone laughed."

I said, "Not everyone, and most importantly not those that run this company."

As for his expense reporting, he said, "Some of those may be inflated."

I said, "I'm not here to examine those. I am here to explain to you the reason the company has asked me to let you know your time as a spokesperson for Stokely-Van Camp is over."

Hank Stram was the first person I ever had to fire. From that year and every year I worked at Gatorade, I'd send a Christmas gift to him and his wife, Phyllis, in Gary, Indiana. I'd always received back a handwritten note from him, thanking me. He was clearly the coach that put Gatorade on the sidelines of the NFL, and for that, he will always be remembered, acknowledged, and appreciated by me. He was a gentleman, an innovative winning coach, and a colorful football analyst.

Gatorade may have made its first appearance in Super Bowl IV, but the Gatorade Dunk wouldn't occur in a Super Bowl until Super Bowl XXI in Pasadena, California, on January 25, 1987, a tradition that in itself is the celebration of victory and triumph. The Gatorade Dunk has occurred at a variety of sports around the world. It has also been copied or imitated in a number of ways.

On January 30, 2021, at the Reese's Senior Bowl in Mobile, Alabama, Brian Flores was dunked with a Reese's logoed cooler filled with Reese's Peanut Butter Cups individually wrapped. Hundreds of them poured over the coach and were being gathered on the field by the participating football players. Certainly a victorious moment of celebration. I want to congratulate Reese's for the incredible job they did with the "look" at the venue. They owned it, colors all coordinated in their motif throughout all the signage and presentation areas. The Dunk was just their crowning glory, and it added to the event.

In some cases, corporations looked to the coolers and cups as mere signage opportunities. Gatorade was on "the field of play" and was being used. H&R Block acquired signage with cups and coolers at an athletic event, and it seemed "out of place." In addition, the colors they used for the cups and coolers were not very visible.

When Gatorade was a sponsor of the NCAA Basketball Tournament, March Madness, we paid less than $1 million and received a variety of VIP Hospitality elements but no Gatorade cups or coolers. My hope was that we could build on this initial sponsorship and eventually receive cups and cooler placement from inside the organization. It also provided me the opportunity to be aware of Coca-Cola's programs and promotions as I sat in these meetings with a representative from Coke.

At one point, Jim Host, of Host Communications and who managed the marketing rights to the NCAA, said, "We'll let you have orange coolers but without any logos. After all, it's an orange cooler, and everyone knows it's Gatorade."

I said, "Until those Gatorade logos appear on those orange coolers, I don't know what's in them. If you give me the logos and cups, I'll give you and the NCAA more money." Our NCAA sponsorship lasted three years, and we didn't get logoed coolers or cups. For the amount of the sponsorship and the bad ticketed seats we received, we could charter a plane, take fifty guests to Las Vegas for the weekend of the Final Four, and it would be money better spent.

On Sunday, January 4, 1987, I was at my home in Glen Ellyn, Illinois, by myself, to watch the NFC Divisional Playoff Game between the New York Giants and the San Francisco 49ers. Friends and associates had told me about what had been occurring at the end of each Giants game after a win. I had yet to see a Giants victory and the game-ending winning celebration. I eagerly watched as the game was about to conclude with the Giants winning 49–3.

As time was winding down and with under two minutes to play, John Madden, the CBS color analyst, started to diagram on the screen what was about to transpire. He used the on screen illustrator, it was an optic yellow, and he preceded to choreograph "the Gatorade Dunk." I remember saying to myself, "Holy shit, I've died and gone to heaven." You couldn't afford to pay for advertising like this.

The next morning at the Quaker Oats Company headquarters and the offices of Gatorade were all abuzz about, "Did you see the Giants game and the incredible Gatorade Dunk?" We all felt we struck lightning in a bottle. The major thought or question was, "What next? Should we do anything?"

After numerous discussions and a variety of ideas, I was able to "sell" my idea that we do nothing. "Let's let it play out by itself." I was firm on my opinion that if we tried to "create" events or moments around the Gatorade Dunk, it would seem phony and contrived. We did not want to do any promotions or events to leverage this serendipitous celebration by the New York Football Giants. It was the "real thing."

The New York Football Giants had one more game to win if they were to make it to the Super Bowl. They were scheduled to play the Washington Redskins on January 11, 1986. While having lunch with John LaSage, CEO of Burson-Marstellar of Chicago, I said, "At some point, the press and media are going to ask Coach Parcells, 'Have you heard from Gatorade?'" I wanted his response to be a positive one as well as being a gracious one.

John and I kicked around a number of possibilities. I decided to go with his idea of a gift certificate from Brooks Brothers. We decided on a nominal amount of $1,000. We also decided to send one to Harry Carson, the Giants linebacker who was dunking Gatorade over Coach Parcells. John purchased those on Gatorade's behalf and had them delivered to my office that afternoon. If I had to have gone back to Gatorade, explain my intent, I might have had a check from Quaker Oats but not a gift certificate from Brooks Brothers. I just wanted to "get it done." They were beautifully placed in white boxes with a gold band around them.

In the letter that I sent Coach Parcells, I stated, "We realize that due to your year-long 'Gatorade dunking' you have been receiving, your wardrobe has probably taken a beating. The enclosed should help remedy this problem. After all, we do feel somewhat responsible for your cleaning bill."

In the letter to Harry Carson, I made reference to the yellow rain jacket he was wearing as he tried to hide from Coach Parcells. His goal was to sneak up on Parcells and do the Gatorade Dunk in a jacket he borrowed from a security guard. I mentioned in the Harry Carson letter, "I saw your impromptu impersonation of Inspector Clouseau, and I hope the enclosed provides you with the opportunity to purchase a rain jacket that is more fashionable and that fits."

Sure enough, Coach Parcells was asked by a reporter, "Have you heard from Gatorade?"

His response was, "Yes, I heard from the CEO of Gatorade."

The reporter dug deeper, "What did he say?"

"He sent me a gift certificate," Parcells responded.

The reporter quizzed him again, "For how much?"

Parcells smiled and said, "Between $5,000 and $25,000." Mission accomplished.

It would be two weeks before Super Bowl XXI was to be played in Pasadena, California. The hype of the New York Giants versus the Denver Broncos continued to grow as did the anticipation of "Would there be a Gatorade Dunk" if the New York Giants won the game. I was concerned because we didn't have "exclusivity" for the NFL sidelines, and the Denver Broncos used coolers and cups with Orange Crush logos on them.

We sent out new shipments of coolers, cups, and squeeze bottles throughout the season. There was nothing more disturbing for me to see than a Gatorade cooler with half the logo missing. For the Super Bowl, we'd drop ship new coolers, cups, and squeeze bottles to the training sites of the team locations for usually a week of practice before the game.

It was a great time to be working on the Gatorade team. It was also time for my mind to spin and think about everything leading up to the game and planning travel, tickets, lodging, etc. I attended the game. The New York Football Giants beat the Denver Broncos, 39–20. Harry Carson did the Gatorade Dunk on Coach Parcells, and the rest is history.

In some estimates, the exposure at Super Bowl XXI with the Gatorade Dunk was valued around $20 million. The media "experts" opinion, not mine. It was now time for me to think of an "appropriate way" to thank both Coach Parcells and Harry Carson.

I worked out a three-year personal services contract with Coach Parcells that paid him $40,000 a year ($120,000). There was some creative language in the contract regarding appearances, etc., but make no mistake about it, we were paying Parcells for his role in the Gatorade Dunk, and this was our way to "thank him."

With Harry Carson, I signed him to a one-year licensing contract for $25,000. It allowed us to use his likeness on a "How to Execute the Gatorade Dunk" poster that we included in every Gatorade cooler we shipped out.

The Gatorade Dunk became a part of Americana. It was sweeping the country from corporate board rooms, to high school games, and television. Bob Weeks, a NASCAR employee in charge of the Winners Circle at the Daytona 500 race, called me to say he had a unique way of providing additional exposure for us. He said, "I put the Gatorade logos upside down on the coolers so that when the drivers were dunked, the logos read right side up." I thanked Bob for being creative but explained to him that it would be viewed as us orchestrating the event and taking away from the spontaneity of the celebration.

Today, in the United States and around the world, "the crowning of a champion" in all sports culminates with an athlete or coach being showered with a cooler of Gatorade. In some cases, it's another product with a different name on the container, but it all started with the New York Football Giants. In addition, we never paid or endorsed anyone to execute the Gatorade Dunk.

There are few things in the history of sports that become iconic and ceremonial moments. The Gatorade Dunk became that, and it continues to be the "crowning of a champion." I smile every time I see it occur.

It was serendipitous from its inception, and I had the honor to see its growth and realizing, "Life's all about celebrations, and none are more important than in sports at any level."

CHAPTER 22

CAN'T WRITE A CHECK

When the Quaker Oats Company acquired Stokely-Van Camp in 1983, the "crown jewel" of the acquisition was Gatorade. Gatorade sales were at $93 million, and Stokely-Van Camp was purchased for $238 million.

I was still working for Stokely-Van Camp when the acquisition frenzy started. William B. Stokely III and his investment group offered $35 per share. It quickly moved to $50–$52 a share. Pillsbury offered $62 a share, only to be outbid by the Quaker Oats Company at $77 a share. Quaker's CEO, William Smithburg, was heavily criticized for "having overpaid" for Stokely-Van Camp. They would eat those words later, following years of double-digit Gatorade growth.

Phil Marineau, a senior executive at Quaker Oats, was named to transition the Stokely-Van Camp brands into the portfolio of Quaker Oats brands with special attention to Gatorade. Sandy Posa would join his team and assist in personnel and product evaluations. Phil Marineau was then, and is now, an analytical individual and the best marketing person I've ever met.

I remember Phil saying, "I'm not sure what Gatorade is." "Is it a belly wash or does it really work?" Phil, with his analysis of the product, found it was formulated correctly, and it did what it was intended to do. There's been little or no change of the formula throughout the years. Phil Marineau would champion my strategies and game plan as we worked together building the Gatorade brand.

Gatorade had limited sponsorships at the time of the Quaker Oats acquisition, and their biggest investment was in NASCAR with the sponsorship of a race car. Minimal dollars were spent with the PGA, LPGA, and the NFL. Most of their sponsorships were through providing cups, coolers, and powdered product. This would provide them sampling opportunities as well as signage with Gatorade banners. Running events and road races were the key focus that involved product but no funding.

Stokely-Van Camp, with its headquarters in Indianapolis, Indiana, sponsored many hometown events. Indianapolis was also the host city for numerous sporting events through the funding of the Eli Lily Foundation, also located in Indianapolis. Gatorade would provide some funding but mainly just powdered product, cups, coolers, and banners.

Gatorade actively pursued running events at all levels, and the main strategy was to have sampling opportunities and gain some exposure. They sponsored Stu Mittleman, an ultra-marathoner who commonly participated in 50, 100, and even 1,000-mile road races. This was also an opportunity to leverage Gatorlode 280, a product developed solely to support the carbohydrate loading craze in the eighties used by endurance athletes.

There was also a small effort to build relationships with a few athletic trainers. These relationships would later become more formalized and emerge as the cornerstone of Gatorade's growth and exposure. John LeGear, a public relations specialist, was employed by Stokely-Van Camp to leverage the Mittleman sponsorship and the resource person with regard to athletic trainers and the athletic training community.

Phil Marineau and the resources of the Quaker Oats Company conducted research not only on the product but also on its demographics. Detailed information that provided insight to the end-user as well as who purchased Gatorade and when they used it, proved invaluable as I developed a sports marketing strategy.

The target audience was eighteen-to-twenty-four-year-old males who worked out at least three times a week. The researched also showed that 25 percent of all product purchased was at a convenience store. Not only was the product purchase there, it was consumed there after the purchase.

Another significant fact was that "soccer moms" were the key purchaser of product in grocery stores. They would buy Gatorade when it was their turn to provide drinks for their kids soccer games. Others, when asked when were they introduced to Gatorade, would respond, "In high school by my coach." It was also noted that once introduced to Gatorade, these individuals were lifelong users. In a few instances, the choice of purchase of a sports drinks was driven by price.

With the research at hand, the goal was to target eighteen-to-twenty-four-year-old males who were sports enthusiasts, introduce them early into the franchise, building loyalty, and making them a lifelong users. Later, the target audience would be expanded to eighteen-to-thirty-four-year-old males. Also, the end-users would be subdivided into "tweens and teens." They used Gatorade, but Mom purchased it.

I was asked to build a strategy for sports marketing, and the research played a key role. I would develop a strategy that would incorporate the facts of the research targeting not only the Gatorade user but also what sports they participated in and watched. The additional research for participation numbers in the various sports I got from *Scholastic Coach Magazine*. The numbers for the demographics, those watching sports, I got from the various ad agencies Gatorade employed. My strategy centered on television sports viewership and the participatory sports numbers.

In the early 1980s, Gatorade wasn't widely known. There was also little information on why you should use it. When I joined the Gatorade team at Quaker, I was familiar with the product through my 1982 World's Fair experience. I was not familiar with the usage aspect of the product. When I competed, there were a few beverages at the trainers' tent, none of them Gatorade. There was Gookinaid, Quick Kick, and water. Bill Gookin, a biochemist, developed his product out of his experience running marathons, and his initial reaction to Gatorade at the 1968 Olympic trials marathon, he consumed Gatorade and got sick. So did numerous other athletes. After this experience, he viewed Gatorade as a "drink designed for beefy football players," so he developed Gookinaid. Quick Kick was a product developed by an athletic trainer and distributed by Cramer, the sporting goods company.

In high school, we didn't have an athletic trainer. My head football coach was against water breaks. You took salt pills with a little water to battle the heat in those two-a-day football workouts. Normally, you'd get sick and throw up, a good reason not to take the salt pills. Dehydration wasn't linked to health issues, athletic performance, or deaths. Education and research would prove that rehydration was essential, and Gatorade was developed for this sole purpose, a fact that I'd build into my strategy.

The five goals of our strategy were to (1) build awareness; (2) utilize implied endorsement; (3) be the expert in thirst quenching and rehydration; (4) utilize new packaging and product at "the point of sweat;" (5) own the sidelines from pee wee (grassroots) to pro. It seemed simple and straightforward. It was now time to build these into programs, packaging, events, and science.

Sampling was the keystone in building awareness coupled with advertising, explaining simply "Gatorade puts back what your body sweats out"—a simple message that was driven by science, science that was proven by independent research and an in-house laboratory, the Gatorade Sports Science Institute. Gatorade became the preeminent experts on the science of rehydration.

The implied endorsement element was significant in that "the pros used it." The professional team organizations and trainers were responsible for millions of dollars of talent on the field, and if they used it, it had to be good. Also, they were purchasing the product, not getting it free. Thousands of recognizable named athletes consuming your product on national television provided exposure and support for Gatorade. At that point, it was decided that we would never hire an athlete to endorse our product. Of course, that strategy changed in 1991 when we signed Michael Jordan.

The research showed that we needed to get our product in appropriate packaging to "the point of sweat," simply getting the product at arm's reach to the athletes where they were competing or working out. Glass bottles were replaced with plastic bottles and fitted with a wider opening so the product could be consumed rapidly. The wide mouth bottle was developed by Phil Marienau, and when he left the Quaker Oats Company to be the CEO at Dean Foods, he introduced the packaging technology to the milk industry. Consumption increased by over 20 percent.

We also increased our flavor offerings as well as vending machine purchase options, targeting schools, playgrounds, and health clubs. Increasing distribution was essential. In the grocery stores, Gatorade was in the juice aisle. The major soft drink companies kept us from being in their aisle. Our sales weren't significant enough to leverage pressure on the grocery stores to relocate us. In fact, some Gatorade advertising was tagged "Look for us in the juice aisle." This was the result from the consumers saying they couldn't find us in the grocery stores.

Our research confirmed that we should focus on five sports: baseball, basketball, football, soccer, and running. These would be the participatory sports and would account for over 90 percent of individuals who played organized sports. Running would be the largest group as it included organized track and field and road racing. The "weekend warrior" would include individuals who played sports solely on the weekends and included organized as well as any physical activity done by an individual.

The running craze was just reaching its peak in the 1980s. Nike footwear and distance running were synonymous and entered mainstream America. Avon, the women's beauty care company, initiated a 10K racing series for women only in 1982 and was instrumental in introducing the women's marathon on the Olympic schedule for the first time in history at the Los Angeles Olympics in 1984. Although Title IX of the Civil Rights Act was signed into law in 1972, few programs existed for women at all levels of competition.

We would target these sports from pee wee to the pros. This would include in ascending order youth sports, high schools, colleges and universities, and professional sports. We would add additional sports throughout the years as the demographics changed and our target audience expanded. Women's sports would later be targeted as would extreme sports.

When reviewing the research, the professional sports provided the greatest exposure, specifically those that were broadcast on one of the three major networks—ABC, CBS, and NBC. The start-up network, ESPN, was in its infancy in the 1980s but would become a major player as they acquired funding and programing throughout all of sports in the 1980s. The Fox network would launch in 1986 and would become a major sports broadcaster acquiring the NFL rights in 1994. No other professional sport could provide the television exposure that the National Football League provided. Its programming delivered our target audience, and even though we didn't advertise in the broadcasts, you couldn't miss those orange coolers and the green cups on the sidelines. The "Gatorade Dunk" would later provide exposure through the "celebration of victory" ceremony that reached its high point in 1986.

Following the NFL, Major League Baseball had the highest television ratings but skewed to an older demographic. The National Basketball Association and the American Basketball Association merged in 1976 and provided limited exposure. That would change dramatically in 1984 when David Stern would become Commissioner of the NBA. The National Hockey League broadcasts were usually local and didn't deliver any real ratings except in those local markets.

College sports, through the National Collegiate Athletic Association, had a limited broadcast schedule. This was mainly football, and those that were broadcast were rivalry games and regionally broadcasted. Most national broadcasts of college football games were the season-ending Bowl Games.

As for youth sports, the most recognizable youth sporting event was the Little League World Series. This was held in Williamsport, Pennsylvania, and showcased boys' youth baseball teams from around the world. In youth football, there was Pop Warner Football, but it wasn't televised. Soccer, often considered "the world's sport," had pockets of interest around the United States but hadn't yet made significant gains in participation numbers. Growth and popularity in soccer exploded after the soccer matches during the Los Angeles

Olympics in 1984. The United States would host the FIFA World Cup in 1994, and the United States Women's National Team would win the FIFA 1999 Women's World Cup at the sold-out Rose Bowl in dramatic fashion as a result of penalty kicks. The women's team created an explosion of girl's participation in youth soccer, and Mia Hamm became an icon in the sport of soccer.

As we executed these strategies, with little or no dollars, I built personal relationships with key people in all of these sports disciplines at various levels. I got to know the decision-makers, event organizers, team owners, league executives, and the athletic trainers.

None would prove more valuable than the athletic trainers as we built the brand.

And as one sports executive, Gary Stevenson, shared with his staff when he introduced me years later, "When you don't have resources to write a check, you have to become very creative, and there was nobody more creative than Bill Schmidt."

CHAPTER 23

BUT IT IS LEFTY, RIGHT?

I had just completed my work at the Los Angeles Olympic Organizing Committee. Los Angeles had staged the most successful Olympic Games in history. We had generated a surplus of $232.5 million. The games ended in August, and after my role in closing facilities, inventorying all sports equipment, and a "thank you" party for 20,000 plus volunteers who worked at the LAOOC, I was headed to Chicago, "the Windy City."

When I arrived in Chicago, I took up residency at the Holiday Inn, Apparel Mart, across from the Quaker Oats offices in the Merchandise Mart. The Merchandise Mart was then the second largest office building in square footage in the world. The Pentagon was first.

The Quaker Oats Company was a $3 billion food company that had diversified into cereals, pet foods, children toys, retail goods, and gift stores. Its brands included Fisher-Price, Quaker Oatmeal, Cap'n Crunch, Brookstone, Joseph A. Bank Clothier, Chewy Granola Bars, Life Cereal, Magic Pan, and Eyelab. With the 1983 acquisition of Stokely-Van Camp, Quaker acquired a vegetable business, Van Camp Pork and Beans, and Gatorade, the "crown jewel."

The president and CEO of the Quaker Oats Company was William D. Smithburg, a forty-four-year-old former advertising executive groomed by Robert D. Stuart Jr., the former CEO and relative of the founding Stuart family.

Smithburg was highly criticized by the financial community for the Stokely-Van Camp acquisition in 1983. Quaker Oats paid $226 million, $77 a share for SVC, who had sales revenue of $598.1

million. Gatorade sales were $93 million. Smithburg, a fitness nut himself, bet the farm and proved the analysts wrong. I was excited to join this company and work on the Gatorade brand.

Two individuals were responsible for evaluating and integrating Stokely-Van Camp personnel after the acquisition, Phil Marineau and Sandy Posa, both longtime Quaker employees. Some SVC employees elected not to relocate to Chicago from Indianapolis. Kent Miller, Doug Stein, and Bob Calvin did elect to accept positions in sales and sports marketing. I would be reporting to Bob Calvin, Director of Sports Marketing. Bob was the VP of Sales Grocery Products Division at SVC.

My title was Director of Sports Development, Foods Division at the Quaker Oats Company. It wasn't common for a director to report to another director within the Quaker organization. This was the first time I realized than a corporation could do whatever necessary and whatever it wanted regarding titles and positions. After all, when I negotiated my agreement of employment, I wanted the title of Director, realizing that a Vice President title was out of the question. I negotiated a $55,000 starting salary, temporary housing for three months, four weeks' vacation, membership at a golf country club in my name with all monthly expenses and fees to be expensed and reimbursed and to qualify for annual bonuses and stock options. The only item I requested and was denied was a company car. I had one while at the LAOOC as Vice President of Sports. At this point, make note that the golf country club membership was in my name and not a Quaker Oats membership. This would play a significant role in my departure from the Quaker Oats Company fifteen years later.

My initial days and months at the Quaker Oats Company, I listened, observed, studied the brand, its managers, their "go-to market strategy," and "how to do business and conduct myself within the corporation." It was a daunting task, but I was eager and threw myself into the deep end of the pool.

I knew about Gatorade's sponsorship of NASCAR and its Gatorade Racing Team as well as its sponsorship of the PGA, running events, and a few carry over events from Stokely-Van Camp that were sponsored in Indianapolis, Indiana, because of their corporate presence in that city and state.

My education of the "other sports marketing expenditures" proved to be eye-opening, and the rationale for these were political in nature and, in some cases, lacked strategy. The most expensive sponsorship proved to be the Gatorade Racing Team that participated in weekly races and primarily in the southeastern United States.

Although there was a loosely defined "category," Gatorade dominated with a 97 percent market share. There were three flavors, Gatorlode 280, a carbo-loading drink, and limited distribution through a network of food brokers. Gatorade was defined as a "electrolyte drink" and a "thirst-quencher." In the running sponsorships, Gatorade was defined as an isotonic beverage.

The NFL promotional agreement with the Quaker Oats Company and Stokely-Van Camp signed September 1, 1984, defined the business category: "Fluid Replacement and/or Thirst Quencher Beverages, High-Energy Carbohydrate Beverages, and Drink Mixes Thereof."

The rights received from the NFL were:

- Use of NFL Marks (NFL Shield) on packing, in advertising, and promotional events to promote the brand. Specific executions to be mutually agreed upon by SVC and the National Football League Properties, Inc. (NFLP).
- On-field use at NFL games of Gatorade product and Gatorade-identified cups and dispensing equipment *at the election of each Member Club.* NFLP will make "best efforts" to solicit the cooperation of the member clubs for their use of Gatorade product, cups, and coolers at NFL games throughout the term of the contract.

Obligations of SVC, (Gatorade):

NFL Tailgate and Super Bowl Media Insert Promotion Events

- Purchase one full-page advertisement in the NFL Tailgate Promotion. This is to be a free-standing insert packaged event with a 38 million household circulation. Year 1.

- Right of first refusal to purchase participation in Tailgate Promotion Event Years 2–5.
- SVC use of NFL Licensed Marks in a free-standing insert advertisement in the months of October and January during the term shall be restricted to use in the Tailgate and Super Bowl Insert Promotional Events respectively.

GameDay Magazine Advertising

- SVC agrees to purchase one full-page, four-color bleed advertisement for the brands in all issues of *GameDay* magazine including Super Bowl and Pro Bowl *GameDay* editions, published during the term.

PRO! Magazine Advertising

- SVC agrees to purchase one full-page four-color bleed advertisement for the brands in all issues of *PRO! Magazine* published during the term.

Designation Status:

"Supplier to the NFL"
Right Fees:

Year 1	$75,000
Year 2	$100,000
Year 3	$100,000
Year 4	$125,000
Year 5	$150,000

The term is the period beginning April 1, 1985, and terminating on March 31, 1990 (five years).

Several areas/items to note:

- Teams were under *no obligation* to use Gatorade, cups, or coolers.
- NFLP would use "*best efforts*" means *nothing!*
- No mention of right to season tickets, Super Bowl Tickets or Pro Bowl tickets, either provided or opportunity to purchase.
- No "Official Status" with the NFL, "supplier" only.
- Does *not* include use of NFL players in advertising.
- No use of NFL films.

These specific items would later drive me to develop a strategy to where Gatorade had "exclusivity," all teams had to use product, cups, coolers, towels and we had individual team deals as well as game tickets and Super Bowl tickets.

PGA Tour

In June of 1982, while I was still working at the World's Fair, Stokely-Van Camp signed a three-year sponsorship with the PGA Tour. It was a royalty and licensing agreement that made Gatorade the "Official Thirst Quencher of the PGA Tour." Gatorade would be provided to all forty-two scheduled events along with cups and coolers.

Tournaments would place the cups and coolers on all tees and encourage tournament directors to sell Gatorade at the concessions. The PGA Tour would also provide youth golf clinics during the scheduled weekly tournaments, usually on Mondays.

This appeared to be a clear strategy to gain exposure on television with the hope of catching the players drinking Gatorade in Gatorade cups before or after their tee shots.

LPGA (Ladies Professional Golf Association)

In September of 1982, Stokely-Van Camp signed a letter of agreement with the Ladies Professional Golf Association and was designated the "Official Thirst Quencher of the LPGA."

The agreement:

- Three-year agreement.
- Gatorade, cups, and coolers provided to a minimum of twenty events.
- $6,000 yearly promotional/implementation fee.
- $400 promotional fee to each participating tournament.

SVC received:

- "The Official Thirst Quencher of the LPGA."
- Use of LPGA name and logo.
- Three Pro-Am spots during the course of the tournament season.
- Five weekly badges for each tournament.
- "Best Efforts" in obtaining product at concession stands.

Stokely-Van Camp had several other contracts. Promotional agreements with the NBA and Major League Baseball (MLB) were in place as well as agreements with the trainers of the NBA, MLB, and the NFL.

The trainers in all professional sports proved to be the gatekeepers for the sidelines, courtside, and dugouts. The relationships with these "gatekeepers" provided the foundation for a strategy that would make Gatorade synonymous with sports.

I decided after several months at Gatorade that I needed to establish a relationship with these trainers, and the first opportunity would be MLB Spring Training.

I did all my research locating training sites for both the Cactus League in Arizona and the Grapefruit League in Florida. I had no staff, so it was me for a week in Arizona and a week in Florida. Now, on the surface, this sounds like a vacation. Yeah, right.

I made my flight reservations, rented a car for the week, and located a motel when I arrived. I had all the trainers names as well as their contact information. I also knew their schedules. They arrived early at the training camps and stayed late.

My goal was to use my athletic experiences with trainers. I knew how important their role was for the well-being of their athletes and build their confidence in me and, ultimately, Gatorade. As one trainer told me later, "Bill Schmidt is Gatorade."

So I'm in Scottsdale, Arizona, and my daily routine was to wake up at 5:00 a.m. and cook breakfast in my room. Yes, in my room. This was 1985, and I was staying at a motel at the site of today's Scottsdale Convention Center. Gatorade didn't have a great deal of travel expense money, so I stayed at the cheapest motel possible, and this one had a "kitchenette." In today's terms, that would be "extended living." This one had a stove, refrigerator, dining area, as well as a TV. I would purchase groceries and ultimately save the company money. I can still smell the blossoms on the fruit trees lining the property.

After breakfast, I headed out to meet with my first trainer at 6:30 a.m. I'd stop along the way to pick up coffee and doughnuts. After all, a visitor bearing gifts had to be greeted with a smile as well as be granted some time. I would repeat this two or three times in the morning, visiting at least two trainers and finishing by 10:00 a.m. The training facilities had other salespeople, league and team administrators, and occasionally an athlete show up by 10:00 a.m. Up until that time, it was just me and the team trainer enjoying coffee, doughnuts, and conversation.

The exhibition games started by 1:00 p.m., but I was back at the motel, working on my schedule as to when I could meet the trainers visiting from Tucson or Yuma. Tucson wasn't a bad driving distance, but Yuma was across the state. I was prepared to make the drive regardless.

I also invited at least two and sometimes four trainers and their assistants for dinner at a local restaurant. Their days were incredibly long, and dinner out on someone else was a welcomed treat. I also learned who to include or, in some cases, not to include. This was about building relationships and understanding what was important to them and their profession.

When you get up at 5:00 a.m., anyone else up at that hour had to be involved with "working" at spring training, not there to see the games. I never attended a game while there.

I noticed these two guys up early every morning. One was an elderly man, gray hair and glasses, and the other one big, dark hair and glasses. He looked like Clark Kent of Superman fame.

So after a few days of noticing them carrying equipment bags early in morning, I decided to approach this large, physically fit Clark Kent-looking guy at the pool in the afternoon.

I introduced myself. His name was Steve Smith, and he worked for Wilson Sporting Goods. He was there to fit baseball players for gloves as well as other Wilson products used in baseball.

Based on his size, I said, "Did you play football?"

He said, "Yes."

He was an All-American at the University of Michigan and played offensive tackle and defensive end. He was drafted by the San Francisco 49ers and played in the NFL for eight seasons. I said, "Didn't you play for the Steelers?"

He replied, "Yes, I did for one season."

I liked him even more, being I was a Steelers fan.

He explained Wilson Sporting Goods' link to baseball and the role they played in outfitting players with gloves and catchers with the necessary equipment. He clearly was there to service the athletes and leverage Wilson's sponsorship involvement with Major League Baseball. They were out early each morning to fit players and had a huge inventory of product in a storage facility at the motel.

I had to ask him, "Who is the older gentleman working with you?"

He said, "You don't recognize him?"

I said, "No."

He said "That's Lefty Gomez."

I said, "Lefty Gomez, the former pitcher for the New York Yankees?"

He said, "Yes, that's him."

I was floored. What a legend!

Vernon Louis "Lefty" Gomez played in Major League Baseball for thirteen years. He was a five-time World Series Champion with the New York Yankees and a six-time MLB All Star. This guy was a stud in his day. He also had quite the sense of humor.

In the evenings, I'd see him at the motel outside, near the pool. I decided to introduce myself. He was gracious, and we became fast friends. Steve Smith mentioned that the players in the training facilities had no idea who Lefty was as he did his daily delivery of bags and equipment. In Steve's words, "These million-dollar spoiled athletes couldn't carry his jock."

One day, as I was walking around the pool, I happened to walk by Lefty's room on the ground level. The door was wide open, so I stuck my head in and said, "Hello." He introduced me to his wife, June, a lovely lady who you could tell was a knockout back in her day. Lefty confirmed my thought when he said June was a former actress on Broadway. I've yet to meet any Major League Baseball pitcher whose wife wasn't gorgeous.

One day, I saw Lefty autographing baseball cards of himself just outside his room. I stopped and said hello. I said, "What are you doing?"

He said, "Making a little money signing baseball cards."

I said, "Really?"

He said, "Yes, I was getting $3 a card, then June renegotiated the deal, and I now get $10 a card."

I also noticed that he was signing the cards with his right hand. I said, "Hey, it is 'Lefty' Gomez?"

He said, "Yes, it is, but you'd write right-handed, too, if the nuns hit you with a ruler as many times as they hit my left hand."

I laughed but also recalled the nuns doing exactly that in one of the Catholic classes my mother made me attend Saturday mornings.

CHAPTER 24

LET'S GO RACING

When I joined Stokely-Van Camp, sponsorships centered around the sponsorship of stock car racing with NASCAR, and Gatorade sales were predominately in the southeastern United States. There were two flavors—lemon lime and orange—and sales were $60 million. Bill Stokely pioneered NASCAR car sponsorship outside of the beer and tobacco product categories. He introduced a green-colored Gatorade-logoed car and won the Daytona 500 twice. Up until then, the drivers considered the color green as "bad luck." That NASCAR sponsorship put Gatorade "in the arena of sports." The sponsorship of the NFL would later provide visibility to millions of fans and provide the foundation that would drive sales and create a new category in the beverage marketplace.

I joined Stokely-Van Camp in February of 1983 and relocated to Indianapolis, Indiana. My first NASCAR race was in the spring of 1983 at Talladega Speedway in Alabama. It was an eye-opening experience and an education in product promotion in the race as well as in the stands. While at the 1982 World's Fair, I had a firsthand experience with the popularity of NASCAR. The Gatorade 88 NASCAR race car on display was the centerpiece of the Gatorade Sports Hall of Fame. After numerous attempts by many fair attendees to climb into the car, we installed "velvet ropes" to keep them at a distance. They wanted to touch the car and have that NASCAR experience. The love of the automobile was extremely high in the 1970s and

1980s. It was also extremely competitive between the automobile manufactures.

I met the patriarch of NASCAR, Bill France Sr., "Big Bill," whose vision moved stock car racing from the beach to super oval racing with thousands of spectators. Bill had been a mechanic and driver himself. He also founded NASCAR, the National Association for Stock Car Auto Racing, the governing body of stock car racing. I also met Bill France Jr., Big Bill's son, and Lesa and Brian France, his grandchildren. It was obvious to me that these two grandchildren would ultimately inherit NASCAR and eventually manage the family interests. I also met Jim France, Big Bill's other son and Bill Jr.'s brother. His role was less defined for me at the time, but he shared in all the interests of the family and would be active in managing various business segments while his brother, Bill Jr., was the face of NASCAR even before Big Bill's death. Bill Jr.'s wife was Betty Jane France, an honest fashionable lady who was extremely insightful as well as influential in NASCAR. It was a family, and they invited me in, and I became a resource for them as well as a supporter and promotor of NASCAR.

The NASCAR race experience gave the everyday fan the opportunity to "touch and feel" the sport. You were in the arena with the drivers, in pit row, and whether you were in the stands, in the infield, or in a hospitality suite, it was an experience you'd never forget. I also learned early on that you could leverage this experience to "drive sales."

Over 24 percent of all Gatorade sales were in the state of Florida. All major grocery store chains expected food companies to deliver promotional events in and around the races at Daytona International Speedway and the Daytona 500. Promotional events included end-aisle displays, in-store stand alone displays, race tickets, and special incentive pricing.

The *big* players, sponsors of actual race cars, were the best at leveraging their brand and their relationship and sponsorship of NASCAR. Winston, the cigarette brand, was the title sponsor of the Winston Cup, the year-long race schedule sponsor of the top division in NASCAR. A high percent of NASCAR fans smoked, drank beer, and visited their grocery stores twice a week. It was also widely promoted that NASCAR race fans were extremely loyal to the products and brands that were sponsors of NASCAR races and events.

Daytona Speedway has been promoted as "the World Center of Racing" and the Daytona 500 as "the Great American Race." It's a race of drama, excitement, American pageantry, thrills, and an occasional crash and caution flags. The track is a 2.5-mile trioval with thirty-one degree banking in the turns and seats over 168,000 fans. Stock car racing moved from the beach to one of the largest outdoor arenas in the United States hosting racing of go-karts, superbikes, drag racing, Rolex 24 Hour Race, as well as car shows, car testing, and various civic events.

My first Daytona 500 Race experience was incredible. Gatorade sponsored the Gatorade 88 race car with Cliff Stewart Racing Team. Stokely-Van Camp had a significant investment in their NASCAR sponsorship and had a former sales representative, Phil Nicholas, manage their interests and relationship with the racing team and NASCAR. He would attend mostly every race and had a Gatorade-decorated van at his disposal. He was on the road most of the time, arriving Wednesday of each race week, and leaving the Monday following each race. June, his girlfriend, traveled with him, and they were both widely known among the racing community of sponsors and drivers—relationships that proved invaluable when working the races for tickets, race credentials, pit tours, photo opportunities, Victory Lane, driver appearances, and customer entertainment. Phil and June were later married and continued to represent Gatorade until the strategy changed from a NASCAR car sponsorship to an integrated program as a contingency sponsor.

Phil Nicholas was introduced to me at the Talladega race, and I shadowed him for the entire week. I met our driver, the race team, NASCAR officials, other sponsors, and had the entire run of the race track that week. I observed, took notes, and asked questions. This was a new sport business experience for me, but I was smart enough to realize the significance of NASCAR and how it could impact the Gatorade brand and, leveraged correctly, drive sales.

Phil Nicholas was exceptional in his role of managing the NASCAR relationship. He was instrumental in providing me with the knowledge, understanding, and inner workings of a race, customer entertainment, and the "unwritten rules" among its sponsors. It was exciting and not without drama on and off the race track. A winning race car would provide the sponsor with additional ways to leverage the brand and its driver. Television coverage, media exposure, driver appearances, and store displays were all leveraged and had significant opportunity to increase sales. A race team that didn't win had fewer opportunities and less impact on sales. Entertainment value was most impactful with a winning team.

My early observations were that Gatorade's spending wasn't significant enough to retain a good driver and provide the necessary funding to obtain the best engines, equipment, and race team management. If you wanted to win on the track and in the grocery aisle, you needed a winning team, and that cost was significant and couldn't be expected on a $1 million investment when other brands were spending in the millions of dollars. Limited investment, limited results.

One of the very first persons I met at Daytona International Speedway was Jim Foster, Vice President of Marketing for NASCAR as well as the Speedway. He had been hired by Big Bill but now reported to Bill Jr. Big Bill had moved stock car racing from the beach to an arena for the public to view. Bill Jr. would move the mainly southern traditional sport to national significance with innovative marketing and negotiated television partnerships.

Jim worked as a sports writer for several newspapers and worked at Chrysler Corporation in public relations. He grew up a fan and was crawling under a fence at the race track in Winston-Salem, North Carolina, to get a firsthand view of the races as a child when he was grabbed by a large man. It was Big Bill who led him to the front gate, bought him a ticket, and told him to "have a good time." Their lives would come full circle, and Jim would be Big Bill's assistant and hold a variety of positions that catapulted NASCAR into a new era and position as a major sport.

Jim Foster was like a big brother to me when it came to me understanding NASCAR, the France family, and how to leverage your brand with a NASCAR sponsorship. I also provided him with a greater understanding on how a corporation views sponsorships, how it budgets for them, as well the expected return on investment (ROI)

Early in my sports marketing career with various employers, I had budget limitations but built relationships that not only educated me on their businesses but that I could also later leverage in negotiating a great deal. With Jim Foster, it was that kind of relationship. I understood his business, and when he needed help or had an opportunity, I'd be there.

Gatorade 88 Racing Team had early success with a variety of drivers. They included Bobby Allison, Donnie Allison, Rusty Wallace, Geoffrey Bodine, Ricky Rudd, and Darrell Waltrip. The Motor Racing Network, broadcast partner of NASCAR, easily announced the sponsor of each car in every race and every turn, providing great exposure and name association with NASCAR and fans.

After we decided at Stokely-Van Camp that we weren't interested in spending the necessary dollars to have a tier one racing team, I set out to meet with Jim Foster to pursue any and all opportunities with in NASCAR. My first goal was to become "the Official Thirst Quencher of NASCAR." My second goal was to obtain the necessary elements to leverage Gatorade at each and every race.

In my initial conversations with Jim, he stated, "All drink sponsorships are broken down into two categories—soft drinks and hard drinks." Soft drink meant sodas, and hard drinks meant beer and alcohol. He considered Gatorade a soft drink. A thirst quencher carried no weight and definitely was not a category as he viewed it.

I built my strategy around. "Hey, we're not a soft drink and we don't want to replace your current soft drink sponsors. We want to give you additional money and expand your position on drinks." In a defining moment, I said, "We're a sports beverage." That decision would put Gatorade in the category it created but hadn't named and develop a strategy that would forever define every relationship and contract.

Jim Foster and I leveraged our relationship to help each other with mutual benefits that solidified our relationship and grew our business and supported NASCAR's growth. There were many a time when Jim made me aware of opportunities before he ever revealed them to the corporate community.

While at the track, Daytona International Speedway, during race week and before the 1990 Daytona 500, Jim Foster told me that 7-Eleven would be dropping their sponsorship of the Twin 125 Races. I didn't hesitate. The next words out of my mouth were, "Gatorade will sponsor them."

His reply was, "I don't even know what I'd price them at."

I repeated, "Gatorade will sponsor them."

On another occasion, as we walked through pit row, Jim pointed to the grand stands and noted where they were going to build four new skybox suites. The first words out of my mouth were, "Gatorade will take one."

He said, "I don't know what we are going to price them at yet."

I said, "Gatorade will take one."

Now, remember, 24 percent of total Gatorade sales were from the state of Florida. Customer entertainment was essential in leveraging our NASCAR sponsorship, and our food brokers were thrilled to have the suite and all the amenities that were also provided. They were able to have access to the garage area, pit row, and Victory Lane. They also had the opportunity to have two Grand Marshalls for the Gatorade Twin 125 races and two starters for each of the races and presentations in Victory Lane. Along with these sponsorships came 500 race tickets for the Daytona 500. This was like gold bullion in the war for shelf space in the grocery stores.

Yet, on another occasion, and during race week at the Daytona 500, Jim said, "The CBS *60 Minutes* film crew will be doing a segment on NASCAR." CBS had requested an interview with one of the sponsors. He and Bill France Jr. had asked me to do the interview from all the list of NASCAR sponsors. Now I remember the old line, "You're not having a good day if a CBS *60 Minutes* film crew is waiting outside your office."

I did the interview with Harry Reasoner in our suite high above Daytona International Speedway. The interview centered around, "Why are you, and for that matter, why would any corporation sponsor NASCAR? What's in it for you and your brand?"

Now this wasn't hard-hitting journalism. It was easy for me to relate the financial benefits for Gatorade's spending money on a sport that was quickly moving from a regional brand to a nationwide phenomenon. I did get a few questions regarding NASCAR, the France family, and its Southern roots as well safety issues and fan demographics. Questions that I reiterated were possible concerns but again emphasizing that "NASCAR delivered our target audience, and we were extremely excited in increasing our involvement as they expanded throughout the United States." Both Jim Foster and Bill France Jr. thanked me.

As Gatorade looked to expand exposure for cups, coolers, and product exclusivity in the driver's garages and pit row, Jim Foster would present a variety of programs. We would become the sponsor of the Gatorade 200, the Saturday race at Darlington, South Carolina, over Labor Day Weekend that partnered with the Southern 500, the Sunday race. Jim also delivered "the Circle of Champions," an awards program that recognized the year end winner in each of the twelve divisions of NASCAR sanctioned racing. We would recognize these winners at a press conference, presenting them with Gatorade green blazers, a commissioned oil painting of themselves, and Gatorade-logoed rings with a green stone and personalized with their names. I would later use the "Circle of Champions" idea to establish an awards program in high school that would eventually become "the Gatorade Player of the Year."

NASCAR and Gatorade's involvement would also come with some surprises and present interesting as well as laughable moments. At the height of "the Gatorade Dunk," Bob Weeks, a NASCAR executive who was responsible managing Victory Lane, called to say he had a great idea. He did arrange a "Gatorade Dunk" at all Victory Lane" celebrations, and he said, "I've put the Gatorade logos upside down on the coolers. So when they are turned upside down when the driver is dunked, they'll read right side up." He had already launched his idea during race week at Daytona. I congratulated Bob on a great idea but told him to stop. I explained to him that this would be too contrived and would hurt the spontaneity of the Gatorade Dunk.

In another incident, Jim Foster called me to say they had traced some Daytona 500 Race tickets that were advertised for purchase in the *USA Today* newspaper as being from our allotment that NASCAR provided to Gatorade.

We had the opportunity to purchase five hundred tickets for the race through our contract, and I provided them to our sales force to leverage for in-store promotions and sales displays.

I learned early in my position at Gatorade to keep an accurate and precise record of all event tickets we received as well as to whom they were assigned. I also required all sales managers to also keep records of their ticket transactions. As it turned out, we traced the tickets to a certain Daytona grocery store manager who received four tickets in exchange for our sales staff erecting an end-aisle display. This was very common in the grocery store business. Slotting allowances were also common. This is where food brokers would pay a fee for a premier shelf location.

Well, every grocery store manager would receive tickets from a number of food brokers to showcase their products. So with all the beer, soda, cereal, and other NASCAR sponsors, the store manager could receive hundreds of race tickets. We found out through Jim Foster's purchasing the tickets advertised by a Las Vegas ticket broker that this store manager had sold over 150 Daytona 500 race tickets and at a premium. He scalped the tickets. There was little we could do, so we let our broker sales staff handle it internally with the specific grocery store chain.

As sponsor of the Gatorade 125s, we had the opportunity to present the winners of our Thursday races with Rolex watches at the Daytona 500 pre-race festivities on Sunday. In my first official duty in presenting these drivers with their watches, I wanted to be certain that when handed the microphone and I addressed the crowd of over 125,000 race fans, I'd recognize the right people and say the right things.

I had the right Gatorade corporate message but wanted to be certain I had the driver's names correct. So I repeated to myself, "Dale Earnhardt, Darrell Waltrip. Dale Earnhardt, Darrell Waltrip. Dale Earnhardt, Darrell Waltrip."

When the moment came and the MC introduced me, I took the mic and said, "Thank you, Jim." "On behalf of Gatorade, the Official Sports Beverage of NASCAR and Sponsor of the Gatorade 125s, I'd like to recognize the winners of the Gatorade 125s and present them with a Rolex watch. The winner of Thursday's first Gatorade 125 race, Darrell Earnhardt." I quickly changed that to Dale Earnhardt.

Dale laughed as he took the watch, and so did Darrell Waltrip, waiting in the wings to receive his Rolex. I was embarrassed but finished the presentation. I did hear some laughter in the background.

What I wasn't aware of was the competitive nature between these two drivers. Maybe even a little dislike. Later, I was ushered to the MRN broadcast booth to be interviewed by Eli Gold, Barney Hall, and Allen Bestwick while the Daytona 500 Race was being broadcast live on radio to forty-eight states and a few foreign countries. These in-race interviews were for all NASCAR sponsors and delivered on behalf of the MRN media buy by the sponsors.

I was still feeling the embarrassment of my pre-race introductions when Barney Hall said, "What a funny and great way to introduce Dale Earnhardt. He loved it, and so did Darrell Waltrip." My blunder had sparked comments of "Genius," "How creative," and "Entertaining." If they only knew.

I became a regular sight at most NASCAR events and at a few races during the forty-two race weekends a year. Ed Shull, a Quaker Oats employee, attended many races on his own, and I later charged him with managing the NASCAR race festivities. I'd cover his expenses and would invite him and his wife as our guests at the NASCAR Awards Banquet at the Waldorf Astoria in New York the first week of December. The NASCAR family loved Ed, and he kept me informed of any issues or concerns regarding our relationship and contract with NASCAR.

Dale Earnhardt won many Gatorade 125 races and, as a result, many Rolex watches. After one Daytona 500 pre-race introduction, he said, "I've won a few of these Rolex watches. Is there any way I exchange this and get Teresa one?" Teresa was Dale's wife.

I responded, "Sure, absolutely."

He then responded, "What do you want me to do with this watch?"

I said, "Keep it, you'll owe me." He laughed.

After winning four straight Gatorade races, I told him pre-race for his fifth attempt to win, "If you win this, I'll do something special with the Rolex watch design." He won, so true to my word, I had diamonds placed at noon, three, six, and nine o'clock on the watch face. He loved it. In the 1998 Daytona 500 pre-race event after recognizing him with his seventh Gatorade 125 win, I said, "If you win today, I'll do something really special with the Rolex design." This was his twentieth attempt to win the Daytona 500. Well, it was his day—he won.

When I got to Victory Lane to do the Gatorade segment of the presentation, he quickly shouted, "Don't forget about that watch!" I had Rolex replace all the numbers with diamonds. He'd wear the watch at all times, and if I was present, he'd shout, "Look at the watch Schmidt gave me!"

I was in Daytona for Speed Week in 2001. I was working on a consulting project for International Speedway Corporation,(ISC) with CEO Jim France. It was also when the France family interviewed me as well as gauging my interest in joining their team on the ISC side of the business.

On race day, February 18, I was in the NASCAR suite, the guest of Bill France Jr. It was an exciting race, and it came down to the last lap as Dale Earnhardt Jr., Michael Waltrip, Rusty Wallace, and Ricky Rudd positioned themselves for the finish coming out of turn four. Everyone was following the results as Michael Waltrip won, just beating out Dale Earnhardt Jr. for the win. There was some focus on a wreck that involved Dale Earnhardt Sr. out of turn four. I went over to Bill France Jr. and congratulated him on an exciting Daytona 500. I also said, "I hope Dale is okay." It just seemed like the usual NASCAR wreck expecting damage to the cars involved but no real injuries to the drivers. Bill had been on the phone. He turned to me and whispered, "I believe we've lost Dale Earnhardt."

I didn't want to believe it. It wasn't until several hours later that his death had been confirmed to the public. A NASCAR icon had been killed, and the racing community would mourn his loss forever.

The programs I started and the opportunities I took advantage with NASCAR would not have been possible without the trust and confidence that both the Quaker Oats Company President, Phil Marineau, and Chairman and CEO William Smithburg had in me. For that, I'm forever grateful. It was this trust and confidence in me that enabled me to help grow the brand and negotiate great contracts throughout my career at Gatorade.

CHAPTER 25

"FORE" ON THE MOON

I, like everyone else at the time, was shocked at the Russian launch of Sputnik on October 4, 1957. We followed it across the night October sky as it orbited the earth. With it came questions as well as panic. "Are the Russian spying on us? Are they planning on attacking the United States?" The space age had begun. I was nine.

In the decade to follow, President Kennedy would vow to land a man on the moon and return to earth. The space race had begun. NASA was formed, and test pilots were transitioning to astronauts.

The idea of space travel was exciting, and I dreamed of what that would be like. I also realized early on that I didn't have the math or science competence to make that a reality. I fell in love with the idea of flying, although I had never been in a plane, a new world, a frontier that made me want to travel and explore.

While at the Quaker Oats Company as Vice President of Gatorade Worldwide Sports Marketing, occasionally, the sales groups would need a speaker for one of their events. They would give me their "wish list" and budget and I'd make it happen. On one occasion, we were having an annual Gatorade divisional meeting and needed a speaker, but they didn't want a sports celebrity.

So at a meeting of my staff and other Gatorade marketing individuals, we discussed all the options. Now, remember, this group of marketing individuals were some of the smartest individuals I had ever been around, some of them recently getting their MBA degrees from an ivy league school or other top institution in the US. Also, if you worked on the Gatorade brand, there wasn't anything we couldn't do or achieve—results-orientated is what we were known for.

After an hour or more of discussing possible speakers, we had no suitable candidates when one of our marketing assistants said, "Maybe my uncle would be available."

"Okay, Cathy Shepard, who's your uncle?"

She said, "Alan Shepard."

I quickly asked, "The astronaut?"

She answered, "Yes, him."

Through Cathy's help and efforts, her uncle confirmed that he would be available, and we made it happen; or rather, Cathy Shepard made it happen. I was excited about the opportunity to meet him and interested to hear him speak.

Now I had competed in the Olympics, won an Olympic medal, worked at an Olympics and, through Gatorade, had been able to interact with some incredible athletes and personalities. This was different. It brought back those thoughts of my youth and the excitement of space travel.

Admiral Shepard had been a naval aviator, a test pilot, the first American in space, and yes, he walked on the moon. It was an event that I was looking forward to attending as I wasn't on the schedule to present. In addition, I wasn't involved in the logistics of Admiral Shepard's visit.

The day before the conference started, I received a call from Cathy Shepard who was planning her uncle's visit, and she asked if I wanted to play golf with Admiral Shepard the next day. He was to speak that evening. I said, "Absolutely!"

The hotel and resort was in the western suburbs of Chicago and had a Pete Dye designed golf course on property. Pete Dye designs were infamous for water holes with plenty of sand, bunkers, and wood railroad ties. One of his most famous designs is the TPC Sawgrass Stadium Course in Ponte Vedra, Florida.

I left my hotel room the next morning, had the buffet lunch with colleagues, and proceeded to the golf course. My golf bag was already on the cart on the driver's side, and a nondescript golf bag was on the passenger's side. I went to the practice range and hit a few balls. Today wasn't about great golf. It was entertaining a great American hero, playing golf. It would be just the two of us together for four and half hours. It would be one of the most incredible experiences of my life. Admiral Shepard showed up with a soda in his hand and quickly checked his golf bag, grabbing his golf glove and a couple of golf balls. I moved to his side, introduced myself, and got in the cart. We proceeded to the first tee.

The admiral was quiet, didn't engage in any conversation, other than the layout of the golf hole we were playing.

On the fourth hole, which had a great number of fairway traps, Admiral Shepard hit his drive and returned to the golf cart. After I hit my drive, I, too, returned to the golf cart. After a few moments of silence, he asked me a question. "Have you ever played La Quinta?"

I said, "Do you mean the golf course in the California desert?"

He replied, "Yes."

I said, "When you look down the fairway at your tee shot, all you see is sand."

He said, "It's like playing golf on the moon."

I smiled to myself and thought, *This guy did hit a golf ball on the moon.* So I said. "You hit a golf ball on the moon?"

He responded, "Truth be known, I hit two golf balls."

I questioned, "How well did you hit them?"

He said, "The first one I topped. The second one was long and straight." We both laughed. We all hit the mulligan, the second ball, always better.

I decided I'd show my knowledge of the event and stated, "It was a five-iron that you hit, and it was on a telescopic shaft."

He quickly stated, "It was a six-iron."

I knew the answer to my next question, but I had to ask it. "What was the make of the golf balls that you hit and that are still on the moon?"

His answer, "You know, a man could make a lot of money if he knew that."

We both smiled.

From that fourth hole on, he was engaging, talkative, and unguarded. He felt comfortable with me. I, of course, shared with him my interest in the space program at an early age. I also realized that the individual I was sitting next to and playing golf with was an explorer like Columbus and Magellan—a pioneer, a test pilot, and an individual who was extremely competitive and wanted to be "first" in everything he undertook. He was fearless, focused, and driven. I was with a true giant of our time.

As our game continued, I said to him, "I have to ask you one question. What was your last thought before they 'lit the candle'?" That in reference to his comment to NASA officials after a four-hour delay on the launch pad and after having to urinate in his flight suit (let's light this candle).

He said, "The Mercury program would have had a man in space before the Russians if it weren't for the NASA delays. I'm sitting on top of this Redstone rocket that had 78,000 pounds of thrust. Attached at the nose was an auxiliary safety rocket to separate me from the Redstone rocket, if there was a problem at launch, a safety system that never worked in testing. We want you to get into to this capsule that was so tight you'd exhaled to enter it. We're going to launch you into space in excess of a hundred miles in altitude and come down range in a 300-mile square area, an area that we can't completely cover with recovery vessels. Oh, and by the way, the heat shield had only been tested to a specific temperature and was uncertain whether it would withstand the reentry into earth's atmosphere. Also, if you reenter the earth's atmosphere at too steep of an angle, you'll bounce off into space and never be recovered.

"If you don't burn up on reentry, you'll need to deploy your parachutes to slow your descent. If they're not ripped off during descent, your capsule will hit the water with the force of a Volkswagen falling off a ten-story building. If you blow the exit hatch too soon, the capsule will fill with water and you'll drown."

After this great shared experience of the challenges of the rocket, it's launch, reentry, and recovery, I was still waiting on the edge of my seat to hear his definitive answer.

He looked me in the eye with those steel focused blue eyes of his and said, "My last thought before they lit the fuse was that I was on top of this powerful rocket with its millions of parts and hundreds of systems that was built by the lowest government bidder." What a sobering thought.

That evening, he spoke about his missions, *Mercury Freedom 7* and *Apollo 14*. His description of looking back at Earth from space on *Apollo 14* was so vivid, you felt like you were there. "A beautiful blue and white marble in a black sky."

Golf and the four and a half hours I spent with this American hero, explorer, test pilot, and astronaut was absolutely incredible. His shared experiences provided me a front row seat with an icon and a legend in American aviation. It, too, fulfilled that early life's desire of being in the space program. In that one afternoon and evening, I sat atop the Redstone rocket in *Freedom 7*, venturing into space, and went to the moon and back on a Saturn rocket on the *Apollo 14* mission.

CHAPTER 26

CONFERENCE AT LAKE COMO

Gatorade's growth in the late 1980s was about 25 percent year over year. In 1988, sales were over $500 million. The brand had great leadership with William Smithburg, CEO, and Philip Marineau as President of Gatorade. They had different leadership styles, but both shared a strong commitment to the Quaker portfolio of brands, the love of Chicago sports, and the excitement of the potential of their newly acquired Gatorade business.

I met Phil Marineau when he visited me in Los Angeles early in 1984. I had taken a leave of absence from Stokely-Van Camp in 1983 to become Vice President of Sports at the LA Olympics. My intent was to return to Indianapolis after the Olympics and resume my role with Gatorade.

Before my departure, Robert Rice, President of the US Grocery Products Group, called me into his office. He said, "I understand you want to leave us to go to Los Angeles to work for the Olympics?"

I said, "Sir, I don't want to leave."

He said, "Then don't go!" Now I didn't expect him to understand what it meant to me having competed in the Olympics in 1972 and now having the opportunity to help organize and run the 1984 Olympics, but I *had* to take advantage of this incredible opportunity.

This was around the time when Stokely-Van Camp was being sought and considered as a possible acquisition by a half dozen companies. SVC stock was at $35 per share, and early inquiries had driven it to $50 a share. Mr. Rice said, "There's no guarantee that the company will even be here when you return."

I said, "Yes, I know, but I want to leave in good standing and return if/when possible." Meanwhile, no matter what happened, Mr. Robert Rice was going to become very wealthy in less than a year, no matter who acquired SVC. The Quaker Oats Company acquired Stokely-Van Camp in July of 1983 for $77 per share. I'm certain Mr. Rice had no concern about his financial future and no concern about me returning.

I received a call from Phil Marineau that he wanted to meet for dinner on his planned visit to Los Angeles in April of 1984. Although the planning for the 1984 Los Angeles Olympic Games was far from over, I wanted to meet with him to hear his plans for Gatorade as they transitioned from Stokely-Van Camp.

We met on a Friday evening at a seafood restaurant along the Pacific Coast Highway in Santa Monica. I made the reservations after finding out seafood was his first choice. Now Friday night is normally a mad house, and it was that evening as well. Let's say that being an executive with the Los Angeles Olympic Committee (LAOOC) had its privileges. I arrived early, and Phil and his associate, Mark Shapiro, were already there. I handed out a few LAOOC pins to the maître d, and we were seated at a prime table overlooking the beach and the ocean. I later found out that this impressed Phil that I came into the restaurant, and it was if "I owned it." His words, not mine.

We had an incredible dinner and great conversation. He made it extremely clear that he wanted me back on the Gatorade team and at the Quaker Oats Company in Chicago. I said, "When I left Stokely-Van Camp, it was a leave of absence, and if you want me back on the team, I'd love to join you in Chicago."

I was impressed with his intelligence, but on my first impression, he knew little about sports but was a sports fan. I could also see that he had the respect of his associate, Mark Shapiro. My intuition told me that I could work with this gentleman. That proved to be correct throughout both our careers. I admired the man, his understanding, and appreciation of what I brought to the brand. He understood what I did better than anyone in sports marketing and provided me with support and resources to do it. For that, I will always be grateful and appreciative. We had so much fun building the Gatorade brand together.

Within a couple of years, 1985–86, we were outselling oatmeal, *the* brand that the company was named for.

Phil Marineau had incredible vision and leadership. Everyone within the Quaker Oats Company wanted to work on the Gatorade brand and with Phil. It was certainly more exciting than oatmeal, pork and beans, and Kibbles and Bits dog food. Now Phil had spent his entire career working at the Quaker Oats Company and on some of these as well as other brands within the portfolio. One of his personal successes was on the "Find the Captain" promotion with Captain Crunch cereal. Here, the 800 call-in system was overloaded and shut down. Phil helped AT&T design a new system and got the promotion up and running, and it became one of the most successful ever.

Phil was also a team guy. Excitement did turn into pride, and Phil was sensitive to the fact that we, on Gatorade, didn't turn pride into arrogance. To help build this "team" approach, leaders from the team came up with the slogan "The Team to Watch (TTTW)." It wasn't about arrogance, it was about understanding the importance of everyone on the team and the job they did in their respective roles. We learned what the roles of various departments and the specific importance they played in Gatorade being successful.

All Gatorade employees, from all disciplines within its business, were divided into five teams—black, green, yellow, blue, and red after the colors of the Olympic rings. There were colored t-shirts for each corresponding team member of each color. We then had an offsite teambuilding exercise over a three-day period that built unity, teamwork, and an understanding of each department's role in the business. Fun and games certainly, but it put names to faces and faces to departments and a collective pride in "Our Team to Watch" at Gatorade. We felt like we could accomplish anything, overcome any obstacle, and meet any challenge.

As with any growing brand, we faced a variety of challenges. We were outselling oatmeal and had a 90 percent market share, but competition in the category was increasing, and we needed to expand our distribution and growth internationally.

Gatorade was originally introduced in Italy in 1987 and was marketed by Chiari & Forte, a food company whose products included Cuore Olive oil, Fido dog food, Felix cat food, and other specialty food items. It's President and CEO was Giulio Malgara. He was also President, Quaker Oats, Europe. The Quaker Oats Company acquired the controlling interest in Chiari & Forti in 1981.

I remember the first time I met Giulio Malgara when he visited the Quaker Oats Company headquarters in Chicago, Illinois, in the late 1980s. He was a tall, handsome, athletic gentleman, extremely well-dressed in Italian custom designer clothing, and who spoke with an accent that left women hanging on every word. He looked and sounded like he was out of central casting from Hollywood. When he entered a room, he "owned it."

As our relationship grew, and I was promoted to Vice President of Gatorade Worldwide Sports Marketing, I became aware of his strategies and the Gatorade-sponsored programs in Italy and throughout Europe. The programs as well as the events sponsored by Gatorade and initiated by him had a different approach than our strategies and execution in the USA.

In the USA, we executed on the "Implied Endorsement Strategy." We wanted the athletes to consume Gatorade on the "field of play" in sports at all levels and specifically those sports that had the greatest visibility in media, especially television.

Now, granted, business is conducted differently throughout the world but it was clear to me as well as senior management at Gatorade, we needed structure and in every instance, definitive guidelines for sponsorships. This necessitated me writing a "how-to" for the worldwide sports marketing groups for Gatorade in their specific countries, titled "Gatorade Worldwide, Field of Play."

Giulio was an expert at getting product placement. How he got it was what I questioned. He would pay cameramen for focusing on capturing athletes consuming Gatorade as well as shots of coolers, cups and signage. In addition, he had a portfolio of athletes that he had under contract as spokespersons. No questioning the caliber of athletes he had, but what I did question was whether the investment had any measurable return (ROI).

My budget on sports marketing was around $3 million on sales of $900 million in 1990. His entire marketing budget was $24 million on $90 million in sales. We also thought that he supplemented his sports marketing expenditures across the other brands that he managed.

In the fall of 1990, we had a Gatorade worldwide meeting in Italy that was hosted by Giulio Malgara. We initially met in Milan, then on to Lake Como, and finally to Venice. Giulio was the most gracious host, and it also provided him with a forum to showcase his businesses and his country. He also used this opportunity to sell his message about his thoughts and marketing ideas.

The last time the Quaker Oats Company had any type of athlete endorsement was in 1934 when Babe Ruth was used in advertising Puffed Wheat and Puffed Rice. I have a framed photo, poster size, of that moment. So, in hindsight, we had the greatest of all time (GOAT) in baseball, and we came full circle with the greatest of all time in basketball.

Giulio took every opportunity to push his athlete endorsement strategy. He had over twenty athletes from a variety of sports signed to endorse Gatorade. In addition, Gatorade sponsored a number of high-profile events through team sponsorship and support. Malgara co-sponsored a cycling team in the Tour de France and The tour de Spain that included three world champions. Sounded great in theory, but the team had to win, and they didn't.

He was extremely proud of a yacht Gatorade sponsored in the Whitbread Round the World Race. He captured the history of the Gatorade 88 race car in NASCAR by using the number and its iconic green color and striping. The race was over 32,000 miles with a variety of scheduled stops for public relations and promotional opportunities. When he showed me the photo of the Gatorade 88 yacht, he proclaimed, "Isn't this awesome?"

I responded, "Beautiful yacht, but how many people are going to be able to see it during its journey around the world?" He never did share with me the cost of the investment, and I didn't have to be a CPA to figure the ROI on that sponsorship. Incidentally, I have a beautiful coffee table book with the Gatorade 88 yacht on the cover with photos and details of the race inside and all in Italian. I also have a poster-sized photo of it with the full spinnaker sail deployed with Gatorade signage in open sea. Impressive, I'll give him credit for that.

While at Lake Como during our meetings at a chateau, Giulio always wanting to impress. We broke for a fifteen-minute recess. When I returned to the room where we were meeting, someone asked me out loud, "Schmidt, if you had one athlete in the world to sign to be the spokesperson for Gatorade, who would it be?"

My first thought was Giulio was working the room in my absence regarding athlete endorsements. My immediate response to the question was, "Michael Jordan."

That was followed by a question from the group, "How much would that cost?"

My response was, "I'll find out."

I left the meeting room to call David Falk, Michael's attorney and agent. Meanwhile, the one-million-dollar number came to mind as I placed the call. Now my goal was to gather information, Michael Jordan's availability, and just to start a dialogue with David, not to exchange numbers or wish lists.

Now I had established a relationship with David Falk previously when Diane Primo, the marketing manager for the Quaker Oats brand, Beanie Weenies, approached me about using Michael Jordan for a cameo appearance in an ad they were creating. So several brands discussed the opportunity of how we could use Michael Jordan to promote our brand. It would also help to spread out the cost of MJ through four or five brands, but Beanie Weenies would be making the commitment for 30 percent of the assumed expense of signing Michael Jordan, around $200,000–$400,000.

Matt Mannelly, brand manager of Gatorade, brought together several thoughts and ideas he'd discussed with other brand managers. Several brands stepped forward. Life Cereal would recreate their iconic ad, "Mikey Likes It." In addition, Gatorade committed to packaging of a Michael Jordan Four Pack utilizing specific packaging for kids lunch boxes. Granola bars, a "Quaker Good for You" product, was in but with no creative or money. So limited funds, but Beanie Weenies was the pitch. Michael's response, "Are you f—king kidding me?" The one thing David Falk did say was that Michael "liked me."

So as I'm waiting to reach David Falk on the overseas call, I'm writing down some questions as well as general conversational points I want to open with. "It's been a while. How's Michael? I'm in Lake Como, Italy, wish you were here." I was always impressed with David, and we respected each other.

David Falk answered the phone, and we started a conversation. After all the "small talk," I told David, "I'm at Lake Como, Italy, at a Gatorade worldwide business meeting." I mentioned that Giulio Malgara, President of Quaker Oats Europe, was in attendance and that I was asked, "If I had one athlete to sign as a spokesperson, who would it be?" I said, "David, that's why I'm calling you."

In our following conversation, we discussed Michael's current sponsorship partners but not numbers. I didn't need to know what companies were currently paying him. I just needed know about his current relationship with Coca-Cola, the only beverage in his portfolio of sponsors. As I shared information with him about the growth of Gatorade sales and the thought that we were interested in employing a strategy of an athlete endorsing the brand and wanted to have additional conversations about what that would cost signing Michael Jordan.

David seemed excited. I tried to measure my level of excitement so as not to overplay my hand. As we talked about money, and it's always about the money, I asked, "Are we talking about high six figures starting out?"

David said, "No. I think we'd have to start at least at a million dollars and a multi-year deal."

I said, "Now I know the starting number. Let me discuss that with the brand group, and let's plan on talking again on my return and after you've shared this with Michael to gauge his interests." My last question to him was, "Is there anything you can share with me about the Coca-Cola contract that wouldn't violate your confidentiality?"

He said, "They don't have a 'right of first refusal' clause in their contract with Michael."

I casually said, "Thanks for that information, and I look forward to talking with you soon."

Holy shit, Batman! I died and went to heaven!

Now when I returned to the meeting, I shared with them my conversation in a calm demeanor. It would have to start at a million dollars and it would also have to be a multi-year contract.

The attendees for this meeting included Giulio Malgara, President of Quaker Oats Europe, Peter Vitulli, President of Gatorade, Peggy Dyer, VP of Gatorade Marketing, John Turley, Manager of Gatorade United Kingdom, Jacopo Marchi, Sports Manager of Gatorade, Italy, and myself, Bill Schmidt, VP of Gatorade Worldwide Sports Marketing.

Well, discussions started, and opinions were voiced and statements made. "Our brand has grown and will continue to grow at double-digit rate."

"Cheaper to sign him now."

"He has at least another five years in the NBA."

"He's led the NBA in scoring the last five years and been named MVP twice."

"The Bulls can win the NBA Championship this year."

Finally, "Bill, what do you think?"

"First, the million-dollar starting number is what I expected as well as the multi-year contract. All of our league and team contracts with the NFL, NBA, MLB, and NASCAR are all structured long-term to benefit from increased sales and to provided precise planning."

Next question asked me was, "So do we enter a bidding war with Coca-Cola for Michael Jordan?"

"Well, the last part of my conversation with David Falk, he confided in me that Coca-Cola didn't have a 'right of first refusal' clause in their contract with Michael Jordan. That would normally give Coke the opportunity to match any offer from a competitor. Not the case here. I think we, Gatorade, should actively pursue signing Michael Jordan as our spokesperson."

Now color me stupid or just confident, but I thought, *I can get this done! In addition, I love a challenge.*

CHAPTER 27

PASS THE COCKTAIL
NAPKIN...PLEASE

I left the Gatorade worldwide meeting in Como, Italy, with one objective: sign Michael Jordan. Sounds pretty straightforward, but I still had to get the "powers that be" at Gatorade and the Quaker Oats Company to bless the strategy and give me their approval.

All the Gatorade brand executives, including Peter Vitulli, Peggy Dyer, and Matt Mannelly endorsed the strategy. One executive thought it had to be more about "team" than just one athlete and continued to question creatives throughout their tenure on the brand.

Phil Marineau, President of the Quaker Oats Company, endorsed and supported the strategy of signing Michael Jordan. So did William D. Smithburg, CEO of the Quaker Oats Company. After all, it was his growth strategy that brought about the acquisition of Stokely-Van Camp in 1983, acquiring the "jewel" of that acquisition, Gatorade. Gatorade was his baby. Bill Smithburg was proud of Gatorade's sales growth and saw the signing of Michael Jordan as great for Gatorade and the Quaker Oats Company. Smithburg was an active sports enthusiast from Chicago who added many "good for you" products to Quaker's portfolio of brands.

Knowing about what Coke was paying Jordan, $300,000 a year, I assumed that we'd have to start or be north of that number. My strategy on all the Gatorade contracts was to have five-year deals. When I was asked what it would take to sign Michael Jordan, my answer was consistent—$1,000,000. The brand and the Quaker Oats Company agreed, and that's where the ceiling had been set.

My conversations and my strategy going forward was a process. I knew I had to make Michael feel special and had to link him to the brand. This was something where the Coca-Cola Company had failed. He was one of a stable of talented athletes, but their creatives never succeeded in connecting him to their brand.

Now I knew we were going into the arena with the "big boy brand," and I knew no matter what number we came up with, they could simply write a bigger check with the stroke of a pen, if they really wanted to keep him. Now if someone says to you, "The money doesn't really matter," there're lying. It *always* matters.

My goal was to put together a package that was competitive but specifically one that made Michael Jordan the centerpiece of the Gatorade brand going forward. He would be the face of the brand.

I knew that Michael loved Gatorade, and based on what David Falk said, Michael liked me. I knew that was not going to be enough to sign him, but it would help.

Based on the feedback from David Falk regarding Michael Jordan's relationship with Coke, I developed my strategy. "Michael didn't feel special. He was one of many athletes they had signed. When pressured, they made a commercial, but the creative was mediocre at best." I took these comments and developed a strategy around them.

1. Michael Jordan would be Gatorade's *only* spokesperson.
2. Gatorade would create a marketing/advertising campaign solely around Michael Jordan.
3. The Gatorade/Michael Jordan relationship would be managed by me.

Now money does matter, and that's what I had to outline next. I was anxious about winning the war to "steal Michael Jordan away from Coca-Cola." The thought of losing it motivated me even more. Now we were willing to spend real money to sign Michael Jordan, but we weren't going to bet the farm.

My communication with David Falk obviously increased. I sold him on Gatorade's strategy for how we'd use Michael. I was a good listener and delivered on the areas that were important to him and his client.

My negotiating strategy was always to have the prospective party that I was negotiating a deal with to send me a proposal. In that way, I knew what their objectives and goals were and their expectations. Everyone has their own desired outcome from a negotiation, and that determines their "negotiating style."

The "Bill Schmidt style" was always a win-win. In other words, each party would feel good about the outcome of the process and essentially achieve what they wanted and was happy with it. I also made it a point that during the term of the contract, I would overdeliver on what we promised. We'd add more programs and delivered more activation dollars, products, and promotions. It was just good business, and it built a relationship.

When the contract was signed and delivered, I was always posturing and positioning myself for the next contract, whether it was three or five years away. I also had built in the strategy of not letting a contract expire. I'd always tried to extend the contract before the full term had expired. This would help me plan and manage a budget with specific timelines and future commitments. Budgetary constraints were determined by Gatorade sales and business planning cycles. These fixed costs provided cost savings as well as a roadmap for our spending.

Most importantly, it kept our competitors from having the opportunity to acquire properties and events. Most times, it became a bidding war and one that we couldn't win. With the trust and support of Phil Marineau, President of the Quaker Oats Company, and Bill Smithburg, CEO of the Quaker Oats Company, I had the ability to take advantage of opportunities as they happened. As an officer of the company, I had the authority to approve an expenditure up to $1 million dollars.

There were times during an event, luncheon, dinner, or presentation when an idea would develop into an opportunity. I was able to make the commitment of dollars at that moment without approval.

Of course, I'd also use a tactic, even if the dollar amount was within my approval amount: "I can't approve that;" "I'll have to check with corporate;" or "I'll have to submit that to our agency for review." This would provide me with more time to review the proposal as well as not making me the "bad guy" in the discussion or the negotiation process.

Now I knew that Jordan's second contract with Coca-Cola would expire in July. The timeline was set, and I had a deadline that was real, and the negotiation process started. It was also imperative that the process move forward with the secrecy of "the Manhattan Project." Obviously, we weren't splitting the atom, but in the world of sports marketing, planning on stealing Michael Jordan away from Coca-Cola was huge.

The 1991 NBA All Star Game was scheduled to be played in Charlotte, North Carolina. I always attended the NBA All Star Weekend activities starting in 1985 when Gatorade began sponsoring the Slam Dunk Contest. David Falk, who represented numerous clients in the NBA, also attended every NBA All Star Weekend. We were both set to be there that weekend, so we scheduled dinner on Friday, February 8 at an Italian restaurant, my favorite food of choice.

As the evening began, David and I exchanged niceties and talked about the NBA All Star Game and the clients he represented who were in attendance. David never missed an opportunity to boast about whom he represented and whom he was recruiting as a client. Some considered him bold and brash. I considered him the very best at what he did and how well he represented his clients. David was Vice Chairman of ProServ, a sports agency founded by Donald Dell, located in Washington DC. It started mainly representing tennis players, including John McEnroe, Arthur Ashe, and many others. David Falk would eventually leave and start his own agency, FAME.

This was the evening that I'd make history by entertaining Michael Jordan's agent and then putting real numbers to securing his client's services. Up until this point, there was nothing but "pie-in-the-sky assumptions." After ordering one of David Falk's favorite wines, I had remembered a comment he made at a dinner he hosted, saying, "This wine is incredible and one of my favorites." I wrote it down that evening and brought my notes to the dinner. I also called ahead and spoke to the sommelier at the restaurant to make sure he had it in their wine cellar.

The mood was relaxed. We talked about the NBA All Star game and the Gatorade Slam Dunk Contest. We both reminisced about the 1988 NBA All Star Game and Michael Jordan's win over Dominique Wilkins in the Gatorade Slam Dunk Contest. Seen as controversial by some, it was incredible. In Chicago, Michael, on his last effort, started at the opposite foul line and took off running full speed. He crossed mid-court. The anticipation was incredible. When he reached the opposite foul line, he went airborne. He reached the basket in full stride, seemingly suspended in air, and made the dunk, and the Chicago Stadium crowd went wild. The judges posted Michael's score, a perfect fifty. He beat Dominique by two points. Michael was also named MVP of the All Star game that weekend.

Michael Jordan made a statement that 1988 NBA All-Star Game weekend with his play. He'd been in the NBA for four years, and this was his "coming out party" in Chicago and putting the league on notice that he was its next big star. I remembered his performance and also noticed how engaged the crowd was in watching him. As I presented him the Gatorade Slam Dunk Champion Trophy and the check for winning, I locked in on that incredible smile of his. It was special.

David didn't have to convince me that Michael was more than an basketball player limited to dunking a basketball. I knew that before he won the 1991 NBA World Championship and was named MVP. I was in New Orleans on March 29, 1982, at the Super Dome when Michael Jordan hit the game-winning shot for the University of North Carolina to beat Georgetown 62–61. I was the guest of Bill Wall, Executive Director of USA Basketball. I was working with him to help me organize an international basketball tournament for the 1982 World's Fair in Knoxville, Tennessee, where I was Director of Sports.

I was also in Los Angeles at the 1984 Olympics, in as the Vice President of Sports, when Michael won the gold medal with the USA Basketball Team. You didn't have to be a genius to see that this kid was talented. At the 1988 NBA All-Star Game, I realized then he had the natural ability to put people at ease, and that smile of his was sincere and engaging.

David Falk didn't have to sell me on Michael Jordan's ability on the court. I was here to find out what was the asking price to utilize him to market Gatorade.

We enjoyed the wine and appetizers, and I took the opportunity to be bold and make the first move. After all, I had invited David Falk to be my guest for dinner, and I was picking up the check. That gave me the latitude to initiate the communication on a proposed contract. This was a very friendly conversation, not hard negotiating. Just a couple of good friends enjoying a great meal and great conversation. I reached for a cocktail napkin, wrote a few numbers on it, folded it, and passed it to David. He reached for it, opened it, and smiled.

My numbers on the cocktail napkin were "$500,000 per year for three years." Total: $1,500,000. I knew he wanted $1 million a year, but this was just the starting point and to get the discussion moving.

We ordered our entrees.

David wadded up the napkin I handed to him, tossed it aside, and wrote some numbers on a napkin, folded it, and passed it to me.

The entrees arrived.

His numbers were "$1,500,000, $1,600,000, and $2,000,000" covering three years.

I wadded up his napkin, placed it aside, and wrote numbers on a new napkin, folded it, and passed it to him.

I had written "Five-year contract, $1,000,000 each year, total $5 million."

Now this became very entertaining for both of us as we ordered dessert. I kept extending the years as well as raising my numbers. I expected him to respond with a five-year deal with new numbers above what I had written.

Desserts arrived.

David smiled as he wadded up the last napkin and set it aside. What he said to me next was totally unexpected. He had just finished a forkful of his dessert and said, "What about a ten-year deal?"

Now the term of the contract might have surprised me, but I quickly responded, "That's intriguing."

In my mind, I quickly thought, *We can't afford him now, but over a ten-year period, Gatorade sales will be large enough to cover the expenditure, if the numbers are right.* I shared this with David and asked him, "What number were you thinking?" In my mind, $1 million a year, ten years, $10 million.

The obvious questions:

1. Would Michael play for ten more years?
2. What if he got injured?
3. What about if he retired?
4. What if he committed a serious crime?
5. Availability for commercial shoots? How many days?
6. Personal appearances?
7. Worldwide rights?
8. Rights to terminate contract?

David said, "$14 million." Quick math, $1.4 million a year.

I'm thinking, *That's doable.* We finished our desserts, and I ordered two glasses of port wine. We weren't celebrating, but we were feeling good about what guidelines we established and the direction we were headed.

I finished our conversation with next steps:

(1) I would sell the management of Gatorade and the Quaker Oats Company on the ten-year term of the contract.
(2) He would structure the annual contract to be flat the first few years and the last few years.

My leverage was around the eight questions I asked regarding the uncertainty on Michael's length of career, possible personal health, and behavior issues. We needed to share this uncertainty equally. Some would call it "sharing the pain." I had to leverage these as I negotiated the contract.

We ended the evening on a handshake and a hug. He said he would share with Michael the details of our dinner conversation. I also knew that this ten-year deal would be monumental for David Falk's career as well as for his ego.

We watched the 1991 NBA All-Star Game that weekend and smiled each time we greeted each other. We both felt great about our new relationship and the magnitude of a relationship with Gatorade and Michael Jordan.

Michael Jordan was the leading vote-getter in the All-Star ballots cast by the public. It was Michael Jordan's fourth All-Star Game, and the East team won, and Michael Jordan led all scorers with twenty-six points.

And, oh, those cocktail napkins were disposed of by the waiter. If he only knew.

CHAPTER 28

THE DEAL OF ALL DEALS

Leaving the 1991 NBA All-Star weekend, I felt certain that I was going to sign Michael Jordan. The groundwork had been laid, the term had been decided: ten-year deal at $14 million. It was now up to me to sell the executives at Gatorade and the Quaker Oats Company that this was a great deal and that Michael was a great fit for the brand.

The length of the contract answered the question as to how long Michael Jordan would be with Gatorade. It didn't answer the question, "How long will Michael Jordan play basketball?" He was twenty-eight years old at this point in his career. There were no guarantees. Michael could suffer a career-ending injury. He could be in an accident. He could be struck by lightning while playing golf. There were any number of reasons and or events that could end or limit Michael's basketball career over the next ten years. We just had to take that risk.

In my role of negotiating the contract, I worked with all areas of need and use of Michael Jordan as it pertained to commercial shoots, photo shoots, promotions, personal appearances, use of his name, likeness, and image with the Gatorade brand.

It may have been impossible to determine how long Michael Jordan's playing career would last, but it was equally impossible to forecast the need and usage of Michael Jordan over the next ten years. I had to structure the contract and cover all the possible scenarios. Fortunately, I had the input from not only the Gatorade brand associates but also from the advertising agency, promotions department, and equally important, the legal department.

I had gained the trust and support of both Phil Marineau and Bill Smithburg during my career at the Quaker Oats company while working on Gatorade. During this challenge, they showcased their support for me and my negotiating skills. I kept them informed, listened to their opinions, and answered all their questions. This contract would ultimately have to be approved by the board of directors of the Quaker Oats Company, and all possible items, terms, and content had be answered to perfection.

The "unknown" scared many of those on the brand and in the company. There were vocal critics of the signing of Michael Jordan by the brand as well as my ability to "do the deal." I never lacked confidence in myself, and I knew what I didn't know. To that extent, I reached out to others to finalize elements of use and needs of Michael Jordan and to protect Gatorade and its risks.

Each and every contact point regarding Michael Jordan's usage of name, image, and likeness had input and signed off on their perspective needs and use of Michael Jordan. We were going to pay Michael Jordan a lot of money and we were looking for every possible way to maximize our investment.

David Falk worked for ProServ as Vice Chairman out of their offices in Washington DC. ProServ clients were primarily tennis players from all over of the world. They had offices in Atlanta, Chicago, Dallas, Los Angeles, New York, Bologna, London, Paris, and Tokyo. Although our contract with Michael Jordan would be managed by ProServ, the contract specified that our agreement was with Jump, Inc.

David had his reasons for the payment scheduled of the $14 million. We at the Quaker Oats Company knew it had to be spread out to lessen the "hit on the business" and to limit the risks associated with the long-term deal. Pay more when we can afford it and pay less when his playing career might be over. Money and terms were set, and we reached a deal.

$50,000 a year would be paid to the Michael Jordan Foundation each year of the contract, and Michael Jordan would be paid $13.5 million over the following ten-year schedule:

Year 1: $1,000,000
Year 2: $1,000,000
Year 3: $2,000,000
Year 4: $2,000,000
Year 5: $2,500,000
Year 6: $1,000,000
Year 7: $1,000,000
Year 8: $1,000,000
Year 9: $1,000,000
Year 10: $1,000,000

Additional contracted rights and terms:

(1) "Contracted Territory," Worldwide Rights.
(2) "Endorsed Products," Gatorade brand and any brand or line extensions.
(3) "Production Days": Six days of availability of each contract year for up to six television and radio commercials and print and advertising materials.
(4) "Right of First Refusal Clause" was included.
(5) "Personal Appearance Days": Two days each year of the contract. One day in the USA and one in Europe at the company's option. If Michael Jordan retired within the term of the contract, appearance days would be expanded to ten days each year of the contract.
(6) "Special Right of Termination by the Company."
   (a) If Michael Jordan were convicted of a felony involving moral turpitude.
   (b) If Michael Jordan were to die during the term of the contract.

There were a few long discussions regarding Gatorade's rights on terminating the contract. Being charged with any crime was deemed not sufficient. It was later changed to "convicted" and to a "felony" level conviction as well as one that involved "moral turpitude."

The original contract also gave the company the right to terminate the deal if Michael Jordan became mentally or physically disabled and couldn't perform the services called for in the contract. The contract was later amended and eliminated this section. Basically, we were going to pay Michael Jordan throughout the ten-year term unless he was convicted of a "vile or depraved act with evil intent which shocks the public conscience" or if he dies. We were locked in.

Now I knew that Michael wouldn't allow this to be a bidding war between Gatorade and the Coca-Cola Company. I stated that up front before we actually started the negotiating process. There would be no going back and forth between us. The one thing I did know, Michael would allow the Coca-Cola Company a "final offer" with the same guidelines that his agent presented to Gatorade: ten years, seven figures per year.

Chuck Morrison was the current head of ethnic marketing at the Coca-Cola Company. I can't confirm that he drafted the original Coca-Cola contract with Michael Jordan. All I knew was that initial contract didn't have a first right of refusal clause. He was now the current man in charge to decide if Coca-Cola kept Michael Jordan in their stable of athletes. The Coca-Cola's offer was $750,000 per year for five years. Their only offer. There was no counteroffer from Michael Jordan and David Falk. At this point, Falk satisfied Michael Jordan's request for a Coca-Cola offer, and we at Gatorade had the green light to move forward, planning an announcement and finalizing the contract.

I had pulled off one of the greatest coups in sports marketing history. The experts' comments after the fact, not mine. I did enjoy the little challenges and "poking the bear" opportunities with the Coca-Cola Company. They could definitely write a check and were huge, but in a lot of cases, they weren't logistically efficient with fulfilling their contracts. I had a few of their clients who couldn't get cups or product contact me. I overnighted Gatorade product, cups, and coolers. Gatorade got all the exposure at a Coca-Cola sponsored event.

We rented a house for a month in Atlanta, Georgia, during the 1996 Olympics. Atlanta was the world headquarters for Coca-Cola. Greg Via, a sports manager on my staff, filled not only the three-car garage but two of the four bedrooms with Gatorade, cups, coolers, towels, and other merchandise. We had contracts with numerous sports governing bodies, but we had no affiliation with the Olympics, its rings, nor its teams. We, however, did have relationships, and Greg Via was one of the best in managing them.

Greg entered the Olympic Village daily with Gatorade towels, merchandise, squeeze bottles, as well as product. He had credentials and entered legally. The individual national teams we supported through contracts of at least five-year terms. Coca-Cola sponsored the Olympic Teams which were every four years. Greg knew the team managers, staff, and athletes. Individuals and team representatives could also pick up larger numbers of items and product at our house by appointment. Greg also purchased tickets in advance for a variety of events as well as opening and closing ceremonies. We offered these to families of athletes as well as sales guests and clients.

While in the Atlanta suburbs, Greg Via and I worked out at a gym about ten minutes from the house we were renting. I met the young lady who I thought was managing the gym. She later turned out to be the owner. I said we'd be here for a month working out and that we were with Gatorade.

She said, "We have executives from Coca-Cola who work out here every day." She also said the Coca-Cola people were arrogant. I found out that one of those executives was Sergio Zyman, Coca-Cola's Chief Marketing Officer.

I was about to have some fun as well as being a pain in the ass to Coca-Cola in their hometown and during their marquee event. I structured a sponsorship with her and her gym. We replaced her entire inventory of towels with Gatorade towels, delivered two Gatorade vending machines, and an inventory of Gatorade squeeze bottles. I also paid her $5,000 included in the sponsorship package. Everyone entering the gym would be offered a Gatorade towel as well as a Gatorade squeeze bottle. A big smile came across my face each time I thought of Sergio Zyman being offered a Gatorade towel and Gatorade squeeze bottle each time he checked into the gym.

Prior to the opening of the 1996 Atlanta Olympics, an executive at McDonald's told me he had a billboard during the Olympics that they decided they weren't going to use. He asked me if Gatorade wanted it. I said, "Hell yeah." I later found that it was located near the Coca-Cola Headquarters. I was excited. I already decided I was going to use a Michael Jordan print ad with the title "World's Greatest."

When I mentioned it to the executives at Gatorade and the Quaker Oats Company, their response was, "We don't want to piss off Coca-Cola." We didn't do the billboard.

On July 25, 1996, William D. Smithburg, Chairman and CEO of the Quaker Oats Company, received a letter from the Chief Marketing Officer of the Atlanta Committee for the Olympic Games. His letter said that the ACOG had been told that Gatorade was going to "distribute large quantities of Gatorade-branded sports bottles or squeeze bottles at Olympic venues beginning this Friday, July 26." The letter further stated that "current research shows that over 80 percent of consumers hold highly negative opinions of companies and products identified as ambush marketers of the Olympic Games."

They were really worried about us "tarnishing our brand by this type of action." The letter ended with, "We will be contacting you shortly to talk about this matter so that we will be able to appropriately respond to questions about your promotional programs in our marketing briefings with 15,000 journalists covering the Olympic Games in Atlanta."

Really? We had no such promotional campaign, but it felt good to know that we pissed off Coca-Cola.

After the signing of the Michael Jordan contract, we brought in our advertising agency, Bayer Bess Vanderwarker, to share their creative ideas in launching the Michael Jordan/Gatorade spokesperson announcement with a commercial. The first commercial they showed us was about a kid in Yugoslavia who wrote a letter addressed to "Michael Jordan, USA." The cut-and-paste footage of Michael dunking the basketball with the voice over was approved.

Meanwhile, Bayer Bess Vanderwarker brought back their former creative chief, Bernie Pitzel. He viewed the already approved commercial idea and thought it lacked creativity, and it really didn't connect the Gatorade brand to the iconic basketball player, Michael Jordan.

I received a call from Steve Seyferth, an account executive from Bayer Bess Vanderwarker. "Bill, we have something we want to show you, and we need your help." Bernie Pitzel came up with new creative that included the song from the 1967 Disney movie, *The Jungle Book*. Having never seen the movie, I was curious. The song was titled "I Wanna Be Like You." They explained the creative. I liked it. They wanted my help to negotiate the rights to use the music.

Most commercial music can be obtained for fees in the $30,000 to $100,000 range, depending on the song, composer, and artist. You also normally have rights that extend for months to possibly a year. When I contacted Disney, they wanted $1,000,000, and we could run the commercial with the music for five weeks. That didn't work. David Falk contacted Disney, and they quoted him $500,000 with five weeks usage.

Bernie Pitzel went to work and scripted his own lyrics around the theme of "Be Like Mike" and not infringing on Disney's music. He did his best creative work at Avanzare, his and my favorite restaurant. He scribed it on a paper tablecloth:

Sometimes I dream
That he is me
You've got to see that's how I dream to be
I dream I move, I dream I groove
Like Mike
If I could Be Like Mike
Again I try
Just need to fly
For just one day if I could
Be that way

> I dream I move
> I dream I groove
> Like Mike
> If I could Be Like Mike

After writing the lyrics, Pitzel faxed them to four Chicago music companies. Ira Antelis and his partner, Steve Shafer, both jingle writers, submitted what they thought would be a hit. It was. The music was cast. Now it was time to put the creative with the music. Oh, yes, one other thing. Michael Jordan was known as Michael Jordan, *not* Mike Jordan. They asked me to get Michael's approval to use "Mike" in "Be Like Mike." Now David Falk had built all campaigns and sponsorships around "Michael Jordan." Everyone assumed it was going to be challenging.

When talking to Michael, I said, "One other thing. I need your approval to use 'Mike' in 'Be Like Mike.'"

He didn't hesitate. "Sure." I'm certain David Falk wasn't excited about it. He did come around later to accept the creative.

Gatorade's announcement of the Jordan relationship also included the hiring of Burson-Marsteller, a public relations firm with an office in Chicago. Its CEO was John LaSage, one of the very best in managing the media, press conferences, and crisis management. John was exceptional, and with his help, we scripted a press conference for the big public announcement. He designed special invitations, room decorations, scripts for the speakers, as well as press releases and quotes. Michael Jordan showed up. I was managing the press conference which included a question and answer segment. All you had to say was "Michael Jordan will be here" and the time, and everybody showed up. Michael made it successful, not me!

Phillip Marineau, President of the Quaker Oats Company, wanted the entire Quaker Oats Company to share in the success of the signing of their local Chicago Bulls star. On August 8, 1991, over 2,000 Quaker employees gathered under a tented parking lot to greet "the man." They also viewed the "Be Like Mike" commercial. Michael was introduced in the same fashion he was introduced at the Chicago Stadium with the same music and by the stadium announcer. It was awesome.

Bayer Bess Vanderwarker also did a $1 million eight-page buy in *Sports Illustrated*, August 12, 1991. It featured an eight-page fold-out starting with the first page stating, "After leading the league in scoring," and it folded open to a picture of Michael Jordan on the left side, smiling. Copy only on the right page, "After taking the Bulls to the Eastern Conference Championship," and fold out the page. Extending arm of Michael on the left with copy on the right, "And after winning the NBA title, what is there left to reach for?" It folded open the last page with more of the extending arm and the last page on the right, a green-colored Gatorade-logoed cup in Michael's hand, arm fully extended. It was awesome.

Initially, Peggy Dyer, Vice President of Marketing for Gatorade, wanted Michael to be in a Chicago Bulls white game jersey. I again received a call from Steve Seyferth, account executive with Bayer Bess Vanderwarker. "We need your help." They needed me to convince Peggy Dyer that a black singlet was the best way to present the ad. I agreed, and eventually, Peggy did too.

Walter Iooss Jr., the renowned sports photographer, did the shoot. Many thought his photo of Michael Jordan in this *Sports Illustrated* spread was very similar to the Michael Jordan's Nike Wings poster. So with a song similar to a Disney song and a photo similar to a Nike poster, we launched our Michael Jordan Gatorade relationship to the world. And as Walt Disney would say when he really appreciated creative that was presented to him, "Good stuff."

David Falk went on to use the Michael Jordan Gatorade contract as a template for all of Michael Jordan sponsorships going forward. In a ninety-day period, David signed ten other sponsors for ten-year deals, each of them paying $5 million a year. So $500 million for Michael Jordan and Jump, Inc. We averaged $1.4 million a year, $14 million total, "the deal...of all deals."

Bill Schmidt professional/ BUSINESS EXPERIENCES

Phil Marineau, President, The Quaker Oats Company, William D Smithburg, Chairman, CEO, The Quaker Oats Company and Bill Schmidt, VP of Gatorade Worldwide Sports Marketing at the Gatorade Windy City Classic at Comiskey Park. Chicago Cubs versus Chicago White Sox.

"Be Like Mike" phot shoot. Standing: Bill Daily, Director, Sports Marketing Gatorade, Peggy Dyer, Vice President of Marketing Gatorade, Matt Mannelly, Director, Consumer/Gatorade, Jane Richtsmeier, Vice President, Sr. Account Supervisor, Bayer Bess Vanderwarker, Bernie Pitzel, Sr. Vice President, Group Creative Director, Bayer Bess Vanderwarker, Steve Seyferth, Sr. Vice President, Account Director, Bayer Bess Vanderwarker, Account Director, Bayer Bess Vanderwarker, Seated: Michael Jordan, Bill Schmidt, Vice President Sports Marketing Gatorade.

Press Conference announcing Gatorade signing Michael Jordan as its spokesperson. Left to right: Bill Schmidt, VP Gatorade Worldwide Sports Marketing, William D Smithburg, Chairman CEO The Quaker Oats Company, Michael Jordan, Peter Vitulli, President Gatorade.

Bill Schmidt welcoming Michael Jordan at the Quaker
Oats Company employees rally after announcing he
was signed as a spokesperson for Gatorade.

James and Deloris Jordan visiting "Casa Italia" while the USA Dream
Team was competing in Barcelona in 1992. They were hosted by
Jacopo Marchi, Sports Marketing Manager, Gatorade Italy. Michael
couldn't attend but we had a MJ life size cutout present.

Bill Schmidt presenting the championship trophy in
Victory Lane at Daytona Speedway to Dale Earnhardt
for winning one of the Gatorade Twin 125 races.

Presenting Peyton Manning with the Gatorade Player of the Year Award on the field at the Superdome during a New Orleans Saints game. Left to right: Eli Manning, Cooper Manning, Olivia Manning, Archie Manning, Peyton Manning, Bill Schmidt, Bruce Weber, Publisher, Scholastic magazine.

Riding through the Black Hills of South Dakota.

Bob and I celebrating our 40th birthday on the 18th tee at
Pebble Beach Golf Club, Pebble Beach, California.

Me and Bob recently hanging out at a bourbon bar in Kentucky.

CHAPTER 29

LEVERAGING THE MICHAEL JORDAN BRAND

When I was negotiating the Michael Jordan contract with David Falk, his agent, I had to anticipate all the possible needs as well as requirements for the Gatorade brand. Worldwide Rights and usage as a spokesman, his likeness, image, and commercials were obvious. The challenge was to put the details in place that would satisfy current needs as well as those during the ten-year term of the contract.

I had numerous meetings and input from the brand, both in the USA and in Europe, as to their specific needs. Asia was a growth market, and although sales were minimal and the business was operated through licensing agreements, it was essential that we plan for the introduction and growth of the brand. The usage of Michael Jordan in marketing and promotions in the region and throughout the world had to be planned and executed. Michael Jordan was quickly becoming a "worldwide brand," and Gatorade's goal was to leverage him to make Gatorade a global brand.

Michael Jordan would be essential in introducing Gatorade to the world. In most places, the consumer had no idea what a "sports beverage" was, but they knew Michael Jordan. The challenge was to build the Gatorade brand leveraging Michael Jordan, not just build the Michael Jordan brand.

Some of the best creative, in my view, came from the emerging markets. All advertising and creative had to be approved through Gatorade USA marketing and Gatorade Worldwide Sports marketing department, which I was responsible for. We, in turn, would be the clearing house and get approval from FAME, David Falk's company, that represented Michael Jordan and other numerous athletes.

These emerging markets were introducing a brand, they weren't protecting a brand. Marketing brands throughout the world is different, and each country and region utilizes different techniques and tools to get their message to their consumer. In addition, some markets have restrictions on how a product is marketed or how a spokesperson is used in marketing a product.

Some of the more unique proposals included signage of Michael Jordan in full layout "dunk mode" on both sides of a city bus. There were also signage techniques utilized on bottles of Gatorade. Many were considered "in-your-face marketing" promoting Michael, not the brand, and were not approved internally. The demands and requests for approval of Michael Jordan advertising along the unending question of which sports our country should sponsor made me develop a "Gatorade Worldwide Field of Play Manual." A "How-To" manual, regardless of country, to choose which sports to target and how to leverage relationships in the sports community.

In the final analysis, I guess we did strike the right balance between building the Gatorade brand and utilizing the Michael Jordan relationship. I, however, would have loved the opportunity to have expanded the use of Michael Jordan along with a budget to accomplish it. Gatorade was creative in a variety of ways, but I would have liked to have "pushed the envelope" a bit further both in advertising and promotions.

Michael Jordan would be advertised and promoted as our "premiere spokesperson," and after retiring from playing professional basketball, he'd be an "ambassador" for the brand. This element was key in the signing of Michael while at Coca-Cola, Michael was one of many athletes in Coca-Cola's stable of athletes. In the negotiation of the contract, I committed to Michael that he'd be the "only athlete we'd sign to endorse Gatorade." Years later, we would receive Michael's approval to use Mia Hamm in a commercial with him. She was a fellow University of North Carolina graduate. This commercial enabled us to broaden the usage to women and was developed around the theme of "Anything you can do, I can do better." It pitted Michael versus Mia in a variety of sports competitions.

Commercial production dates per year would be six. Each commercial shoot would be two four-hour days. Most commercials require the "talent" to be there on set for twelve hours. This was usually "sitting around time." We needed to be more efficient. We'd have a Michael Jordan "lookalike" on set for the entire pre-and post-process for lighting purposes as well as activities that didn't necessitate using Michael. In addition, I hired Michael's favorite chef, who had her own trailer. She'd cook his favorite foods as well as make his favorite chocolate chip cookies. I'd also show up on the first day of shooting with a box of Michael's favorite Cuban cigars, Montecristo's #2. They cost me $500 a box, and I couldn't expense them. A few years later, Phil Marineau, then President of the Quaker Oats Company, approved reimbursing me for these cigars in my expense reports.

I negotiated two "personal appearance days" per year with one being in the United States and one in Europe. These were also based on Michael's availability and limited to four hours, exclusive of travel time. If Michael retired during the term of the contract, personal appearances would be ten per year for the remaining years of the contract.

David Falk and I had agreed early in our negotiations that the term would be ten years. We also agreed the total compensation over the term would be $14 million. My goal was to spread the payments over this period that would best suit the growth of sales of Gatorade, a "pay as you grow" strategy—greatest endorsement contract ever! The Quaker Oats Company/Gatorade would be average paying $1.4 million per year, and the other Michael Jordan endorsement contracts that followed paid $5 million a year for ten years or $50 million in total. In my separation package from Gatorade, I still regret not having negotiated a "Gatorade for Life" clause for me, just on the Michael Jordan contract. I still purchase and consume Gatorade daily.

On July 22, 1991, we signed the contract with Michael Jordan and Jump, Inc., his company represented by David Falk and ProServ, Inc., located in Arlington, Virginia. David Falk would later leave

ProServ and form FAME, his own company—Falk Associates Management Enterprises.

Our Quaker Oats Company worldwide entities, partners, and licensing groups continued to have great growth, and Bill Smithburg's strategy to divest or sell off the slower growth businesses proved successful. His strategy in finding another acquisition that would rival Gatorade failed. The acquisition of Snapple proved to be disastrous and cost him his job. Snapple had Wendy, the Snapple Lady, and Gatorade had Michael Jordan—conflicting cultures and different strategies as well as distribution systems. The Quaker Oats Company acquired Snapple for $2.1 billion and ended up selling it for $300 million. Somebody had to lose their job.

We were able to leverage Michael Jordan's success with the Chicago Bulls and the six NBA World Championships that he won and grew Gatorade sales. In addition, our partnership with the NBA enabled us to grow internationally with USA Basketball and the Dream Team at the 1992 Barcelona Olympics. We were also able to be proactive with advertising and the use of Michael Jordan when he retired from the NBA and basketball to pursue a baseball career.

At the 1992 Barcelona Olympics, Gatorade purchased a broadcast sponsorship with NBC Sports. Housing was at a premium, but with the NBC purchase, we had several cabins on a cruise ship docked in the Barcelona harbor. With unbelievable excitement worldwide regarding the "Dream Team," we had an opportunity to leverage Michael Jordan and USA Basketball without paying the exorbitant price of an Olympic sponsorship. We really didn't need the Olympic rings. We had Michael Jordan.

We invited Michael's mom and dad, James and Deloris Jordan, to be the guests of Gatorade. They, in turn, invited Michael's aunt to join them. In addition to seeing all the USA Basketball team's games, they enjoyed other Olympic events as our guests.

I needed to have Michael sign several of his #9 USA team jerseys and one document. I had to reach out to Director Barbara Allen at FAME. Barbara Allen was absolutely the *best*. She managed all requests as well as approvals for advertising, promotions, graphics, and appearances for Michael Jordan. She managed other athletes for FAME and was exceptional at her job.

Barbara was extremely efficient, intelligent, straight to the point, organized, as well as protective of Michael Jordan, her client. Barbara would reply to all requests with a sense of urgency. I loved the professional relationship that we shared.

The Dream Team, the 1992 USA Olympic Basketball Team, was staying at the Hotel Ambassador in Barcelona. I did receive clearance with the help of BA, to visit and enter the hotel. It was an armed encampment surrounded with barbed wire, an army of guards, as well as an armored personnel vehicle strategically located in the courtyard. The courtyard was gated, and admittance was gained by clearance through a variety of checkpoints and undergoing numerous screening devices.

Once I cleared security, I met with Michael in the lower lobby level. We were by ourselves, except for David Robinson, who was practicing playing a saxophone in the far corner of the room. David Robinson played for the San Antonio Spurs in the NBA and was a top player in his own right. Michael signed a few jerseys as well as the document I needed him to sign.

Gatorade had several Michael Jordan promotions with him being on the USA Team. We could advertise the USA Basketball Team but not the Olympic Team or use of the Olympic rings. We did several promotions with Michael Jordan "Pop a Shot" machines with Michael Jordan's action photo on the bank board in his USA Team jersey. We also did a promotion giving away a Michael Jordan signed USA Team jersey. I completed my mission. Michael thanked me for inviting his parents, and I wished him good luck during the Olympic Games. They didn't need luck. They beat their opponents by an average of 43.8 points. I was there for the gold medal game against Croatia along with Michael's parents and aunt.

During the medal ceremony, everyone thought how great it was that Michael had an American flag draped over his shoulder. I, too, thought it was patriotic, but I also knew immediately, it was to cover the Reebok logo. Michael Jordan was extremely loyal to his sponsors, one of which was Nike.

Michael Jordan was a sponsor's dream. His endorsement of any product brought immediate recognition and an increase in sales. This was true for Gatorade then and throughout the ten-year contract I negotiated in 1991.

As we did for every Gatorade event, we supplied swag bags to all our guests. Our Italian team provided Gatorade-logoed bags with a variety of Gatorade-logoed shirts, hats, pins, squeeze bottles, and towels. We had about a hundred bags. A variety of people in addition to our guests requested and even offered to purchase the bags. The USA Basketball pins and logoed items were a big hit.

Ira Harris, a friend of mine from Chicago and a merger and acquisitions specialist for Solomon Brothers Investment Bank, requested a bag for him and his wife. He was a guest of Coca-Cola and on the cruise ship that was adjacent to ours. He told me he caught some dirty looks when he boarded the ship that evening. The next day, I gave him an additional six bags and told him to give them away on his ship. Ira Harris was responsible for the Quaker Oats acquisition of Stokely-Van Camp that included Gatorade.

I tried never to miss an opportunity to let Coca-Cola know that Gatorade was present and visible. Coca-Cola paid hundreds of millions of dollars for their sponsorship of the Olympics, and a $200 gift bag got us visibility in their backyard. It felt like we invaded their castle. Small moral victory, I know, but a victory no less.

CHAPTER 30

AUGUSTA WITH THE GOAT

Golf is a game that I love, and I've been fortunate and blessed to have played some of the most prestigious golf courses in America and in the world. It's also a game that tests an individual in a variety of ways. I've always said you can learn a lot about an individual when you play golf with them for four and a half hours.

How do they handle adversity? Are they honest? What type of a competitor are they? How do they manage risk? How well do they communicate? Do they have integrity? Believe me, in a little over four hours and normally after nine holes, I can determine if I want to do business with this individual and even ever play golf with them again.

Now I'm far from being perfect, but the Lord has blessed me in a variety of ways. In two specific areas of my first impressions and intuition, the Lord really blessed me. I trust my intuition or as some people like to refer to it as "that deep down in your gut feeling." I don't remember the exact first time I decided to trust it. I'm certain being raised Catholic and the instilled learnings of right from wrong did influence me.

It wasn't until my athletic career ended and the starting of my business career was I conscious of this inert competency. It was also about the same time that I trusted my first impression of people. Now I promise you it went beyond how the person looked, dressed, or talked. Using this criteria alone would seem to be shallow.

My mind works in a unique fashion. It's as if I could take in a multitude of information, process it, and make an accurate assessment. I found that I paid particular attention to details. My mind would process as my eyes would rove. The information included but not limited to body language, eye contact, stature, voice, facial expression, how they interacted with others, and the first few words that came out of their mouth. People can quickly tell you a lot about themselves without saying anything.

I found this roving eye assessment ability to be extremely valuable in my business career. I could "eye" a situation, venue, or problem, assess it, realize opportunities, and capitalize on it or seek solutions and resolutions. This was definitely an asset.

A colleague of mine in the sports business industry, when introducing me to his company staff, stated, "Bill's an individual who can not only develop great creative. He can follow it through with how to execute it. That's rare."

I was flattered.

Also in my business career, I was credited in numerous situations or instances with "That's genius," when all along, it was common sense to me. As they say, common sense isn't common to a lot of people. Street sense falls somewhere in there as well. Experience helps too.

My love of golf and not taking myself too seriously enabled me to meet a variety of influential people and build great relationships, some that shaped my career and influenced my reputation. John LaSage was one of those.

When I first met John, it was at a charity fundraising event. Later, I would see him at his best when he managed the crisis management of a Gatorade recall for tainted product in California. Long's Drugstores voluntarily recalled lemon-lime Gatorade from its 198 stores in Alaska, Arizona, California, Hawaii, Nevada, and Oregon. The California Attorney General threatened to pull all Gatorade product from all grocery stores in the state.

A firefighter had purchased some product, consumed it, and became severely ill. California health officials investigated and later discovered urine in the product but not before Gatorade product had been pulled from the shelves in numerous grocery stores throughout the western region of the United States. This was August of 1985.

Tampered product in grocery stores was highlighted by the Tylenol scare in 1982 when seven people died in Chicago from ingesting Tylenol that had been laced with potassium cyanide.

It was discovered that at the store, where the tampered lemon-lime Gatorade product was purchased, two stock clerks had removed the caps and urinated in several bottles. The implication of not only empty shelves in numerous states but the public's perception of bad product translated into a public relations nightmare.

John LaSage's management of this crisis, his plan, and its execution was exceptional. Product was back in the stores within days, and the public was made aware of this being an isolated tampering incident. The product was safe, and all communication from Quaker Oats, the manufacturer of Gatorade, and stores in the western region reassured the public Gatorade was safe to purchase as well as to consume.

John's client list read like a "Who's Who" in corporate America. Crisis management isn't all that he focused on as CEO of the Midwest Regional office of Burson-Marsteller, the world's largest public relations and communications company. Their services included developing public relations campaigns, new product launches, press conferences, corporate imaging, CEO training, and media training, to just name a few, and are legendary. One time, there were nearly fifty-four Fortune 500 companies headquartered in Chicago. He personally knew the CEOs, their boards, and was connected not only to the business community but Chicago's social/philanthropic community as well. He knew everyone. To say he was connected is an understatement.

John LaSage had an individual on his staff, a senior consultant named Irving Seaman Jr. Irv's background was in a variety of leadership roles in the banking industry. He spent over fifty years in the field and lived in Lake Forest, an upscale community north of Chicago. His contacts and reputation in the Chicago business and charitable organizations were endless. A graduate of Yale, he served on numerous boards and knew everyone. I'd say between John LaSage and Irv Seaman, they had Chicago covered as well as the New York City area.

There was also another area where Irv Seaman proved to be most valuable. Not only was he a member of the most prestigious golf clubs on the Northshore, he was a member of Augusta National in Augusta, Georgia. Yes, that Augusta where the Masters is played.

Now I played with John in a variety of corporate golf events in Chicago as his guest. I also reciprocated and invited him to a variety of Gatorade events, including golf, baseball, as well as the Bulls games. This included NBA and Major League Baseball games. He was quite the sports fan and very knowledgeable as well.

John worked on the Gatorade account personally. I took Burson-Marsteller's media training seminar, and it proved valuable throughout my career. We also hired him to organize our campaign, announcing the signing of Michael Jordan as our Gatorade spokesperson. He managed everything form the press conference, press releases, interviews, follow-up, and provided us with exceptional leadership and a great "Be Like Mike" campaign.

We employed John LaSage throughout my time at Gatorade and the Quaker Oats Company. He not only provided great campaigns, but he provided great crisis management strategies. That included everything from tainted Gatorade product to allegations of Michael's gambling, the Dream Team, and Michael's retirement and return to basketball.

I don't exactly remember the first time he invited me to play at Augusta, but I believe he had an individual who canceled at the last minute, and he needed a fourth. I thought, "I've died and gone to heaven." Now I know what you're thinking. "Why would anyone cancel a trip to Augusta?" I believe it was due to a death in his family. Either way, I was there!

Throughout my personal relationship with Michael Jordan, John LaSage was there. He was at our MJ commercial shoots, personal appearances, promotional campaigns, and, yes, the NBA Finals. I had negotiated a great contract with Michael Jordan, and John brought "added value" through his area of PR and communications expertise where we were able to leverage that contract.

Frankly, I think John LaSage floated the idea of Michael playing golf at Augusta at one of our MJ commercial shoots. Of course, we had to work it around Michael's schedule and ultimately through Irv Seaman, a member at Augusta and an employee of John's at Burson-Marsteller.

Now, I'd never if rarely talked to Irv Seaman on the phone. I'd see him at the airport as well as throughout my visits to Augusta National with him to play. So I was surprised when my assistant said, "There's a gentleman, Irv Seaman, on the phone for you." Of course I took the call.

Now Irv was a man of few words, and he got right to the point.

"Smitty, I've received a call from Augusta National Golf Club, and their concerned about Michael Jordan's allegations of high stakes gambling on the golf course."

I told Irv that while I was aware of those allegations, I assured him that there would be no gambling of any kind with Michael Jordan when/if we played Augusta National Golf Club.

Within weeks, Irv Seaman communicated through John LaSage that we had a date scheduled for us to play Augusta National Golf Club. We now had to confirm the date through Michael Jordan's assistant at FAME, which was David Falk's Agency, and his agent. Within a week, we had it on Michael's schedule, and we were good to go. John LaSage said that Irv Seaman was extremely nervous about the event, but Irv was relying on me to manage Michael as well as his behavior.

We arrived at the "hallowed grounds" and checked in at the reception area and were assigned to the California Cabin. It was named for the group of California members who had it built for the club. There were four bedrooms with a common living room as well as a small kitchen.

There was a buzz around Augusta National Golf Club about MJ being there. Irv assured us that the word was out and that members, guests, caddies, and workers were informed about their expected behavior.

Normally, when playing at Augusta National Golf Club, a member's caddie would place a ball next to the tee markers to indicate the order to tee off. Sidney was Mr. Seaman's caddie, and it was rare that Mr. Seaman's ball wasn't first in the lineup; again, no tee times. I remember once when it was in second or third, but when got to the tee, the other members would let Mr. Seaman's group tee off first.

It was extremely important for the first group out to set the pace for the day and for the following groups. Irv stressed how important this was. A trip to Augusta National Golf Club meant you played eighteen holes with caddies, have lunch, and play eighteen more with maybe one cart. Then we'd play the par 3 course. A long day, but we were in heaven. We'd be there usually for three days with the same routine except for the last day. One round of eighteen holes, lunch, shower, then off to the airport to catch a flight.

We had breakfast delivered to the California Cabin, where Michael introduced us to his special concoction of scrambled eggs with grits. He called it "Greggs." Seemed natural to me. After breakfast, we headed to the range to hit some balls and meet our caddies. Then to the first tee.

Every time I played Augusta National Golf Club, I had the same caddie, MacArthur Williams. He went by Mac. Now Mac, over the years, attended an NBA Finals game in Chicago, the NBA All-Star Game in Miami, and a Super Bowl in Atlanta, all courtesy of me.

Now we arrived at the members tee box, and we looked back, and MJ was at the tips or the farthest set of back tees where the professional golfers tee off. John and I looked at Mr. Seaman, and we did the Michael Jordan and hunched our shoulders when a three-point shot goes in unexpectedly. "Why not?" As the older members watched from their forward tee, we teed off over them, and our adventure had begun. Mr. Seaman said he'd never been back here before. Irv at this time was near eighty years old.

Now it might have been my imagination, but it seemed like the "flotilla" of mowers were in front of us throughout the first several holes. We were all having a great time and loved the challenge of playing from the tee box location that MJ selected.

When we got to the seventh tee box, a par 4, there was a plastic envelope and a Sharpie pen tied to it and a note that said, "MJ, please?" We all hit, and Michael didn't notice it, but I pulled it out of the ground and asked him to sign it. He did willingly. When we approached the green after our second shots, a number of carts with only women in them surrounded us. They were excited and asked for photos and autographs. Michael loved it, and he was very gracious. Irv wasn't moved by the incident.

Practices changed over the years, and we were able to order dinner and have it delivered to our cabin as opposed to eating in the dining room which required a coat and tie. That evening, we— John, Irv, MJ, and I—were invited to the Butler cabin to have cocktails with the Chairman of Augusta National Golf Club, Mr. Jack Stephens. Irv said he'd never been invited for cocktails before. John and I joked that maybe Mr. Stephens was going to invite us to join Augusta National Golf Club.

We were also informed that our attendance would require a coat and tie. Now Mr. Seaman's green jacket was in his cabin in the closet upon his arrival, as was customary for all members. John LaSage and I had jackets as well as ties. MJ had a jacket but no ties. I invited him to select from the assortment of ties that I brought. None suited him. I did bring a tie, an MJ tie with a design of his hand with three championship rings with great color. He mumbled an obscenity but put the tie on. I previously had him autograph it. He wasn't excited about wearing it, but he had little choice.

We arrived at Butler cabin and were greeted by Mr. Stephens's assistant who welcomed us. He introduced us to Mr. Stephens, and he was very gracious. An employee, a bartender, made us drinks, and we had about two hours of conversations along with a professional photographer taking photos. A lot of photos. Individually and in groups. Mostly of MJ and Mr. Stephens. John I realized quickly that this was about MJ and Mr. Stephens and not about our invitation to join the club.

After golf the next day and before we departed, Michael wanted to go by the pro shop. I've never seen a larger collection of Bobby Jones Signature Collection of clothing before or since. The golf shop professionals, both from Chicago, preordered all the designs and colors of every shirt and vest made by Bobby Jones available in XXL sizes, MJ's size. Now he couldn't purchase them. They had to charge to Mr. Seaman's account, and I asked Irv if it was okay, and we'd settle up when he got his monthly statement.

I again received an unexpected call from Mr. Seaman weeks later. "Smitty, two things. The charges from the pro shop are in, and they're a little over $4,000."

"No problem, Irv, Gatorade will pay it. Send me an invoice."

Irv also said Mr. Stephens had sent a few pictures for Michael to sign. I said, "Send them over too."

Irv said, "There are a lot of photos, and they have Post-it notes on each one as to who they are for." I was thinking, *How bad could it be?*

I received the invoice as well as the pictures. Irv was right. About a hundred-plus photos with notes on each one to whom they were for. This was going to be a challenge. I rarely asked Michael to sign anything except at our commercial shoots. A few balls and a few jerseys. Mostly charitable causes. I brought out the stack of photos from Mr. Stephens with individual Post-it notes attached. Michael said, "You've got to be shitting me!"

I looked at him and said, "You want to ever play Augusta National Golf Club again?"

He signed them all and signed them to the individuals Mr. Stephens had directed.

CHAPTER 31

IT WAS THE BEST OF TIMES; IT WAS THE WORST OF TIMES

Charles Dickens was right in his opening line of *A Tale of Two Cities*. Gatorade had experienced tremendous growth, and sales had exceeded $800 million by 1993. We signed Michael Jordan, the most recognizable athlete on the planet. He and his "Dream Team" had won the Olympic Gold medal in the Barcelona, Spain, Olympics in 1992. Michael Jordan and the Chicago Bulls had won their third consecutive NBA Championship defeating the Phoenix Suns, 4–2, in the best of seven series finals in 1993. Michael averaged 41 points per game and was named MVP for the third consecutive year. I had had been promoted to Vice President of Worldwide Sports Marketing for Gatorade. Life was good.

I learned that in addition to Benjamin Franklin's certainties of "death and taxes," you could add "change." Times do change, things happen. To say that 1993 would be a year of change is an understatement.

In July of 1993, James Jordan, Michael's dad, was murdered along US Highway 74 while sleeping in his car. "Pops," as he was known as, had been reported missing for weeks. Those of us close to Michael shared in the anxiety of the times for him and his family. James Jordan's body had been found on August 3 in a swamp in McColl, South Carolina. It was not identified until August 13,

1993. The body had been in a state of decomposition, and the coroner cremated the body, saving the jawbone and fingers for future identification purposes. Michael's life changed as did those who had a relationship with him.

James Jordan's funeral was on August 15, 1993, in Teachey, North Carolina. William Smithburg, CEO of the Quaker Oats Company, made the corporate jet available to the family. I, along with family and friends of Michael and Juanita Jordan, flew to North Carolina for the service. Upon arriving in Wilmington, North Carolina, we assembled with Michael Jordan, Deloris Jordan, and other family members. Dean Smith, legendary basketball coach from the University of North Carolina, embraced Michael and gave his condolences.

We then proceeded to disperse into six limousines that were waiting our arrival. With a North Carolina Highway Patrolman leading us, the caravan headed out for the forty-five-minute drive to Teachy, North Carolina. We were traveling at a high rate of speed, and about twenty minutes into the drive, the North Carolina state policeman pulled off, and we were on our own.

When we reach the road leading to the Rockfish AME Church, each side of the road was lined with television satellite trucks. This was news to the world, and the world was there to cover it. Our vehicles pulled up and parked next to the church. The church was already full as we entered through the side door. As David Falk, Michael's agent, Ahmad Rashad, renowned sports broadcaster, and I were ushered into a pew, Michael went forward to embrace his mother and other family members. There were about 200 people in attendance.

There were four ladies from the church or provided by the funeral director, dressed in all white, offering water and hand fans to all those present. It was hot, and there was limited air circulation. For a moment, it reminded me of a movie set. It was surreal.

As the minister welcomed everyone, family members spoke and related stories of James Jordan's humor and importance as a man, husband, father, and Air Force veteran. All the while, those in attendance were wondering if Michael would speak. What would he say? Michael approached the podium with his dad's casket draped with an American flag between him and the audience. We all held our breaths.

As he stood at the podium, he hesitated, then smiled, and said, "I always wondered what it would be like to be up here."

We all laughed and exhaled.

He went on to say how important his dad was in his life and the lives of his four siblings. As I listened intently and viewed the flag draped casket, I thought, *The body of James Jordan isn't in the casket.* His remains consisted of his jawbone and fingers. His body had been cremated before having been identified. Michael ended, saying, "Don't dwell on his death, but celebrate the life he lived." A very moving and heartfelt emotional moment.

The six pallbearers, including George Koehler, Michael Jordan's confidant and close friend of James Jordan, carried the casket out of the back of the church to the cemetery nearby. After a few graveside comments and hugs of Deloris and family members, we were back into the limousines and headed to the airport. We made a "pit stop" along the highway at a rest center. Michael was identified by a seven-year-old who said, "You're Michael Jordan!" I can only imagine how that then seven-year-old tells that story today about his encounter with Michael Jordan at a rest stop in North Carolina.

The Chicago Bulls, fueled by the success of the team with Michael Jordan and three NBA Championships, were building a new facility across the street from the Chicago Stadium. It would be a new state-of-the-art facility shared with the Chicago Blackhawks of the NHL. Michael's final game at the Chicago Stadium was June 18, 1993. It had been his home for the first nine years of his career.

Worldwide sales of Gatorade were increasing at double-digit rates, and the Quaker Oats Company was at $6 billion in sales. Prosperity was everywhere. The Quaker Oats Company would he hosting a worldwide meeting at Laguna Niguel, California, in late September of 1993. It would be a time for celebration and recognition of the various successes throughout the portfolio of Quaker Oats brands worldwide. Management accompanied with spouses from all over the world would be attending. We would be staying at the Ritz-Carlton, Laguna Niguel.

As the event organizers were creating the program and developing a list of activities, there was a request to explore the possibility of having Michael Jordan attend this function. I had my challenge and immediately formulated a plan to make it happen.

Our contract with Michael Jordan stated that we had two personal appearance dates in addition to the six commercial filming dates. I had to first call Barbara Allen, Director at FAME and who managed Michael's calendar requests. The dates appeared to be open. Now it was up to me to sweeten the pot and make it happen.

In the Southern California area where we were located, there were numerous theme parks, water parks, and amusement areas—Disneyland, SeaWorld, Universal Studios, Knott's Berry Farm, and Six Flags Magic Mountain, to name a few. My strategy was to sell the trip as a family vacation for Juanita, Michael's wife, and the kids. Michael would fulfill his obligation by making an appearance, play golf, and socialize with all the Quaker Oats officers and directors while Juanita and the kids would be attending the various parks with VIP treatment.

I personally made the call to a select number of parks, with Juanita's input, to set dates, attendance, and VIP status. With VIP status, most celebrities get private tours in addition to select seating and entry to rides. There would be no waiting in lines and no waiting in food and cueing areas. The first call I made was to SeaWorld where my old roommate and fellow alum from the 1984 LA Olympics, Ed Litrenta, was Vice President of Marketing. He was more than gracious. In fact, the Jordan children would be involved in the main water show with the porpoises and the killer whales. They loved it.

I had only one park, Disneyland, that wouldn't provide VIP treatment for the family. When I spoke to the lady in charge of "Park Services," she said if Michael Jordan was attending, she could. But for the wife and family only, she couldn't. I passed it off as the widely known fact that Disney was extremely difficult to work with. It also made me recall Disney's demands on the use of the music from the *Jungle Book* film back in 1991 when we were doing our first commercial with Michael.

So Michael's appearance dates confirmed, golf was set, Juanita and family booked, and the entire Quaker Oats family worldwide would be meeting Michael Jordan. Excitement was everywhere.

I thought it necessary to include Juanita Jordan in some of the activities where she wanted to be involved. I also extended an invitation to dinner for her and Michael to join me at a fine-dining restaurant in Laguna Beach. I invited Gina Salazar, a friend from Southern California who was also a former LA Raiderette cheerleader.

Gina was not only gorgeous, but she was also intelligent, self-assured, and confident. She wouldn't be intimidated having dinner with Mr. and Mrs. Michael Jordan. She also wouldn't embarrass herself or me, for that matter. She wasn't just "arm candy." She was sincere and down to earth.

Dinner was exceptional. Michael and I had established a great personal relationship by this time, and this helped me build my relationship with Juanita. The next day, I said to Michael, "You were really quiet at dinner last night."

He said, "Did you see all the dirty looks Juanita was giving me?"

A few years later, I got engaged to Gina Salazar. I called off the wedding six months prior to the event over Thanksgiving. She was a lovely, intelligent women seeking a career in broadcast journalism, but I just knew that it wouldn't have worked. She was successful and married the Fox news anchorman at the station in Phoenix where they both worked. She has three children and is still in the broadcasting industry.

The next morning, we were scheduled to play golf at Monarch Beach Golf Links. We left the hotel with Michael driving a Mercedes Benz 600 Series Sedan. There was me, Bill Smithburg, and Denny Banner who was a close friend of Bill Smithburg's and also piloted the jet that Michael chartered.

As a foursome, we partnered up with Bill Smithburg and I playing Michael Jordan and Denny Banner. In all my life, I've *never* met anyone more competitive than Michael Jordan whether it was golf, poker, or even the in stadium races on the giant screen during the Bulls games at the United Center. There he'd get the scoreboard programmer to provide him the results, and he would bet teammates on the outcome. Our golf game was just a friendly game with no wagering.

We beat the Jordan-Banner team and were now headed back to the Ritz-Carlton in Laguna Niguel. Michael hated to lose. On the drive back, he asked, "Do you play tennis?" He had now challenged Bill Smithburg and I to a game of tennis with his partner, Denny Banner.

As we drove through Laguna Beach, the traffic slowed, and we noticed the plethora of beautiful women on both sides of the two-lane street. I also noticed that there were basketball courts near the beach that were fully packed with players. I asked Michael to pull over. He pulled into an area and stopped. I then said, "Wouldn't those guys shit if we showed up to play?"

Michael said, "I'm not ready."

We arrived at the hotel, had some lunch, and headed to the tennis courts. Bill Smithburg was also a very competitive guy. He was part of the A Team, a group of gentlemen in Chicago who were very active in a variety of sports that included golf, tennis, and heli-skiing. I was not a member of that group, but I was still competitive.

Michael and Denny Banner lost in straight sets. Michael then said, "I'm ready. Ready to play basketball at those beach side courts that we passed."

Smithburg had to attend a dinner and entertain the attendees. He excused me from the social functions that afternoon and evening and said, "Your job is to manage Michael."

I said to Michael, "We are going to make this an eventful day." I asked the hotel van driver to take us to a bike shop in Dana Point, California. I rented three mountain bikes, three helmets, and purchased three sets of riding gloves. I asked the van driver how far it was to the basketball courts in Laguna Niguel. He said, "Twelve miles."

Now this was a two-lane road with narrow shoulders on either side. It was also a very hilly area that was going to require multiple gear-shifting, given the change in the terrain. I told the van driver to drop us off about four miles from the courts. Denny Banner was now a permanent fixture in whatever the rest of the day and evening would bring.

As we started our four-mile bike ride, Denny Banner led with Michael next in line and me bringing up the rear. I guess our subconscious told us that was the best way to protect Michael. As these cars and busses passed us, a few left very little space for us. My life was passing before me as I thought of the newspaper headline: "Michael Jordan Killed Along Beach Road in Biking Accident." It was subtitled, "Two Other Cyclists Killed but Not Identified." Hell of a way to meet your demise as a footnote.

When we reached the basketball courts, Danny quickly jumped from his bike and interrupted a game in progress. He came back to where Michael and I were straddling our bikes. I said, "Denny, what did you do?"

"I told them I was with Michael Jordan, and we wanted to play basketball."

I then asked, "What did they say?"

"The guy said, 'Whitey, we don't care who you have with you, you can't play.'"

I said, "Denny, it's backyard basketball. All you have to do is call winners."

Denny proceeded to interrupt the game again but he did call "winners."

Now Michael had on sunglasses, a helmet, and you couldn't recognize him. Before the game ended, he said, "Pick the guy in the gray shirt." He realized it was four on four and there was only three of us. As we prepared to take the court and challenge the winners, Michael took off his helmet and sunglasses. One guy who saw this happening said, "It's...It's...It's *the man!*"

A small crowd started to gather as word had gotten up and down the beach that Michael Jordan was playing basketball nearby. We kept the court, playing for three hours until it got too dark to play. There were about 5,000 people crowded around the court, and they surrounded us as we left, pushing our bikes across the street through the crosswalk. One driver was distracted and rear-ended another car.

People were asking for autographs, and I said, "Give me your address, and I'll send you an autographed photo." Some did, and others didn't believe me.

I located the White House Restaurant just up the street and asked to talk to the manager. I told him I had Michael Jordan with me and that we needed to get something to eat and drink. "And by the way, could you put our three mountain bikes in your office?"

He did, and we sat at a booth, and again, Michael was sandwiched between Denny Banner and myself. I said, "No photos, but if you give me your name and address, I'll send you an autographed photo of Michael." Now, remember, this was before smartphones.

Now I've been around Michael enough to know that if he wanted someone to join us at our table and they asked, he'd give me the okay sign, and they'd join us. Our waitress who did get off work two hours later wanted to join us, so MJ said, "Sure."

Now Denny and I were there to protect Michael, but when he headed to the dance floor, all bets were off. He wasn't dancing with one person. He just hit the dance floor by himself and started to dance. Everyone joined in. I laughed until tears came to my eyes. We had fun, drank about a case of beer each, and tried to rehydrate—sure. I paid the billed and generously tipped all the waitresses who waited on us.

We were there until the placed closed. It was a Sunday night, and they closed at midnight. I used the manager's office phone to call the hotel to have the van pick us up. We retrieved the mountain bikes from the manager's office and met the van outside.

As we headed back to the hotel, Michael said, "This was the best day of my life."

I said, "Michael, imagine how I feel." That would be an understatement.

He then said, "Let's go back to the hotel, clean up, and head back out." We didn't.

It was September 26, 1993.

*****

The next morning, the waitress who sat at our table showed up at the golf outing and asked for Michael. I saw her and asked, "What are you doing here?" She said she didn't think she got a big enough gratuity the night before. "And after all, Michael invited me here today."

I first doubted he invited her, but there she was. I quickly asked her to join me in my cart. I said, "I tipped everyone very generously." Rather than create a scene in front of the entire Quaker Oats world-wide attendees, I gave her an additional $300, and she left. Everyone assumed she was with me.

Within the Michael Jordan spokesperson contract with Gatorade, there was a clause that we would make a $50,000 dona-tion to the Michael Jordan Foundation each year of the contract. That was $500,000 over ten years. After three years, the foundation was dissolved, and the annual payment was then made to the James Jordan Boys and Girls Club.

It was at one of the Michael Jordan Foundation's black-tie fund-raisers that William Smithburg bid and won, "Golf for you and a friend with Michael Jordan and Fred Couples." Mr. Smithburg raced over to me and said, "Get ready, Schmidt, we're playing golf with MJ and Fred Couples." He paid $20,000 for this opportunity, and I tried to tell him to "take a customer." He declined.

As the word got out, many private golf clubs offered to act as host for the event. This was all handled by Michael's agent's staff. They decided on a private golf club in Vero Beach, Florida. The Windsor Club had a British motif. We arrived on Sunday and were to play on Monday when the course was closed to its members as well as the public.

Fred Couples arrived with his girlfriend and her son. William Smithburg arrived that evening by private jet. I found my way to the club after a commercial flight or two. We stayed in housing on the property. The accommodations were luxurious.

We met the next morning at the Windsor Club clubhouse. We had a light breakfast and headed out to play golf. I was partnered with Fred Couples, and Bill Smithburg was teamed with Michael Jordan. We stopped for lunch at the clubhouse. The Couples/Schmidt team were plus-one on the front and minus-one on the back. The match ended even. Couples shot 72, me 90, Jordan 83, and Smithburg 91.

After a sales pitch to the group on joining/purchasing property, we headed out for our second eighteen-hole match.

The Couples/Schmidt team finished plus-one on the front, and we were minus-two on the back when we pressed and essentially started another game within the existing match. We finished the back nine, minus-three and minus-one, meaning we won one bet and lost three. Fred shot a 73, me a 92, Jordan a 78, and Smithburg a 97. I think we lost $10. Well, William Smithburg did spend $20,000 for the day's experience. I was just glad to tag along.

When David Falk's office called and made us aware of the location and date of the golf event, I quickly checked the Miami Dolphins home game schedule. The Dolphins were schedule to play that Monday night on national television. Gatorade had a sky-box suite at Joe Robbie Stadium, home of the Miami Dolphins. I quickly notified the sales manager in that area who managed the suite that I would need six tickets. The Gatorade sponsorship of the Dolphins included the suite and was paid out of the Gatorade Sports Marketing budget that I managed. I also told him Michael Jordan, Fred Couples, and the Quaker Oats CEO, Bill Smithburg, would be attending. In addition, he could have his guests bring a few items, and I would get Michael Jordan to sign them.

After finishing the thirty-six holes of golf, we showered and headed to the airport to board a private jet to Miami, Florida. When we landed in Miami, I scheduled a limousine to take us to Joe Robbie Stadium. It was a short ride of about forty-five minutes. I had one last challenge. I did not have a parking pass, so the limo driver thought he'd leave us off right at the gate where we needed to enter. I decided to throw a Hail Mary. I used the limo driver's cell phone and called security at Joe Robbie Stadium. I reached them and asked to speak to the VP of Marketing/Sponsorships. I explained my dilemma, and they had our limo escorted to the ground level parking area beneath the stadium. They then ushered us to the Gatorade suite in time for kickoff.

As the word traveled throughout the stadium, a few people tried to enter our suite. We had to place a guard at the door. One occasion, someone claiming to be Michael Jordan's friend or a sports celebrity from the skybox level we were on wanted to say hello to Michael. Michael determined who he wanted to see or if anyone was really his friend.

The then named Washington Redskins were playing the Dolphins. It was the perfect end to a perfect day. I was the golf partner of one of the best in golf, playing in a foursome with the greatest of all time (the GOAT) in basketball. It was the best of times.

As we got comfortable in the suite, I was facing the buffet at the back of the suite. Michael reached over my shoulder to grab a sandwich. At the same time, he whispered in my ear, "Billy"—he called me that—"I'm announcing my retirement from basketball on Friday, but you can't tell anyone."

I said, "Congratulations, you've accomplished everything you wanted." I then hugged him and said, "I love you, man!" He did say I could tell Bill Smithburg.

It was October 4, 1993. In the last week, the seven-day period started with an incredible day with MJ on the golf course, on the tennis courts, and ending with teaming up with Michael on the basketball court to beat "all-comers." Incidentally, when Michael was asked about what kind of basketball player I was, he stated, "He threw up a lot of air balls."

I quickly answered, "Michael, those weren't air balls, they were passes to you."

Everyone laughed.

I was one of only a few in the entire world who knew that Michael Jordan was going to announce his retirement on Friday. I didn't mention it to anyone—family, friends, or even those who worked on the Gatorade brand. I'm certain they wouldn't have been as positive as I was. After all, we had the greatest basketball on the planet with eight years left on a ten-year contract, and he was retiring from the sport. Word finally leaked, and Michael's press conference was moved to Thursday, October 6, 1993. Michael Jordan retired. It was the worst of times.

Sidenote: The Miami Dolphins won the game, 17–10.

CHAPTER 32

MJ TIMES TO REMEMBER

From the time I signed Michael Jordan in July of 1991 and the release of the "Be Like Mike" commercial, on August 8, 1991, Michael never disappointed us or me personally. We had an exceptional relationship. He welcomed me into his "inner circle" as he trusted my opinion, and he knew I didn't want anything from him. It was a relationship of mutual respect, and we would do anything for each other. The relationship I had with his agent, David Falk, was also exceptional. In addition, Barbara Allen, who managed and coordinated his interaction with his sponsors, was absolutely the best.

The "Be Like Mike" commercial was shot at a playground on the northside of Chicago. It was my first introduction into the "megastar" status of Michael Jordan. We had to control the film site and deal with a variety of issues, including securing the site, limiting Quaker attendees, public access, catering, pre-and post-shoot meetings, wardrobe, and "making it enjoyable" for MJ. Having his favorite cook and his favorite Cuban cigars cemented our relationship. It was my first time being involved in a commercial shoot as well as my first time with Michael. I'd be actively involved with all MJ commercials from that point on.

Bayer Bess Vanderwarker was the advertising agency of record for our introduction of Michael Jordan and Gatorade. That encompassed print as well as television, consumer packaging, and in-store promotions. They were a great creative shop that had just hired Bernie Pitzel as Sr. Vice President and Group Creative Director. "Be

Like Mike" was his idea, his baby from its inception, and as well as the music. He was assisted by Steve Seyferth, Sr. Vice President and Account Director. Steve was a University of Michigan graduate, who was exceptional at managing the Gatorade account and the creative talent of the agency and the brand executives that included Peggy Dyer, Vice President of Marketing/Gatorade, and Matt Mannelly, Director, Consumer/Gatorade.

My role as Vice President, Sports Marketing, was unique. I negotiated the Jordan contract, but I also solely managed the Michael Jordan relationship. That included all requests, creative use, and review of materials. Greg Via, one of my staff of sports managers, produced a document, "Jordan Rules," that was a template regarding protocol for everything Michael Jordan. Greg's work was exceptional.

We found that we got most of the best shots and film of Michael Jordan when he was unscripted. We just let the cameras roll after each shot and got some of the best footage ever. Later, at other commercial shoots, I could read Michael quite well and easily determined when he was ready to move on after the director may have wanted more takes of a particular scene. He rolled his eyes and gave me "that look." I'd step in and say, "I believe we've captured it. Let's move on."

I also had the dubious responsibility to present Michael with shaving cream and a razor when the goatee he grew all summer had to be shaved off, per agency request. He never complained.

Although the "Be Like Mike" commercial was iconic, one other commercial was also worth referencing. Michael had taken a retirement from basketball in 1993 to play baseball with the Birmingham Barons, a farm club of the Chicago White Sox. He played for two seasons. At the end of his second season, a baseball strike loomed on the horizon. It was thought that these minor league players would be used doing the strike season, if there was one. There was never a question of Michael's loyalty. He would not be used as a pawn or cross a picket line.

This left many people questioning, "What would Michael do?" The agency developed creative around the premise of Michael seeking out possible answers to that question for himself. In this commercial, Michael would seek the guidance and insight from a Tibetan monk. It appeared as if Michael had climbed the mountains and trekked across various terrain to reach this holy man. Once there, he was able to ask the monk that one question.

As is in some cases, well-known producers and directors, if they're not filming a movie, will take on the project of producing or directing a commercial. It's short work and pays well. That was the case in this instance. The agency hired Ridley Scott and his production company to produce the spot. Now this was *the* Ridley Scott, film director of movies like *Alien, Blade Runner*, and *Gladiator*. Not many directors with bigger credits.

The location of the commercial was in eastern California near Death Valley in Inyo County. We stayed in an area, Alabama Hills, known for being the site of various western movies. The snow-covered Sierra Nevada Mountains would be the background for the filming. The entire construction of a "temple" as well as the surroundings had a Tibetan feel to it. It felt like we were filming a movie.

After one day of shooting—we had four days of actual filming—Michael grabbed me and said, "Let's go for a drive." We got into his rental car, and he drove. We headed out of this small town out toward the desert. We entered an even smaller town where we made a U-turn after going down the main drag. We noticed a hole-in-the-wall bar. MJ pulled over and said, "Let's check this place out."

Now there couldn't have been more than a few store front businesses, and some of them were boarded up. Now I said to Michael, "Let me go in and check this place out first." I was thinking that this place hadn't seen a black man in some time. I wanted to see if it would be safe.

Michael said, "Hell, let's go in." So we did.

Michael followed as I pushed open the doors. I was prepared for a western watering hole with the locals. Upon entering, we got immediate stares. There was a long wooden bar with barstools and a few tables scattered throughout the place. It felt like a movie set. I kept waiting for someone to say, "You aren't from around these parts, are you?"

Michael smiled, and that eased any tensions in the place. He quickly engaged the locals in conversation, and he was their new best friend. We ordered a few drinks and moved to the end of the bar, near the tables. As we glanced at one table, there was this guy smoking a cigar. Lo and behold, it was Ridley Scott. We sat down with him and proceeded to light up our cigars. Mr. Scott was smoking the same cigars that I brought for Michael—Montecristo Cuban Cigars #2.

Our conversation, bourbon, and cigars lasted a few hours. Now I've been fortunate enough to have met a few individuals that I said afterward, "That man is a genius at what he does." I felt that way about Ridley Scott. The commercial could have won an Oscar for Best Cinematography.

When Michael Jordan first came back from his retirement from the NBA, he did it with a press release on March 18, 1995. It read "I'm Back." It was just two words that the entire world was waiting to hear. He was to play the next night, March 19, 1995, at Market Square Arena in Indianapolis against the Pacers.

I got the call from Michael. "Billy, I want you to be at the game." I said, "Great, I'll be there."

He said, "I want you to fly down with me."

I said, "Absolutely."

The next day, I met him at the Palwaukee Airport, north of Chicago, and headed to Indianapolis, Indiana, along with his long time security guard, Gus Lett.

When we arrived, a limousine was there, waiting to transport us to Market Square Arena. When we arrived at the arena, the driver asked me, "Who is paying for the limo?"

I asked him, "When they made the reservation, who did they say was going to pay for the limo?"

He said, "Michael Jordan."

I thought Michael had more important things to be concerned about, so I pulled out my company American Express Card and paid the $475.

As we arrived about three hours before the game, nobody was in the visiting locker room but MJ, Gus Lett, and myself. Michael opened his travel bag and said, "Billy, check this out." He opened the bag and pulled out a jersey. It had the number #45 on it. I thought, *I'm the only person besides John Ligmanowski*—the Chicago Bulls equipment manager—*who knows beforehand that Michael won't be wearing his usual #23 jersey*. He said, "That number is retired."

That comeback game was surreal. It was if Elvis Presley and Jesus Christ were returning, and they were both at the arena that night! Crowds were everywhere, looking for a sighting. It was an electrifying environment. Michael scored nineteen points that evening in a loss, in overtime, 103–96. He wore the #45 jersey for twenty-two games and returned to wearing the #23 jersey in his twenty-third game back.

When individuals find out that you know Michael Jordan, the first question is usually, "What's Michael really like?"

Now my first comment is usually, "He's the best!" Now if I were to elaborate on the subject as having been in his inner circle, you see sides of Michael that most people don't. Sure, he's competitive, but he's also generous, kind, considerate, and sensitive. Above all, Michael is extremely loyal.

I invited my twin brother, Bob, to attend a NBA Finals Game, June 4, 1997, at the United Center against the Utah Jazz. My Gatorade seats were the first two seats to the left of the visiting team at the scorer's table. We arrived early, watched warm-ups, and enjoyed the atmosphere and excitement in the stadium. Michael is always so focused, and players as well as the Bulls staff know to stay away from him.

The Bulls won the game, and Michael scored thirty-eight points as the Bulls took a 2–0 lead in the best of seven series. As the game ended, MJ came by our seats and said, "Come back to the locker room." Now he had never invited me back to the locker room. As we walked through the tunnel, Michael saw us coming and shouted out, "Hey, Bob!" Now I never introduced my brother to Michael. MJ remembered his name from a conversation we had where I might have mentioned his name. It amazed me. He then said, "Join us for dinner."

I said, "Sure."

Bob looked at me and said, "Was he serious?"

I said, "Absolutely."

Now Bob was sure that we'd be two of many people joining Michael for dinner that night. When we showed up, there were six of us—Michael, George Koehler, his confidant; Gus Lett and John Michael Wozniak, his longtime security guards; and us. Aside from Bob, these were the individuals that knew Michael the best.

The next morning, *USA Today's* front page of the sports section had a picture of Michael driving on Jeff Hornacek. You can clearly see Bob and I in the background at the scorer's table. I contacted the photographer and acquired a few prints of the photo. I had Michael sign them and sent one to Bob within the week. Bob shared his experience with his friends in Lexington, Kentucky, when he returned home. The signed photo validated his story.

Michael was also extremely generous. He'd often drop off tickets before the game to the kids outside at the housing development that was in the neighborhood of the Chicago Stadium/United Center. No hoopla, no cameras, just Michael being Michael. There were numerous examples, too many to mention.

During the pregame of the fourth NBA Championship season, George Koehler came over and gave me a box. He said, "Michael wanted you to have this." I opened it up, and it was a championship ring, a ring Michael designed and had made. It commemorated the Bulls' third NBA Championship. Although the Chicago Bulls had a championship ring, Michael had these made for himself and a few close friends. I felt special.

At the Quaker Oats Company, there was a corporate policy that you couldn't accept gifts from a supplier for more than $80. Knowing the ring's value exceeded that amount, I reported the gift to Tom Howell, Quaker's General Counsel.

Quaker's Code of Conduct states that as a general rule that employees should not accept gifts from suppliers. Michael Jordan is a "supplier" to Quaker in that he was paid for his advertising and promotional services. There are some exceptions to this general rule, however. The Code goes on to state: "In some cases, it may be appropriate to accept a gift because of protocol, courtesy, or other special circumstances. However, all such gifts must be reported to your supervisor and the Corporate Law Department, which will determine whether the employee may keep the gift or return it. In some cases, the Law Department may determine that certain gifts or awards should become the property of the Quaker Oats Company."

Bill Daily, my Director of Sports Marketing, also received a ring. In a "draft" for a Quaker Oats in-house communication article, mid-week, the following was stated:

> Members of Quaker's Ethics Council have deter-mined that, under these circumstances, it is neither required nor advisable for the rings to be returned to Jordan. They were given to Bill and Bill as expressions of close personal friend-ship and respect. These personal relationships are important to the Jordan-Gatorade rela-tionship, which, in turn has been beneficial to Quaker. Because, however, of the unique nature and value of these rings, it has been determined that these rings should become the property of Quaker. As Quaker property, consideration will be given to displaying them for Quaker employ-ees, and perhaps other Quaker constituencies. Notwithstanding the fact that the ownership resides in Quaker, Bill and Bill will have custody of the rings from time to time.
>
> Keep your eyes open for news regarding the location and time for displaying these rings!

I met with Phil Marineau, President of the Quaker Oats Company, and the individual who hired me to review this "draft." I said, "This was a personal gift from Michael Jordan and had nothing to do with any additional services or supplier benefits. His contract states exactly what he's to provide over the ten-year term, nothing more. Returning the ring to Michael would be an insult." I also said, "Gatorade has the best deal ever with Michael. We're paying $1.4 million a year while his other sponsors are paying $5 million a year." I also said, "I don't want the rings to be displayed."

He said, "I need your help."

We agreed, and I signed an agreement where we were custodians of the rings, but they were the property of the Quaker Oats Company. We further agreed that we would take ownership of the rings when/if we left the company.

A year later, after the Chicago Bulls won their fourth NBA Championship, George Koehler again presented me with another gift-wrapped box. I was sitting with Bill Smithburg, CEO, in our floor seats at the baseline in the United Center. I opened the gift. It was Michael's own designed championship ring for the fourth NBA championship. I showed it to Bill Smithburg. He said, "That's impressive." I reminded him of the situation with the last ring Michael gave me. He said, "Just take it and don't tell anyone."

Today, I have both rings. I wear them on occasion during the NBA finals each year. I also wear one of them every February 17, Michael Jordan's birthday.

Michael Jordan was obviously known as a basketball player. Sure, his love may have been baseball, but the love he has for golf is difficult to convey, unless you've played with him or seen him at the Ryder Cup Matches. His enthusiasm for a game he can play and the appreciation he has for the players who play it at the highest level is amazing.

I've played golf with Michael Jordan on numerous occasions. We played Augusta National and Butler National in Chicago, and it was incredible. We didn't wager anything on any of these occasions, just pure fun and relaxation.

The 32nd Ryder Cup matches were contested at the Valderrama Golf Club in Sotogrande, Spain, September 26–28, 1997. Gatorade's sponsorship of the PGA (Professional Golf Association) and our purchasing of advertising with *Sports Illustrated* gained an invitation for me and another colleague from Gatorade.

We flew with the US Ryder Cup Team out of New York on the Concorde, an incredible plane and an even more amazing flight of three and a half hours to Europe. The US Team was seated at the front with their wives, then the officials of the PGA, and then the sponsors. It wasn't like we were at the back of the plane. It seated about a hundred passengers in twenty-five rows of seats, two on each side of the aisle. We reach an altitude of 60,000 feet and traveled at Mach 2, twice the speed of sound or around 1,330 miles per hour.

Now I'm not an engineer, but I understood the reality of the plane's surface expanding and contracting when it reached this altitude and speed. In my mind, twenty years of this contraction and expansion had to take its toll on the structure and integrity of the plane. I told anyone and everyone when I returned home to book a flight because I wasn't sure how long they would be flying that plane. The last actual fight was November 26, 2003.

While in Spain, we stayed about forty-five minutes from Valderrama Golf Club at a resort with a golf course, spa, and all the amenities you'd want. I, along with my Gatorade colleague and with our hosts from *Sports Illustrated*, played golf every day. We noticed that each morning, adjacent to the first fairway, a jet helicopter would land at a hangar facility. It was loud and it was new and expensive.

I received a message from Barbara Allen from FAME, Michael's agency, that Michael would be in Europe and that he wanted to attend the Ryder Cup matches. They also wanted me to secure transportation for Michael from the airport to Valderrama Golf Club. My first thought was the jet helicopter we'd seen every day.

The next morning, while in the first fairway, I heard the helicopter approaching to land. I quickly climbed the hill and shouted to the pilot to come over to the fence that surrounded the hangar facility. I said to him, "I want to charter your helicopter."

He said the owner didn't charter it out.

I said, "I have a special guest, Michael Jordan, coming from the United States, and I need to get him from the airport out to the Valderrama Golf Club and the Ryder Cup Matches."

Now I had no idea what it could cost, but I knew that I would be reimbursed by his agency. The next day, I received word that the owner of the helicopter agreed we could use his helicopter at no cost. Now nothing is free. So I knew there had to be a catch. The catch, Michael would have to sign a few items for the owner when he arrived at the Ryder Cup Matches in Valderrama. Now define "a few." I would have preferred to have paid for the charter.

That afternoon, I met Michael at the airport. We quickly were routed to the awaiting helicopter on the airfield nearby. It was raining as we boarded the aircraft. We then ascended to about 500 feet and proceeded to follow the coastline to the Valderrama Golf Club. The steady rain hampered our vision, but we stayed close to the shore.

Michael and I both had headsets on, and that helped silence the noise from the jet engines that propelled the aircraft. Michael nudged me and asked, "How deep is the water that we are flying over?" Michael was concerned about the possibility of crashing in the water. I had to admit, the visibility was like a hundred feet in front of us and a hundred feet below us. I also remembered that Michael couldn't swim. In his childhood, he witnessed a friend's drowning.

I pushed my communication microphone button to ask the pilot to get the answer to Michael's question. The pilot answered back to me, "Six feet."

I then said to Michael, "It's just six feet, and you could walk in the water and have plenty of room over your head if we had to land." I didn't say crash, and Michael was six feet, six inches tall.

We landed on the Valderrama Golf Club grounds and were immediately met by the owner of the helicopter. He ushered us to his hospitality tent nearby. I immediately noticed hundreds of items, including game jerseys, shoes, and basketballs waiting to be signed by Michael. Again, I would have rather paid for charting his aircraft. I didn't wait for "that look" from Michael. I told the gentleman we were very appreciative for the use of his helicopter, but Michael would not be signing all these items. I told him to pick out about thirty items and Michael would sign them. This man was not excited to hear that.

When Michael arrived on property, it was if a rock star had landed. He was quickly greeted by the officials of the PGA and later the US Ryder Cup Captain, Tom Kite. He later embraced President George H. W. Bush and his wife, Barbara. He was given a headset and credentials to walk inside the ropes with the players. I was left to walk outside the ropes and find my own way. The reality: he was Michael Jordan, I was not.

I know that experience ignited Michael's love for the Ryder Cup matches, and he rarely misses the event, which is held every two years.

CHAPTER 33

THE NFL WAS THE GOLD STANDARD PARTNERSHIP FOR GATORADE

When I completed my responsibilities at the 1982 World's Fair, in Knoxville, Tennessee, I joined Stokely-Van Camp in Indianapolis, Indiana. Gatorade sales were around $80 million, and the marketing of Gatorade was handled by a staff of about eight.

I left Stokely-Van Camp in July of 1983 and started in my new role as Associate Vice President at the Los Angeles Olympic Organizing Committee (LAOOC) on August 15, 1983. With my entire focus on the goal of preparations for the 1984 Olympics which were to open on July 28, 1984, I kept a close eye on what was happening with Stokely-Van Camp. After the Quaker Oats Company acquired Stokely-Van Camp, I was invited to Chicago, Illinois, to meet the group that was going to manage the transition. I had been invited by Bob Calvin, my former boss at Stokely-Van Camp and now Director of Sports Marketing for Gatorade.

After my meetings with Phil Marineau, Sandy Posa, both employees of Quaker Oats, and managing the "transition team," which included Scott Dissinger, Kent Miller, and Doug Stein from SVC, I met with Bob Calvin. He asked me to let him know about my thoughts after my meetings.

I responded with a letter dated February 6, 1984. In it, I said:

> The Quaker Oats Company can and will sup-
> ply Gatorade with resources that were not avail-
> able at Stokely-Van Camp. However, Quaker is
> relatively unaware of sports promotions and the
> significance and importance of personal contacts
> and tie-ins. The individuals with whom I met,
> made me feel that they are excited about having
> me as an employee. They know that I have many
> personal contacts and a great deal of experience,
> but they are not sure how we need to operate in
> their organization. We require greater flexibility
> than what they are accustomed to. Both you and
> I know of the personal contact and entertain-
> ment necessary in promotions. Yet, It's all new
> to Quaker. We operate much like salesmen in the
> field. We build credibility with influential people
> through our contacts with them at dinner, on the
> golf course, etc.
>
> I've roughed out some ideas and concerns
> when I returned from Chicago, which I'd like to
> share with you.
>
> Sports Marketing and Promotions should:
>
> 1. Function to increase visibility, product iden-
>   tification and credibility.
> 2. Function separately and independently from
>   retail marketing but rely on good communi-
>   cation to keep each other informed.
> 3. Work together in developing promotional
>   tie-ins with retail media: reintroduction of
>   Gatorade in the North.

4. Communicate with the marketing group regarding the status of certain sponsorships to insure the timeliness of media tie-ins.

We need to take advantage of all the opportunities that are available to us.
Major concerns:

1. Lack of clear definition of the role of the sports promotions group.
2. The necessity for a clear division of responsibilities within the sports promotions group.
3. Sponsorship evaluation should be centralized; develop check list/or outline.
4. Product premium budget established with flexibility to add different items as deemed necessary.
5. Total lack of experience in marketing as to how promotions should be handled. Sports promotions are not retail promotions and should all be handled by the sports promotions group.
6. The importance to have the authority to make decisions and the ability to implement without committee approval.
7. Institutional Gatorade should center around sales and service. The actual sponsorship proposals and negotiations should be separate.
8. At sponsored events, we should have a task force to work on signage visibility, product distribution and event planning. If a task force cannot be deployed from Quaker, then the event budget should reflect monies to implement this group at the location.

Little did I know that I had outlined my future position and career at the Quaker Oats Company. Substitute sports marketing for sports promotions, and that was what and how I built the Gatorade Sports Marketing group. Institutional sales was the sales group that targeted sales to all professional teams, colleges and universities, workplace entities, and penal institutions. Yes, we sold to penal institutions as well as road crews.

The professional teams and colleges *purchased* the products. In total, $1 million in sales. I grew it to $20 million when I relinquished those responsibilities. It was the 3 percent of sales that drove the other 97 percent. In addition, it was the key relationships and contacts within this group, the athletic trainers, that provided Gatorade visibility and placement on the "field of play." Without them, Gatorade had nothing. With them, we owned the "field of play."

Today, it's common to see Gatorade on the sidelines of all thirty-two NFL teams. That was not always the case. Stokely-Van Camp had established a relationship with the NFL back in the early 1980s. They had an advertising agreement with National Football League Properties (NFLP), the marketing arm of the NFL, a "promotional rights agreement" that mainly centered around advertising in the print properties owned by the NFLP. It also included the national FSI (Free Standing Insert) for the Super Bowl each year in newspapers and magazines nationwide. It was the cost of using the NFL "Shield."

The 1982 NFL season was a strike year. The NFL played only a nine-game season. Stokely-Van Camp had an "NFL Playbook Promotion," and after publishing thousands of playbooks, they were left with limited time to promote a product that was deemed too complex for the NFL viewer. In fact, when I joined Quaker in 1984, there were still copies in storage at our Indianapolis warehouse. We couldn't give them away. We eventually threw them away. The other strike season was 1987, when there was a fifteen games season. Fortunately, we had no product promotion during that season.

Stokely-Van Camp was in the process of negotiating a new NFL agreement when Quaker Oats acquired them. It was finalized on April 1, 1985, and expired March 31, 1990. The rights fees per year were:

Year 1: $45,000
Year 2: $100,000
Year 3: $100,000
Year 4: $125,000
Year 5: $150,000

It also included advertising in the NFL publications, *NFL Tailgate*, $380,000, *Gameday*, $93,670, and *Pro Magazine*, $39,042. Historically, the magazine elements were always being debated. It may have been advertising for the NFL season, but it wasn't in our advertising season for Gatorade. We'd occasionally find another Quaker product to purchase the space with the approval of the NFLP. With this contract, we received the designation as "Supplier to the NFL" of "Electrolyte Beverages, High-Energy Carbohydrate Beverages." This was the NFL contract I inherited.

When I developed "the field of play" strategy, I focused on two areas. First, the sports that provided Gatorade with visibility; and second, on those that provided high participatory numbers. Simply, it was visibility, those on television, and those sports that would make up the number that would be targeted for opportunity for users through sports organizations. After I determined the sports, I focused on the various opportunities and organizations of these sports. Wherever there were sports, Gatorade had an opportunity, and in our mind, a right to be there. Our science and research proved that.

Now, with limited budgets, I'd target the sports of football, baseball, basketball, running, and soccer. These sports were targeted from top to bottom based on visibility, professional, college and university, high school, and grassroots. From the participatory numbers standpoint, it's these same sports but prioritized from grassroots to pro. Numbers don't lie. Whether it was television ratings or those listed for participants in sports in the United States and at all levels, these numbers would be the biggest determining factor in our "road map" for sponsorships. Sales in respective areas and partnerships would also be factored in.

The NFL was a must-have property. Now, with a growing business, you also had growing budgets. Growth of Gatorade was at double-digit in sales, year over year. I couldn't sponsor all the NFL teams, so my strategy was to target those in the "Sunbelt" and those that had championship history and pedigree. Other criteria that factored in was if they had a history of or a possibly of hosting a Super Bowl in their venue. That was a plus. Bottom line, I'd budget one-third of the teams in the first selected group and add one-third each year, and at the end of the third year, I'd have them all. They would be $40,000 per year with all of them having a five-year term.

There were some teams that had existing contracts, and eventually, my goal was to have exclusivity and be on the sidelines of all the NFL teams. With only the possibility of a third of the team's contracts expiring at one time, the NFLP couldn't offer or sell them to a competitor. Some say, "Genius," but honestly, it was determined by what I was budgeted. I later employed this strategy and extended contracts with two years left on most contracts. I extended contracts; I didn't renegotiate them nor let them expire. This strategy made it difficult for the competition to gain any foothold on the sidelines. That, coupled with the relationship with the Professional Football Athletic Trainers Society (PFATS), who displayed our product on the sidelines, we owned the sidelines.

We never told the trainers what to do. Through John LeGear and Timothy Communications, we provided basic public relations materials and programs to further their objective to professionalize their organizations. We never paid them nor did we provide them with free product. I would later provide them a rebate where we would reimburse them for up to $2,500 of product purchased. This was a small amount when you consider some teams purchased $100,000 of product annually. We did provide cups, coolers, squeeze bottles, and Gatorade towels.

The Gatorade logo was most noticeable on everything we provided. The Gatorade cups were of a specifically designed green color, and when a player made an exceptional play or scored a touchdown, the trainers would meet them as they exited the field with two cups of Gatorade, "Celebration time." I have some issue with the current "G" on the coolers and packaging. As for signage, the current display of Gatorade coolers on the sidelines in the NFL looks like an "end-aisle display in a grocery store." Obviously, the "G" isn't working because they spell out Gatorade where possible. The product is distributed with mainly squeeze bottles that are colorless.

We'd utilized the sidelines to enforce our "implied endorsement" by the players. Gatorade is paying the NFL hundreds of millions of dollars a year, so I can understand their objectives for sideline exposure.

One of the most successful items that was ever developed was the Gatorade towel. This came from Sandi Finlinson and her company, FINCORP. I met Sandi through Leo Dumas when I worked at Stokely-Van Camp in Indianapolis, Indiana. She and her company provided embroidered hats, shirts, jackets, and numerous other items. When I joined the Quaker Oats Company, Sandi provided all our premium-logoed items. Everyone wanted apparel with the Gatorade logo on it. Sandi created a Gatorade Premium Catalog. Instead of my department carrying an inventory of product, she handled all inventories and sales. She was the best. She started her own company located in Greenwood, Indiana. I used her company exclusively. We would provide numerous entertainment opportunities for the NFL trainers as well as other trainers of the various professional and amateur sports. They'd be Gatorade's guest at Super Bowls, the Indianapolis 500, Daytona 500, the Final Four, and a variety of other sporting events. It was just "good business" and managing great relationships.

One of the most epic behind-the-scenes Gatorade moments at a Super Bowl occurred at Super Bowl XXIII at Joe Robbie Stadium in Miami, Florida, on January 22, 1989. The Cincinnati Bengals were playing the San Francisco 49ers.

I and my staff of four would arrive at each site of the Super Bowl early in the week of the Super Bowl Game. We'd had to distribute tickets to Quaker Oats sales guests as well as sports marketing invited guests. We provide Gatorade-logoed items as well as the Super Bowl XXIII logoed premiums supplied by the NFL. It was detailed work but necessary. Each guest had to feel special, and my staff was the best at it. We managed a suite at the host hotel for ticket and premium pickup. It was furnished with food as well as beverages.

The Super Bowl teams worked out at local college and university sites.

I received a call from Kevin O'Neill, a longtime friend and current trainer at the University of Miami, Florida. Kevin had previously been an athletic trainer at the University of Tennessee and, like me, from the Pittsburgh area. It was his responsibility to provide the visiting team athletic trainers with all their needs and necessary services in the host city.

I called Kevin back. He said, "I've received these Diet Coke coolers for the sidelines. What do you want me to do with them?"

I said, "What the hell?"

He said, "They have the Super Bowl XXIII logo on it, and I've also received cups with both the Super Bowl logo and Diet Coke logos on them."

I said, "I can't tell you what to do. If they said they are there to replace the Gatorade coolers, I have a problem with that." Somehow, those coolers got lost but were quickly replaced by another shipment.

I scheduled a meeting with the NFL properties staff that were there for the game at their suite that afternoon. I had also contacted Gatorade and the Quaker Oats Senior Vice President and General Counsel, Luther McKinney. Luther was a tough litigator, and he threatened an injunction that could halt the game from being played, at least in theory. The Gatorade case centered around the fact that you would have Diet Coke coolers, but Gatorade would be in them as well as being distributed in Diet Coke cups. Luther and the law stated that whatever product was on the coolers and cups had to be in the coolers. This practice was called "passing off." In theory, you were passing off your product as something else. There was no way Diet Coke was going to be served on any sideline of a sporting event, let alone the Super Bowl.

I had given my staff the afternoon off as they had worked their asses off and needed to enjoy the day. I knew in the meeting there would be at least three individuals from the NFLP. I didn't want to go to the meeting by myself. I drafted two executive salespeople to go with me. I instructed them to just sit there, act pissed off, and occasionally grunt.

I explained to the NFLP executives, John Flood, Rick Dudley, and Jim Schwebel, the "passing off" legal ramifications and the threat of an injunction. We had to reach a compromise. It was mutually decided that Gatorade cups and coolers would share the sidelines equally with Diet Coke cups and coolers. Furthermore, water would be in the Diet Coke cups and coolers, and Gatorade would be in the Gatorade cups and coolers. Coca-Cola was a major sponsor of the NFL, and they were paying millions of dollars in sponsorships while we were paying $150,000. NFLP had to placate them in some fashion.

Super Bowl XXIII turned out to be one of the most exciting Super Bowls in history. The Cincinnati Bengals made a forty-yard field goal with 3:20 left in the fourth quarter to take the lead over the San Francisco 49ers, 16–13. After the kickoff, the 49ers were on their own eight-yard line, ninety-two yards away from winning the Super Bowl. Of course, they could get close enough to try a game-tying field goal.

While everyone was watching history unfold with "the drive," I was watching what was unfolding on the sidelines. There was a group of individuals on both sidelines, removing all the Gatorade cups, coolers, and squeeze bottles. Then there were noticeably two Diet Coke coolers staged on both sidelines, ready for a Diet Coke Dunk on the winning coach. I wanted to leap onto the field, but I had to restrain myself.

As Joe Montana began "the drive," with 190 seconds in the game, from his own eight-yard line, everything for me was focused on the sidelines and what was to occur after the game. Montana skillfully drove his team down the field and scored with thirty-four seconds on the clock. Cincinnati failed to score, and the San Francisco 49ers were Super Bowl XXIII Champions, winning 20–16. As I looked to the San Francisco 49ers sidelines, I noticed two individuals hoisting a Diet Coke cooler and trying to dunk Bill Walsh, the 49ers head coach. He moved abruptly and received a half shower of water. It was poorly staged and executed.

At a PFATS meeting in the spring of 1989, Lindsy McLean, head athletic trainer for the San Francisco 49ers, said he did something at Super Bowl XXIII that gave Gatorade more TV exposure. He related to me that because his players drank more water than Gatorade, he filled the Diet Coke cups and coolers with Gatorade and the Gatorade cups and coolers with water. Now on one hand, I was disappointed that they preferred water over Gatorade, but I applauded his efforts for the TV exposure, especially when a thirty-second TV commercial was costing $675,000. The irony, the Diet Coke dunk was done with Gatorade.

As the Gatorade contract was going to expire on March 31, 1990, the "dance" for negotiating an extension had begun. There could not be a repeat of what happened at Super Bowl XXIII. I was smart enough to know that the NFLP wanted to renegotiate a new contract and tear up the existing one. In all my contract negotiations, I wanted the opposing party/group to submit a proposal first. That way, I knew their starting point. I didn't want to show my hand.

Now the success of the "Gatorade Dunk" during the New York Giants run to Super Bowl XXI was going to drive up the cost of doing business with the NFL. I knew that and was preparing to make a larger Gatorade commitment. I also had tied up the sidelines where they couldn't offer but a third of the teams, given the structured contracts I had in place. There were twenty-eight NFL teams in 1989, but they would expand to thirty teams in 1995, thirty-one teams in 1999, and thirty-two teams in 2002. I wanted a long-term contract of at least five years, and I needed to stress the fact that Gatorade would increase our commitment, and that would have to include exclusivity with the current teams and any expansion teams going forward.

Prior to receiving our initial proposal from NFL Properties, Inc., on April 4, 1989, I received a copy of a fax that was sent out to all twenty-eight NFL member club presidents, general managers, marketing directors, and public relations directors on March 27, 1989. It stated that the NFL club owners, the week before, and the

NFLP were "evaluating the isotonic/Hypotonic beverage category for a possible league-wide endorsement of a sideline beverage." It further stated, "While the NFL Properties evaluates the category, the NFLP Executive Committee asks that all NFL Clubs suspend any current negotiations with Gatorade or any other sponsor or local associations involving sideline cups and coolers. Please direct inquiries to NFL Properties."

The fax was sent out by John Bello, then President of NFL Properties. I'm certain that he never gave it a second thought that my relationships were so great with the various clubs that they would share this information with me. So I had information that they had no idea I was aware of—advantage Schmidt.

The first proposal I received from NFL Properties was on April 4, 1989. There were some significant details in this document that gave insights as to the intentions of the NFLP.

They were:

- The term was for three years, this included the last year on our current contract. So only two years. I wanted at least five years.
- Exclusivity with all twenty-eight teams in year 2. I needed this.
- Spending level with each club, $50,000, $10,000 more than what I was currently spending with a 10 percent increase per year.
- NFL Television spending $5 million per year of the contract. There was no way Gatorade was going to spend any monies on TV. It was out of our primary selling season and considered unwarranted.
- There were two items listed under "Other." Quote: "NFLP is interested in developing with Quaker a line extension of Gatorade to establish a branded NFL sideline drink. Royalties accrued to the NFLP by this program could have offset, in part, the above rights fee." Were they serious? Develop a brand by Quaker to compete with Gatorade? *No way in hell!*

- "In addition, NFLP would like to explore and test with Quaker the commercial viability of a line of NFL Training Table Foods to include a cereal, granola bar, bread, juice, etc." On the surface, this might sound like a "good discussion." The NFL had no way of developing brands without partnering with a current producer of such brands. Again, Quaker would be competing against its own brands. Not happening.

I now had the details that were important to the NFLP. It was now my job to communicate Gatorade's and the Quaker Oats Company's needs and counter NFLP's wants. There were certain "must haves" as well as "items we wouldn't do."

While I continued to voice the importance of a long-term contract, we decided to invite the NFLP to Chicago. Our goal was to have them meet the Quaker and Gatorade executives and educate them on the science of Gatorade. It was our hope to deter them from wanting to develop a "NFL sideline drink" by us or by anyone else.

After arriving in Chicago, the NFL Properties group that included President, John Bello; Vice President of Marketing, Rick Dudley; Executive Vice-President, Legal Business Affairs, John Flood; and Promotions Director, Jim Schwebel, met us for lunch at Arnie's Restaurant. Joining us for lunch was William D. Smithburg, Chairman and CEO of the Quaker Oats Company; Mike Callahan, Executive Vice President-Grocery Specialties; John Breuer, Vice President, Product Management, and myself.

Arnie Morton was the owner of the restaurant. He was also the owner of Morton's Steakhouses, which were nationwide. I became friends with him during my time in Chicago. The first time I visited Arnie's, I noticed there was a table with a Colts NFL helmet as a centerpiece. I had to ask him about the significance of that table and the helmet. He said, "That's Robert Irsay's table, the owner of the Indianapolis Colts."

I said, "Is Mr. Irsay going to be here for lunch?"

He said, "No, but I set the table each and every day in case he does come in for lunch."

I thought, *What a great place to take the group from the NFL Properties, Inc.* It was perfect. I told Arnie that I would be bringing an NFL executive group in for lunch. Arnie Morton had our table and introduced himself to the group as well as mentioning his relationship with Mr. Irsay.

After Mr. Smithburg's "meet and greet," and him confirming Gatorade's commitment to the NFL long term, we had a limousine transport the group to Meigs Field. There we had a helicopter waiting to transport us to Barrington, Illinois, site of our research facility and home of the Gatorade Sports Science Institute. On the lighter side, when we made our ascent, the helicopter pilot asked, "Does anyone know the way to Barrington?"

John Breuer quickly answered, "Well, you head north on the Kennedy Expressway." Now that was the driving route. I thought we'd fly a direct path to Barrington. We didn't.

Our group at Barrington, headed by Dr. George Halaby and assisted by Dr. Robert Murray, had displayed an NFL Shield on the grounds so we could locate the facility from the air. It was perfect. Dr. "Bob" and his group did a Gatorology 101 presentation to the group. I had asked Bob to show the number of "me too Gatorade products" that had been developed and failed. They totaled over seventy-five. That did register with the group, and I was hoping to move their focus away from developing a "NFL Sideline Beverage." We had dinner that evening at Ditka's Restaurant, keeping with the NFL tie-ins.

The next morning, April 4, 1989, we met with the group and presented Gatorade's strategic plans for 1990 as well as the history and analysis of Gatorade. I presented Gatorade's current sponsorships with the NFL clubs. We had a period of open discussion before they left for Chicago O'Hare Airport. I decided not to go into detail about their proposal they had given to us. I would negotiate these terms and details at a future meeting in New York City.

I scheduled a meeting with the NFLP for April 26, 1989, in New York City. I was expecting, and it was confirmed by Rick Dudley, that I would be receiving a new proposal before that date. We scheduled our flights and awaited the proposal. That proposal came by way of fax on April 25 at 4:00 p.m. I was initially pissed. I later summoned Hank Steinbrecher, my director of sports marketing, and Jackie Leimer, attorney at the Quaker Oats Company, to share with them my strategy. My initial response was to cancel the meeting. After removing my emotions from the equation, I said, "We are going to New York, but I don't know how long the meeting will last." I said, "We may get there and we may decide to walk out of the meeting."

As I always do, I wanted to be prepared for this meeting. I met with Hank and Jackie late into the evening. We finished our discussions around 10:30 p.m. Our flight was at 7:00 a.m. the next morning. My last instruction to Hank and Jackie was direct and focused. I assumed that the meeting would be in a conference room and not in someone's office at NFL Headquarters on Park Avenue. I told Jackie that I wanted her to sit across from me and a few seats from the middle of table. I told Hank I wanted him to sit next to me on my right side.

I told them both as I did with all my staffers who were in meetings with me, "As I go through my discussions, it may appear that I jump all over the place. Just remember there is a plan, and I'll circle back." I did this consciously to disrupt the focus of those with whom I was negotiating with. I also told Jackie if I needed a break in what I was discussing, I'd tug on my left ear. Jackie then would refer to her prepared responses and interject an appropriate comment. I told Hank who would be sitting to my right, "I'll kick you under the table." Hank was going to be the "bad guy."

We arrived at the NFL Headquarters early and were ushered to a conference room. I then told Jackie and Hank where to sit as I positioned myself in the middle of the table. It was their meeting, but I would determine how the meeting would go and eventually end.

Now I was still steaming by the proposal that Rick Dudley had faxed to me the day before, especially these comments:

His opening paragraph, "To make tomorrow's meeting as productive as possible, the attached represents our latest, and probably final renewal proposal. Specifically, this position represents a significant change in four key areas."

1. We have backed off requiring NFL network television as part of your media plan. It is our understanding that significant fourth-quarter spending is inefficient given the seasonality of the brand.
2. Except for 1989/90, we are no longer requiring your participation in our October FSI. Again, this seems inefficient given the seasonality issue.
3. As requested, we have extended the term of the agreement.
4. We recognize your desire to maintain local relationships with the clubs and agree this can be an important element in our overall association. Therefore, we will structure the program to allow for revenue to flow from Quaker to both NFLP and the clubs. As you know, our executive committee would prefer all money coming directly to NFLP.

The last paragraph read:

> Bill, we strongly feel the NFL has compromised significantly in coming to this position. With this kind of package, we are confident we can sell this to club ownership. Falling short of this might mean we would have to pursue other options available to us.
>
> I look forward to seeing you tomorrow and further discussing our position on this important matter.

First, Gatorade still had another year on the contract with the NFLP with rights fees of $150,000 and another $500,000 spending toward *Gameday* and *Pro Magazine*. Rick's proposal structured that remaining year to $3 million in rights fees with $3 million in rights fees for an additional four years. He also added a $500,000 marketing fund for all five years as well as $1.5 million spending with the clubs each year.

The Marketing Fund can be applied against Tailgate, ticket purchases, special events, local promotions and NFL media, (i.e., GameDay, Prolog).

The Local Club spend will cover all twenty-eight clubs with a minimum payment of $40,000 per club. Free product and coolers and the trainer's association fee can be applied against this fund. Sideline exclusivity is guaranteed, except in New Orleans and San Francisco in Year 1 (current).

I had succeeded in registering several keys goals in the negotiating process: A long-term contract, exclusivity with all twenty-eight clubs, dropping the media buy each year, elimination of a NFL branded sideline beverage, and continued support of the local clubs. There was still the over-escalated increases in rights fees that needed to be reduced.

I knew it was Rick Dudley's meeting, and my goal was to take him out of the equation. As John Flood, Rick Dudley, and Jim Schwebel entered the room and said their welcomes and hellos, Rick Dudley opened the meeting.

I stopped him at mid-sentence. I said, "There was some question as to whether we were coming to New York, based on the tonality of the proposal we received last night. And frankly, I don't know how long we are going to stay. We've showed the willingness to negotiate in good faith and for a long-term agreement. We will not be intimidated into an agreement with such terms as 'probably final renewal proposal' or 'falling short of this might mean we would have to pursue other options available to us.' We have an agreement that is legally binding through March 1990.

"Furthermore, we have twenty-four club agreements in 1989, twenty-two in 1990 and seventeen in 1991. You can't shop this to anyone else now, legally or realistically. I'd also request the opportunity to present our proposal directly to the NFL executive management committee."

John Flood stood up; Rick Dudley sat down. Mission accomplished. Rick Dudley would enter back into the conversation, but it would involve a major concession by the NFLP.

As John Flood and I talked through the details, I grabbed my left ear twice. Jackie answered with appropriate and timely comments. I kicked Hank twice. His comment on "good faith" and how the NFLP wasn't quite there yet. He also replayed the Super Bowl incident from earlier in the year.

Here's what we ultimately agreed to:

- Six-year agreement. I doubled the rights fees on the last year on the contract to $300,000, then $3 million in rights fees each year for five years.
- We received exclusivity with all twenty-eight teams, starting Year 2.
- The "category" had been redefined as "sports beverages."
- We'd receive a suite/skybox for each Super Bowl.
- 150 Super Bowl Tickets at various and premium seat locations for the game.
- 150 NFL Super Bowl tailgate party tickets.
- 12 tickets (a table of 12) at the Commissioner's Party. This area is usually reserved for club owners.

Again, I circled the room with a variety of issues, then focused back on exclusivity. I said, "I want to institute a penalty if one team has an incident where they didn't use Gatorade cups, coolers, and squeeze bottles."

John Flood responded, "What do you think the penalty should be?"

I responded, "A third of the rights fees for every incident."

Now Rick Dudley had been a spectator throughout all these conversations and negotiating details discussed by John Flood and me. With no lapse in time and almost immediately, Rick Dudley asserted, "We can do that."

I thought to myself, *Thank you, Rick.*

Now in Year 2 of the contract, I had received reports that the San Francisco 49ers had used Powerburst cups and coolers during a game. I notified NFLP about the incident and noted this was a violation of our agreement and a penalty would be assessed ($1 million, a third of the $3 million rights fee). The 49ers violated this exclusivity agreement two more times at two home games. The NFLP was duly notified and put on notice.

Early that Monday morning, after the third game violation, I received a call from John Flood. He said, "I need your help putting this San Francisco 49ers issue to rest."

I said, "Sure, John, what do you want me to do?"

He said, "I want you to call Carmen Policy, the Executive Vice President of the 49ers, and execute a five-year, $125,000 a year marketing agreement with the team."

Without hesitation, I said, "Sure." He said Carmen Policy was expecting my call.

Now, on average, I was spending $50,000 with the NFL Clubs. In some cases, Gatorade was a suite holder, so costs could exceed $100,000. Now the San Francisco 49ers won Super Bowl XXIII, and that Diet Coke incident loomed large in my memory. I had no qualms about doing the agreement. It built a stronger relationship with the NFLP and one very influential owner, Eddie DeBartolo Jr. As for the penalty that grew to $3 million for the three incidents and equaled our rights fees for the 1990 season, I said to John Flood, "For the benefit of Gatorade's relationship with the NFL and the NFLP, I'll forgive you of those penalties *in good faith.*"

I received a fax from Carmen Policy on November 3, 1990, with the cover sheet from the Radisson Inn, Green Bay. Attached was a one-page handwritten agreement, signed by Carmen Policy, from the San Francisco 49ers and Richard Strayer from Powerburst Corp. It outlined the rights of Gatorade moving forward and "indemnified" us of any action from Powerburst, its shareholders, Board of Directors, or anyone connected with Powerburst. Crisis avoided, relationships protected.

In Year 3 of the agreement, John Flood contacted me and said he needed my help. I flew to New York and met with him at his Park

Avenue offices. By this time, he'd been promoted to President of the NFLP. We chatted for a while, and he said, "Let's go to lunch."

John and I got in one private vehicle, and Tom Fox from my department and Jim Schwebel got in another vehicle, and we met at Peter Luger Steak House in Brooklyn. It was a famous and expensive steak house, cash only. We were NFLP's guests. While there, we discussed his and NFLP's needs as Tom and Jim listened in.

On the way back to his office, he and I agreed on an extension of the Gatorade contract with expanded worldwide rights and broader category uses. It would be a seven-year deal with rights fees of $5 million for four years, then $6 million for the last three years.

In addition, I wanted to bring back an event I remembered from my youth, the NFL Punt, Pass, and Kick Competition. It would be titled The Gatorade Punt, Pass, and Kick Competition (PP&K). It would involve all twenty-eight clubs and included signage, local and halftime competitions, and the presentation of national age group winners at the American Conference Championship Game. It was open to boys and girls, ages six to fifteen years of age. The PP&K would cost an additional $1 million per year of the contract. It was that simple, but he said he wanted his associate, Jim Schwebel, to get major credit for structuring the new deal. I said, "Sure." Honestly, I didn't care who got credit.

This locked up a new long-term contract with the NFL from 1992 through 1999, and the Gatorade Punt, Pass, and Kick Competition satisfied a new initiative to target youth, specifically girls, from the Gatorade Marketing Group. This was betting on the gold standard of professional leagues, the origin of Gatorade's TV exposure.

I negotiated my last contract with the NFL in January of 1998. They outlined their rights fees proposal at:

- Year 1: $18 million
- Year 2: $27 million
- Year 3: $29 million
- Year 4: $31 million
- Year 5: $33 million
- Year 6: $35 million

I negotiated the rights fees to:

- Year 1: $9 million
- Year 2: $11 million
- Year 3: $13 million
- Year 4: $15 million
- Year 5: $17 million
- Year 6: $19 million

I saved Gatorade and the Quaker Oats Company $89 million from the $173 million asked for in rights fees alone over the six years of the contract from the NFLP. There were other elements in the contract, but their increases were in the 10–20 percent range and not significant as the rights fees.

I say I left Gatorade in great shape for the future with the NFL, the brand Gatorade absolutely had to have and couldn't afford to lose.

CHAPTER 34

KEY PROPERTIES AND PROGRAMS

Major League Baseball (MLB)

In implementing the Gatorade "field of play" strategy of owning the sidelines, dugouts, courtsides, and gain exposure from the professional sports to peewee leagues, the National Basketball Association (NBA) and Major League Baseball (MLB) played important roles. No one delivered exposure like the National Football League (NFL), and as they did in the NFL, the athletic trainers were key in our relationships, contacts, and visibility for the brand.

Gene Gieselmann, the head athletic trainer for the St. Louis Cardinals Baseball Team, was the reason Gatorade not only entered the MLB, but he was also the reason we were successful. Gene was already working with Gatorade at Stokely-Van Camp in the early 1980s. Gene was exceptional at building relationships with other team trainers, and he had provided Gatorade with incredible television exposure in the Cardinals dugouts during all their games. He was very proactive in gaining us exposure in all their broadcasts and was the conduit to Gatorade's access to the team's marketing directors.

We'd worked with the marketing directors of selected teams to sponsor "Gatorade Day" or a premium giveaway day along with providing cups, coolers, and towels in the dugouts. In addition, through Gieselmann's assistance, we provided program funding for the professional baseball trainers. As they organized the Professional Baseball Athletic Trainers Society (PBATS), Gatorade provided Public Relations programs that were administered by John LeGear of Timothy Communications. John LeGear and his agency became the "key developer of programs" and Gatorade's relationships with all athletic trainers in all sports disciplines at all levels, nationwide.

LeGear would develop PBATS Media Guides, press releases, and schedule interviews and appearances. Athletic trainers in general received little or no publicity on their professions. They were well-educated, certified "healthcare professionals." John LeGear was the best at developing a strategy and communicating that to the sports world and the public.

While the athletic trainers were providing Gatorade with exceptional exposure, and we had a handful of MLB teams sponsored, I wanted to approach Major League Baseball and the commissioner's office to explore sponsorship of MLB. This would make Gatorade a fully licensed partner, and it would also leverage our relationship with PBATS.

When I arrived at the Quaker Oats Company in the fall of 1984, Gatorade was already sponsoring a Home Run Hitting Contest with Major League Baseball. It involved a selected player of each team facing off against each other at a selected game during the season. These contests would be before the game, during batting practice. There was a bracket for the American League and the National League, and the winner would advance throughout the season culminating at Game 5 of the World Series that season. It seemed very popular with the fan base and the teams.

At the end of this season-long elimination tournament, Greg "The Bull" Luzinski from the Chicago White Sox won the American League, and Jeff Leonard of the San Francisco Giants won the National League. They would face each other in a final contest at Game 5 of the World Series in Detroit in 1984. I was asked by Mark Shapiro, Brand Manager of Gatorade, to travel to Detroit with him for the culmination of the Home Run Derby.

The Detroit Tigers had taken a 3–1 lead in the series over the San Diego Padres and could clinch the series with a win on Sunday night, October 14, 1984. The Home Run Derby final contest was in a "flex" scheduled date. It was originally scheduled for Game 4 of the World Series but was moved to Game 5. I was attending as a guest and was there to observe. Mark Shapiro told me to meet him in the lobby of the hotel that morning.

We met in the hotel lobby that Sunday morning at 8:30 a.m. Along with us were Greg Luzinski and Jeff Leonard. We boarded a van along with a few MLB marketing personnel and headed to Tiger Stadium. After a brief warm up by both hitters, the Home Run Derby began.

Each player brought their own pitchers. Luzinski's pitcher was his dad, and Jeff Leonard brought a coach from the San Francisco Giants. As I recall, each hitter had three innings to hit or a total of nine outs. They would alternate after every three outs.

In the end, Greg Luzinski beat Jeff Leonard and won the $50,000 first place prize and the trophy. The trophy was a Blair Buswell commissioned piece and a composite of five famous Major League Baseball home run hitters—Babe Ruth, Ted Williams, Mickey Mantle, Hank Aaron, and Roger Maris. It was eighteen inches high, weighing forty pounds.

This was my first Major League Baseball World Series. It was also Peter Ueberroth's first World Series as MLB Commissioner. Peter had been President of the Los Angeles Olympic Organizing Committee, the most financially successful Olympics in history. Peter was to be the savior of Major League Baseball.

As Mark Shapiro and I traveled back to our hotel, I graded the event in my mind. When asked by Mark, "What did you think?" I said, "It was an event that lacked exposure. After all, we're at the 1984 Baseball World Series, and our culminating event was before an empty stadium at 9:30 in the morning. We got no bang for our buck!"

We were both so disappointed with the event we left Detroit before the game started and returned to Chicago. We both thought Detroit would win the game and win the 1984 Baseball World Series.

Weeks later, I was with Mark in his office at the Merchandise Mart and noticed the home run trophy on the floor by his door. He said, "We commissioned Blair Buswell to do two trophies. This is the second one." He said, "If you want it, you can have it. We don't plan on doing another MLB Home Run Derby."

I still have that trophy. It may be the best Home Run Derby Trophy that the public never saw. It's beautiful and too good to be used as a door stop.

There would be five seasons of us working with PBATS as well as the individual Major League Baseball clubs in securing dugout exposure and exclusivity. As we expanded to having twenty-two clubs with marketing agreements and promotional days, I continued trying to negotiate an overall deal with MLB Properties. In the 1990 season, I was able to finalize an agreement.

It was a five-year agreement, and MLB granted Gatorade:

- Isotonic product category exclusivity on a national and regional basis.
- Product category exclusivity to conduct national and regional premium promotions utilizing MLB-licensed merchandise (single-market premium promotions subject to club approval).
- Rights to provide and display product in dugouts during All-Star Workout Day, All-Star Game, and World Series and League Championship Series (LCS), the latter subject to club approval.
- Collective use of club marks and MLB logo in advertising and promotion (individual use of club marks subject to club approval).

The research by Bayer Bess Vanderwarker, Gatorade's advertising agency, provided me with information that had me focused on the marquee event of Major League Baseball, its mid-summer All-Star Game. The researched showed that the demographic of those watching baseball were male and over the age of forty. The Gatorade user demographic was eighteen-to-twenty-four-year-old males who were "physically active enthusiasts" (PAE), meaning they worked out at least twice a week. The demographic for the MLB All-Star was near thirty years of age and male. This would be my focus.

I would receive dugout, bullpen, and signage exposure for the MLB All-Star Game where the marquee players would be seen drinking Gatorade, a page out of our "implied endorsement" strategy. Best of all, we wouldn't be paying the players to drink it. I wanted more than that. I wanted an event during that All-Star Workout Day, an event within an event.

My thoughts ran back to my youth when I watched a black and white television broadcast of some of the greatest sluggers in the game face each other in a nine-inning "Home Run Derby." It was a thirty-minute broadcast filmed in Los Angeles, but like the final of the Gatorade Home Run Derby in 1984, it was held in an empty ballpark. I could do better. I would do better!

I would finalize the new MLB sponsorship before the start of the 1990 season on March 20, 1990. It included an expanded category of "Sports Beverages" and "the Gatorade Home Run Derby."

We would receive additional signage during the workout day with additional tickets for the MLB All-Star Game, LCS, and World Series Games. We committed to program ads and an FSI national promotion and sponsorship of the MLB Fanfest.

The Gatorade Home Run Derby had tremendous success at the MLB All-Star Games in Toronto in 1991, San Diego in 1992, and Baltimore in 1993. Several head-to-head finals with double-digit long home runs punctuated its growing popularity. As the broadcast of MLB games changed, so did Gatorade's strategy on advertising purchasing. We'd purchase time within the Gatorade Home Run Derby and did national promotions around the event.

In 1994, Gatorade became one of the original sponsors on the Baseball Network. Ken Schanzer stepped away from NBC Sports to be the CEO of the network that MLB owned and produced broadcasts and brokered them to ABC and NBC. Gatorade made a three-year, a $3 million a year commitment. The network was dissolved after two years.

The broadcast landscape would change again after the 1994 MLB Strike and the canceling of the 1994 MLB World Series. FOX and ESPN would enter the broadcast bidding wars and bring new blood and new technology to its broadcasts. NBC owned some late playoff season games, but those would later go to FOX, and NBC would be out of MLB after the 2000 season. Gatorade's advertising buy strategy at the time was to purchase spots in local markets and with local market TV programing and rely on sports marketing to acquire and control team dugout exposure.

In the final analysis, MLB was in our prime selling season, May-August, but never delivered on our target audience.

National Basketball Association (NBA)

In February of 1985 and my first year at the Quaker Oats Company, I was in New York City at the invitation of David Stern, the newly named Commissioner of the NBA. David Stern had been General Counsel to the NBA and Executive VP before being named NBA Commissioner on February 1, 1985.

David was an attorney who inherited the NBA at a time of cocaine and "free base" use. Drug use in the NBA was a real problem. In the early 1980s, cocaine and drug use were estimated to be about 70 percent of the league players. There were NBA players charged with possession, use, and some higher profile incidents of automobile wrecks that resulted in death. There was a stigma of the NBA being the "Drug League." David Stern had real challenges going forward.

There were three other sponsors represented at this meeting besides Gatorade. There was American Airlines, Schick Razors, and Spalding, the basketball and sporting goods company—four NBA sponsors and the NBA Commissioner in one room.

David opened the meeting by welcoming us to New York and thanked us for taking the time to make this meeting possible. He was very open and honest about the challenges in the NBA and the hurdles that faced him as the new commissioner. Drug use was the biggest problem along with promotion of a game that had little television exposure. Most of the early games were produced and broadcast at a later time. The NBA had nowhere to go but up.

David made this statement: "I'm going to build this league, but I can't do it without your help and support." He outlined changes that would be occurring soon. A new television broadcast partnership, league-wide drug education programs with the NBA Players Association, and league expansion.

David delivered on what he said, and he was loyal to those that were there in those most difficult and challenging times. In my opinion and through my sixteen years in working with him, Rick Welts, and the NBA, David Stern was the best sports commissioner of any sport.

He cleaned up the "Drug League" and grew the NBA into a global brand. He launched the Women's National Basketball Association (WNBA) in 1991. I remember him saying, "You will be involved with the launch of the WNBA, and it will be a three-year commitment of $3 million a year." There was no discussion. We made the commitment.

He moved the television contract from CBS to NBC where he partnered with Dick Ebersol, President of NBC Sports. Ebersol was the NBC genius who "owned the Olympics." He knew how to build television viewership. A new NBA Playoff schedule extended the season broadcasts into late June, well into Gatorade's selling season. They also delivered on our eighteen-to-twenty-four-year-old male target audience.

David Stern knew he wanted the NBA to be global. He established NBA Regional offices in Asia, Europe, Canada, and China. He saw the increased number of the international players playing in the NBA and built a strategy to welcome them into the league. He, in turn, would partner with FIBA, the international governing body of basketball, to grow the sport. He utilized McDonald's worldwide business to build an international tournament in Paris, the McDonald's Open. He, along with FIBA, allowed professional basketball players (NBA) to compete in the Olympics.

The "Dream Team" was one of David Stern's greatest achievements. The NBA partnered with USA Basketball, the governing body of amateur basketball in the United States, to manage their marketing rights. Up until this time, USA Basketball had little if any marketing staff. Bill Wall, then the executive director, welcomed the NBA and its marketing expertise.

So you had USA Basketball, who determined what players were on the USA Olympic Basketball Team, the NBA, its marketing and the best basketball players in the world, and FIBA, the international governing body working together to grow the sport. David Stern brought them all together. They weren't a close rival to world soccer, but they now had a strategy and a plan. David Stern made players in the NBA superstars and the foreign athletes who played stars in their own countries.

David Stern was extremely loyal, and I had a great personal relationship with him. In all my negotiations with the NBA, I worked directly with Rick Welts, President of NBA Properties, David's lieutenant. Rick and I were able to meet and satisfy all the needs of both the NBA and Gatorade. These contracts were historical in term length, television advertising commitment, and rights fees.

After completing a new five-year agreement, David, Rick, and I toasted with champagne. Later, David confided in me that he had been approached by one the highest executives from the Coca-Cola Company. David said, "He laid a blank check on my desk and said, 'You fill in the amount, we want Gatorade out of the NBA.'"

David's response to them was, "Where were you when I needed help?"

Gatorade remained a very visible partner with the NBA, and David was still able to acquire fees from the Coca-Cola Company, and he made it clear Gatorade was here to stay.

Those four sponsors who met with David Stern back in February of 1985 became the sponsors of NBA All-Star Saturday, the diamond of the NBA All-Star Weekend. American Airlines sponsored the Three-Point Shootout, and Gatorade sponsored the Slam Dunk Contest. It was the American Airlines Three-Point Shootout and the Gatorade Slam Dunk Contest. Later, Schick would become the sponsor of the Three-Point Shootout.

In addition to increased talent and creativity in the Gatorade Slam Dunk Contest, we looked for additional ways to engage the crowd. One year, we introduced "Rating Cards" for the spectators. They were handed out as people entered the arena, two cards with the numbers 7, 8, 9, and 10. After each participant's dunk, the fans would show how they scored the dunk, 7 through 10.

Now, when it came to the NBA, Gatorade had the trifecta. We sponsored the NBA, we sponsored the Chicago Bulls, and yes, we had the greatest basketball player on the planet, Michael Jordan. This was showcased at the 1988 NBA All-Star Game played in Chicago. The duel between Michael Jordan and Dominique Wilkins in the Gatorade Slam Dunk Contest was legendary.

Dominique had beaten Michael in the Slam Dunk Contest in 1985. This 1988 Gatorade Slam Dunk Contest would have Dominique Wilkins against Michael Jordan for the second time. Dominique took the lead on his last dunk, 145–97. Michael had one dunk left.

Michael Jordan started his approach from beyond the baseline at the opposite end of the floor. He moved across center court and took off from the foul line, fully extended, to make the dunk. Michael scored a perfect 50 on that last dunk and edged out Wilkins, 147–145. As I presented Michael Jordan the trophy, I thought then in 1988, if Gatorade ever wanted to sponsor an athlete endorser, this was the guy. Three years later in 1991, I signed Michael Jordan.

Michael Jordan left an incredible legacy in basketball. That 1988 NBA All-Star Game, Michael scored forty points and was named MVP. It was a great weekend to be Chicagoan. The entire NBA All-Star Weekend was held at the iconic Chicago Stadium. Michael's success powered the Chicago Bulls to a dynasty in the NBA with six NBA World Championships, a new arena, the United Center, and millions of fans around the world.

Gatorade Player of the Year

There were numerous award programs honoring athletes at all levels of sports in the USA. Some, like the Heisman Trophy, were awarded to "the most outstanding player in college football." Others were named after outstanding athletes and focusing on a variety of sports. The John Wooden Award, named for UCLA's outstanding basketball coach, John Wooden, honored the most outstanding men's college basketball player. The Wooden Award would later add the honor to include the most outstanding female colligate basketball player.

In my "Gatorade Sideline Strategy," I was still trying to fill the gap from Peewee to Pro. I established relationships with various youth sports organizations and, in most cases, a sponsorship. My relationships with the collegiate athletic trainers enabled me to sponsor seventy-five colleges and universities over time. Some had great football programs, others exceptional basketball programs. Later, after the implementation of Title IX Legislation, the exposure increased as women's programs developed and received greater visibility.

The remaining gap was in high school sports. Gatorade had no programs or sponsorships outside of a Quaker employee providing cups and coolers to their local high school. So I was intrigued when Bruce Weber, publisher of *Scholastic* magazines, scheduled a meeting to discuss a new program that involved his target audience, high schools.

We met in my office in Chicago at the Merchandise Plaza. Bruce started his presentation informally and walked me through the proposal. I learned to hold my questions to the end. In some cases, it took patience that I wasn't sure I had. I also didn't refer to the last pages of the proposal as I wanted Bruce to have my undivided attention. His *Scholastic* publications were in every school throughout the United States. He reached the target audience that I needed.

Bruce Weber's proposal to me that day was the sponsorship of "The High School Heisman Award." It would recognize the most outstanding high school football player in the country. The award would have the similar format of the collegiate Heisman Trophy Award, and the individual would be honored at an awards banquet. My first response was, "Bruce, this is a great idea, but we don't want to mimic the Heisman Trophy Award." I also said, "This is just for the sport of football and only targets males." I also said, "The only winner in this award is the caterer." I then remember saying, "What about a Heisman Trophy award for all sports, including girls sports?"

He kind of laughed, and I got that "Where is Schmidt taking this?" look.

As I thought out loud, I asked him, "What sports in high school have the highest number of participants?" I could guess what they were, but I wanted to engage Bruce in this open creative discussion. He responded, "Football, basketball, baseball, track and field, and soccer for boys. Basketball, volleyball, softball, track and field, and soccer for girls."

I then said, "How can we recognize a national winner in each of those without the caterers winning? Also, how can I best leverage this award with our existing sales regions and staff?"

Bruce was at his best. He said, "We can have a winner in each state, then from those states, we could have twelve regional winners, culminating with a Gatorade National Player of the Year."

I said, "Perfect."

Bruce said he had a staff of sports writers across the country that could provide the names or candidates. I added one caveat. I wanted academics to be part of the criteria in the determination of the winners.

He said, "We can do that."

And with that discussion, Bruce Weber headed back to New York to determine how *Scholastic* was going to price the cost of running the Gatorade Player of the Year Award. I heard from him three days later with the cost. I said, "Bruce, that's great, but there's one more thing."

He said, "What's that?"

I said, "I want the winners to be featured on the cover of your *Scholastic* magazine when we make the announcements."

He said, "That would involve more advertising in the magazine."

I said, "That's to be expected."

He said, "Let me call you back."

By the end of the week, we had The Gatorade Player of the Year Award. We would provide award certificates to each state winner and ideally present them to the winner at the winner's high school in front of his/her student body. Plaques would be presented to the regional winners, and we would hold a press conference in the national winner's hometown and present them with the award, inviting local press, family, coaches, teammates, and dignitaries to attend. It would follow with dinner with the winner and his/her family, coaches, and high school administrators.

The plaques, certificates, and trophies were all produced by Bardach Trophies in Indianapolis, Indiana. Tom Bardach was the best. He mailed out all awards and certificates when necessary and handled all printing and engraving.

In the first two years of the program, the Gatorade National Player of the Year would be our guest at the championship of that sport for the professional sports. The football winner would our guest along with a guest to attend the Super Bowl. The basketball winner would be our guest at the NBA Finals, and the baseball winner would be our guest at the MLB World Series. The logistics and NCAA oversight became too challenging, so this component was eliminated.

Bruce Weber was a dear friend, and I loved him dearly. He always had a story to share. He made you laugh so hard you'd cry. He and his wife, Annette, were our guests at many Super Bowls, World Series, and NBA Finals, Final Four, and other events, when/where Gatorade was involved. He could play the piano, and if we had a function and a piano was nearby, Bruce entertained us. He passed away on May 25, 2018.

It was our hope that years down the road, the list of winners would be a "Who's who in Sports," national champions, world champions, and Olympic champions. Mission accomplished. Thank you, Bruce Weber.

CHAPTER 35

THE OAKLEY EXPERIENCE

I became familiar with Oakley eyewear at the various sporting events that Gatorade sponsored. My first introduction to the brand was at the Gatorade Ironman World Triathlon Championships at Kona, Hawaii.

This was a very fertile market for Oakley. You weren't considered a serious triathlete unless you wore Oakley glasses on the bike and running portions of the event. The eyewear was everywhere. Winners Mark Allen and Paula Newby-Fraser were showcasing Oakley's throughout the event and at the finish line. Oakley catered to an edgy audience with a flair for design and technology mixed in.

David Duval, PGA golfer, noticeably wore Oakley's on the golf course while playing golf. This was at a time when very few golfers wore sunglasses. He'd win, and the glasses became a staple for young golfers everywhere who wanted to "be like the pros."

Oakley had a solid base of consumers with an underground following in the ski, skate, and extreme sport disciplines. Any products this audience used had to be ultra-cool and not worn by "mainstream" consumers. They set trends; they didn't follow them.

After a phone interview with Jim Jannard, I was extended an invitation to join Oakley's board of directors in October in 1997. I was recommended to the Oakley board by Michael Jordan, himself an Oakley board member. The other independent board members were Irene Miller, Vice Chairman and Chief Financial Officer at

Barnes and Noble, and Orin Smith, President and Chief Operating Officer at the Starbucks Corporation.

After conferring with William Smithburg, Chairman, President and CEO of the Quaker Oats Company and the legal department of Quaker Oats, I was given permission to accept the board position with Oakley on October 12, 1997. This would be a new growth experience for me. The Oakley board and Jannard had reached out to me because of my marketing skill and expertise in building a brand, so they said.

The other internal Oakley Board Members were Jim Jannard, Chairman, Founder; Mike Parnell, Vice Chairman; and Link Newcomb, CEO. Oakley went public with an IPO in 1995 raising $230 million. Now, I wasn't intimidated by this new "boardroom" experience. Again, I knew what I didn't know. I listened intently as financial numbers were being discussed. Sales projections, sales performance numbers, along with marketing I could understand. I had been around sports and sports enthusiasts all my life. That only increased during the time I was at Gatorade. I also relied on what I was blessed with: street smarts and common sense.

As board members, you have the various presentations made by the CEO, the Chief Financial Officer and with Oakley, the sports marketing department. Now everybody loves the "glitz and glamor" of a brand, and with Oakley, that was understandable. The brand was becoming synonymous with sports. There were incredible similarities with Gatorade and Oakley. Now I knew that I might not have been the smartest person in the room, but when it came to understanding a sports brand and defining its audience, I was the only person in the room who had that kind of experience and success.

Jim Jannard was quite the pitchman. He was passionate about the brand and its potential. He rallied his employees around a "defiant anti-culture," and no one questioned his ideas nor, for that matter, his opinions. He had the most loyal following within the workplace.

His staff lived in a creative technology fishbowl. The technology was incredible, and they searched for ways to describe it with adjectives that seemed superfluous and, in some cases, meaningless. It didn't matter if the consumer didn't understand it. Oakley would define it. They'd tell you what you needed and what price you were going to pay for it. This all occurred at the self-proclaimed "Interplanetary Headquarters" in Foothills Ranch, California.

Jannard ran the place as a self-proclaimed "benevolent dictatorship." He was affectionally known as the "Mad Scientist," coming up with "mind-blowing creativity." There's no question about the creative and "edgy" culture at Oakley. What they were missing was a general business "go to market skillset." As someone said, "You can have the greatest product in the world, but unless you get to market, it doesn't matter."

Certainly, they had success, but to me, the ceiling seemed higher and the opportunities limitless. Incorporating a defined business strategy with production timelines and committing to retail delivery dates would make Oakley a billion-dollar brand in three years. I was certain of that. Jannard would showcase the new models and products at Oakley board meetings. The technology and especially the design elements were core competencies for Oakley. They owned it. Oakley was expected and did deliver "new news" each year and set the standard for "chic, stylish, and design-driven eyewear."

After the showcase of new products and listing of various successes in sports marketing, the conversation would ultimately center around "projected sales and revenue for the quarter or the year." The conversation about "soft sales" and not meeting projections were basically discussed away by "The new product introductions would be more than enough to make up for the difference."

One specific area that I noticed about Oakley was its sports marketing department. As an outsider and someone who understood "product placement and implied endorsement," I knew what relationships were all about and how to reach endorsers for your product. Oakley did it extremely well. What surprised me was the size of the sports marketing staff and the monies paid to an extremely large number of athletes. It reminded me of Giulio Malgara, President of Quaker Oats, Europe, who had an abundant number of paid athlete endorsers.

At Oakley, it was not only the number of athletes they were paying to use their products but also the number of staff people employed to manage these relationships. As a board member, I couldn't review department staffs or structure. That would change when I became the CEO.

There was also "low-hanging fruit," areas that begged the question, "Why not expand into that specific market?" Prescription glasses were always questioned by the board as were "polarized sunglasses." It was normally answered that production issues and current sunglass model production projections made it impossible to consider at this time. No way of confirming the effort necessary for either production opportunity. We were told what they wanted us to know.

At Oakley's first quarter board meeting of 1999, we had just come back from a break, and I noticed that Link Newcomb, the CEO, was conspicuously absent. As the meeting renewed, Jim Jannard, Oakley's founder and chairman, looked at me and asked, "How would you like to run this company and be its next CEO?" Now that explained Link's absence. I responded to Jim Jannard after he mentioned that he and the other board members thought I'd be an exceptional CEO.

I said, "Why would I want to do that when I had an incredible position at Gatorade?" Jim proceeded to proclaim my area of expertise and how I would be an asset for Oakley, and they could make it beneficial for me. Board members, Irene Miller and Orin Smith, echoed Jim's comments and endorsed me being the next CEO.

I stated to the group that I had to get back to Chicago and consider this opportunity and I'd have an answer within a week. I also needed to have in place the specifics of the offer. There would be salary, bonuses, stock options, relocation packages, etc. I left John Wayne Airport on my flight back to Chicago, thinking, *What a great new chapter in my career.*

The atmosphere, climate, and culture at the Quaker Oats Company had changed since the departure of William D. Smithburg, former Chairman and CEO. His departure was considered eminent after the fiasco of the acquisition of Snapple. Bill Smithburg was a friend and a corporate executive who understood my importance to the Gatorade brand and the relationships that were so important to

Gatorade's success. I knew I'd have to reeducate my new chairman and CEO.

Robert Morrison was named the new chairman and CEO of The quaker Oats Company on October 24, 1997. It ushered in a time of uncertainty throughout the headquarters of the Quaker Oats Company. Change is the only certainty in life in addition to death and taxes, and change would be coming.

My associate, Sue Wellington, VP of Gatorade Marketing, asked me, "What changes do you think will happen?" I was VP of Gatorade Worldwide Sports Marketing, and we both reported to the president of the Grocery Specialties Group. I said, "'This guy will come in, eliminate the level above us, and promote you to President, and you'll be my boss."

She then said, "What will you do?"

I said, "I'll quit."

Now it wasn't that I couldn't work for Sue Wellington. We had established a great relationship as we worked collectively to build the brand. It was my intuition that told me that this new Chairman/CEO wouldn't want me around. I sensed that I was too visible, and no one was going to be more visible than him.

As I predicted, Morrison came in and did exactly what I said. The entire level of executives above us were eliminated in a "restructured" company memorandum. I was now reporting to Sue Wellington. I looked forward to continuing the success of the sports marketing department as my direct report had changed.

The next one and a half years were extremely significant as I was renegotiating the contracts for the NFL, NBA, MLB, and NASCAR. The strategy was clear: sign them all with realized savings to Gatorade.

My first noticeable sign that things were changing occurred on two fronts. I was questioned about my position on the Oakley board and my membership at Butler National Golf Club. These questions came from Sue, but I know she had to be directed by Morrison.

They didn't ask me to resign from the Oakley board, but I would be losing my membership at Butler National. Ms. Wellington stated, "The membership at Butler National is the Quaker Oats Company's membership, and Quaker will be terminating it."

Now I explained to Sue that Butler National didn't have corporate memberships, and I negotiated this in my contract when I joined the Quaker Oats Company after the Los Angeles '84 Olympic Games. Quaker was to pay for a membership for me, in my name, at a country club. They would also pay all fees and reimburse me for any work-related entertainment/expenses. I would be responsible for my own personal expenses.

Sue Wellington told me to resign from Butler National. Butler National, at the time, was a 100 percent equity club. Quaker Oats paid the $36,000 initiation fee in my name when I joined in 1986. Butler wrote me check for $100,000. This was the current initiation fee in 1998. The Quaker Oats Company then issued me a Form W-2 for the $100,000. The message was clear.

I completed the renegotiation of the National Football League contract and saved the company $89 million over the seven years of the contract from the asking amount of the NFL's $173 million. In addition, I finalized contracts with the NBA, MLB, and NASCAR with costs savings of $50 million. That would be considered incredible in any performance review or year's accomplishments.

I had to get Robert Morrison's signature on all these contracts as we wanted to execute them as soon as possible. The respective parties for the NFL, NBA, MLB, and NASCAR had already signed them. I went to Mr. Morrison's home in Lake Forest, Illinois, a northern suburb of Chicago, to have him sign them on a Saturday morning. His wife answered the door. She was warm, friendly, and very cordial and invited me in. When Mr. Morrison appeared, he said nothing. I reviewed the contracts with him regarding the terms, length, and importance of having these major contracts in place and completed for the next five to seven years.

In this competitive environment, these contracts were significant. As I left for the door, I decided to say to Mr. Morrison, "The Quaker Oats Company has always rewarded me in some fashion with bonuses or stock options when I negotiated these contracts in the past. I just wanted to make you aware of that."

Never did I make that comment to Bill Smithburg or Phil Marineau during my time on Gatorade while at the Quaker Oats

Company. They knew my value and my negotiating skill and rewarded me unsolicited and without prodding. I just felt like I was the FedEx guy delivering a package and the recipient signed for it and I left. My intuition was saying the end of my career at Gatorade was near.

Months later, in my annual review conducted by Sue Wellington, I was informed by her that my performance for the year was unsatisfactory and that I'd be put on review for the next six months. It was now obvious that I wasn't wanted at Gatorade or the Quaker Oats Company, no matter what contracts I negotiated or the amount of money I saved the company. By the way, I never received anything but an "Exceeds Expectations" in the fourteen years previous annual reviews by my supervising manager.

I looked right at Ms. Wellington and said, "If you don't really want me here, why don't you offer me a package?"

She said, "You'd take a separation package?"

I chose my words carefully and said, "I'd entertain a separation package."

She closed her notebook and walked out. In fifteen minutes, she was back with a separation package in detail. They had it prepared and were letting me go. It was now or in six months. The result was the same: You're out! That cold fact was hard to swallow. Ms. Wellington was just doing what she was told to do. I guess I expected more from her. It was disappointing. The real disappointment was that I didn't negotiate "Gatorade for Life" in my separation package. After all, I had plenty of "sweat equity" in the brand.

Now this coincided with the opportunity presented to me by Oakley. The Oakley board had no idea that I was going to be out at Gatorade. They thought they were hiring me away from Gatorade, and so did I. I made no mention of my situation, all the while assuming I was going to continue at Gatorade. I worked out all the details before and after my annual review with Sue Wellington. Ms. Wellington had no idea I was in the process of leaving. Leverage is a wonderful thing. My first official start date as the Chief Executive Officer (CEO) of Oakley was May 1, 1999. I signed a three-year contract with a $250,000 signing bonus. I received a car of my choice, a membership to a country club, and options on 900,000 shares of stock with a $350,000 annual salary. Timing is everything.

My only perspective on Oakley was as a board member. As it's said, "You have a completely different view when you see the sausage being made." My view in the next six weeks would define what I thought needed to be done and whether I would be able to accomplish it.

I had several areas I felt certain that needed improvement as well as other initiatives that needed to be implemented. I first wanted research on the Oakley consumer. Jim Jannard was telling me and the board about his view of our consumer, but I wanted my own research and facts. I also needed to talk to our retailers. Sunglass Hut accounted for over 40 percent of all Oakley sales. We needed to have a great relationship with them and, at the same time, try to find new partners to help our distribution, increase sales, and rely less on Sunglass Hut. Most of the research I could acquire by interviewing advertising agencies and inviting them to "pitch the business." They'd have to research Oakley to understand how to reach and target our consumers. In addition, I offered a public relations firm the opportunity to present a public relations campaign for Oakley. I would later compare their research and "target our consumer." All this research, and I received it for free.

We had more than one advertising agency present an advertising campaign, although I was favoring one agency that I wanted to have the account. The amount of $8 million would be spent on advertising and $2 million on the PR campaign. After meeting with the agencies and having them present their campaigns for Oakley, I was ready to decide. Jim Jannard stepped in and said he wasn't ready to take that step. It was a little embarrassing and disappointing.

My plans included establishing a mission statement, vision statement, and define our purpose and our primary objectives. My goal was to have managers along with key members of my senior staff with the help of a professional facilitator to develop these key elements. I learned earlier in my career that buy-in was more successful when the group had input in developing these.

I hired Michael Cohen, a former employee of the Quaker Oats Company. Michael had been the facilitator for many of Gatorade's strategic planning sessions. He was exceptional. I gave Michael the background on the attendees and the current culture at Oakley. I told him it would be challenging. That was an understatement if there ever was one.

Michael had all the necessary tools that he requested—whiteboard, colored markers, tape, easels, and a list of attendees. I started off the morning with an agenda followed by an introduction of Michael Cohen. His reception from the assembled group was less than warm. It was downright defiant and disrespectful. Jim Jannard added no leadership or assistance in the process. Neither did Link Newcomb, who had been demoted to Chief Operating Officer when I was named CEO.

Trying to develop Oakley's mission statement/vision statement was totally torpedoed by Jim Jannard and his loyal cronies. Jim sat in the back of the room and took offense to everything Michael was trying to pull from the group. Michael would take two steps forward, then an "F" bomb would come from Jim Jannard's mouth.

There was little I could do. I'd step in and mention how important this exercise was in determining the future of Oakley and its success. I felt like the substitute teacher in a room full of class clowns and bullies. After the lunch break, I dismissed the group, saying, "There is little need to continue this exercise when a few of you have disrupted the process." I paid Michael Cohen double the rate he quoted and told him I had some real challenges before me. This would not be the last time I would be undermined by Jannard.

Oakley had a clothing line and had started a shoe brand. They would later start manufacturing watches. On the surface, they all seemed reasonable brand extensions. They were creative designs and had the Oakley "edge."

I decided to try the shoes on and wear them throughout the day. They were made of Kevlar, the product that bulletproof vests were made of. They allowed little air circulation, I had worn blisters on my feet, and the sole had become detached from the shoe. I joked, "If I get shot in the foot, I'll be ready."

There was about $4 million in shoe inventory and equipment, and I sold Jannard on the idea that if he was so set on having footwear, we should have it manufactured offshore. He agreed. I made a contact with Joe Lin, a friend of mine who help me establish a weight equipment company with manufacturing located in Taiwan. We started the process, sold off the inventory, and scrapped the shoe manufacturing equipment. It cleaned up our balance sheet. When I inquired about who purchased the Kevlar shoes? The response was, "The Chief of Police of Mexico City." When I asked for how much, they said, "$25,000." When I asked where the money was, no one could tell me.

The watches were attractive and had a perpetual timing device. Jannard had named his latest watch extension the "Time Bomb." He partnered with the Tourneau watch store in New York City to launch the watch. The watches were sent through the US Mail in boxes that had "radioactive type" wrapping. It also said "Time Bomb" on the outside packaging. What could go wrong? Well, the boxes were held at the US Postal Service and were later cleared but were late for the launch.

With Sunglass Hut accounting for 40 percent of Oakley sales, I thought I'd contact the CEO of Sunglass Hut and schedule a meeting. Internally, he was despised by the former CEO, Link Newcomb, and Jannard had nothing nice to say about him. This seemed so ass-backwards. Our biggest retailer was our most despised and worst treated customer. Sunglass Hut had threatened to pull all Oakley inventory from its stores. I needed to visit them ASAP.

I called John Watson, the president and CEO of Sunglass Hut, within the first thirty days of me being at Oakley. He was cordial and said he looked forward to our meeting at his headquarters in Miami, Florida. I also discovered that Link Newcomb had never visited Sunglass Hut. That was, again, difficult to believe.

By contract, Oakley was to manufacture a Sunglass Hut seasonal catalog featuring all Oakley offerings for the coming Christmas season. The catalog had already been laid out but hadn't been mass-produced yet. I had our production people identify each item in the catalog that we would not be able to deliver for the season. Out of the hundreds of items, about 30 percent would not be delivered.

When I arrived for the meeting with John Watson, he welcomed me with open arms. He said his people wanted to pull all

Oakley inventory from their 1,200 stores. When he heard that I was named the new CEO at Oakley, he told them to wait. He told me if anyone could turn Oakley around, it would be me. It seemed John had an appreciation of what I accomplished at Gatorade. I told him, "I come on bended knee asking for some time to right the situation at Oakley." He said he would give me all the time I needed. Establish a relationship, rule number one, accomplished.

As I researched the manufacturing process at Oakley, products rarely got out of design on time, and this made delivery late or impossible. I implement project managers to closely monitor the design process. Computer Assisted Design programs (CAD) were used, and it seemed that the design group continued to design with no sense of urgency or deadlines. I used a term made famous by Ed Keen when he was the Chief Project Engineer at the 1982 World's Fair and Chief Construction Engineer at the 1984 Los Angeles Olympics, "We have to break some pencils." Stop designing and get the job done or, in this case, get the design to manufacturing. I later was aware that Jim Jannard continuously monitored all design efforts and their completion.

Jim Jannard may have been one of most visionary designers in the world, but he had a flaw. He couldn't execute or complete the project or product when there was a timeline. Jim Jannard needed adult supervision. Sometimes you have to "color within the lines" or "stay on the tracks." Link Newcomb provided that to him for years. Link's reward: Jim turned on him and hired me. Jim Jannard told me I could fire Link if I wanted to. I elected to retain him as a valued resource, and there was plenty I could learn from him. Oakley had four CEOs in five years. That's saying something about Jim Jannard's management style.

At my first Oakley shareholders meeting, Jim showed up in a black trench coat, orange Oakley shoes, a beret, and sunglasses. I guessed that was Jim Jannard being Jim Jannard. But when he showed up to the opening of the O Store, Oakley's first retail store, he wore a black trench coat and a gas mask. I thought, *Holy shit, this is different.* He then tried to address the attendees with a handheld megaphone. Of course, his speech was muffled, and they couldn't understand him. I tried to get him to remove his gas mask, but he wouldn't. By the way, the store build-out was budgeted for $300,000. That moved to $600,000 and finally built at a cost of $1.2 million. Jim made it difficult to manage costs. He still ran this now public company as if it were still his private company. No accountability, no defined strategies, objectives, or delegation of power.

After six months, Jim Jannard called me into his office and said, "This isn't working out. You haven't provided the leadership that I expected you to provide."

Now leadership is one of my core competencies as listed by anyone I've ever worked for. I smiled and elected not to provide chapter and verse as to where he undermined my decisions and limited my efforts. That would have been a waste of time.

He said he'd honor my contract. Like he had a choice. My stock options hadn't vested, and I had to return the leased car. From the day I walked into the "Interplanetary Headquarters" of Oakley, I had hope that I'd have the time, effort, and support to make it a billion-dollar brand. I wasn't given the time, but I did leave an impact on the brand. They eventually hired an advertising agency and expanded the brand to include prescription glasses and polarized sunglasses. A small victory.

When I stood up to leave Jim Jannard's office, he extended his hand to shake mine. I refused. It was a matter of respect. He also told some people that I refused to shake his hand. They said that surprised him. He may be worth billions, but I had no respect for him then or now.

Meanwhile, I had two companies paying me not to work. The separation packages from the Quaker Oats Company and Oakley. *What a country!*

Chapter 36

Pegasus Sports Marketing

My departure at Oakley didn't surprise a few people. After all, Oakley had four CEOs in five years. It worked for me at the time. I continued to live in Irvine, California, taking a break from the corporate world. I was a member of Dove Canyon Country Club, provided by my contract with Oakley. I played golf each and every day. I played over 300 rounds of golf in 2000 and got my handicap down to a 2. I'd hit the practice range before and after each round. I met some great guys and had a lot of fun.

Throughout my life, the idea of a healthy lifestyle had been instilled in me when I was at the Quaker Oats Company. I had a complete health physical and exam each year. In 2000, that would be no exception. I had been monitoring my PSA score. It had been climbing about a half point each of the last three years. It had reached 6, and I was referred to a urologist. A biopsy of my prostate was called for, and the results confirmed I had prostate cancer.

The urologist never mentioned the C-word. He just said, "How do you want to handle this?"

I said, "Handle what?" I finally asked, "Do I have cancer?"

His reply was, "Yes."

My first thought was, *Oh f—k, I'm going to die.* My next thought was, *Cut it the f—k out of me.* I was fifty-one. That day, I scheduled a prostatectomy, a surgical procedure where the entire prostate is removed. It was scheduled for September of 2000.

I decided to clear my head by taking a trip. I jumped on my 1997 Harley Davidson Heritage Springer and headed north from Irvine, California. My only plan was to meet some Quaker friends in Sturgis, South Dakota, for the Black Hills Rally. I had no definitive plans. I rode, stopped when I saw some picturesque views, and slept and ate along the way.

I traveled north on US Highway 1 along the Pacific coast. It was beautiful crossing the Golden Gate Bridge and traveling the Columbia River Gorge between Washington and Oregon. When I crossed into Idaho, I headed south through Montana, thinking what a beautiful country I live in.

I arrived in Yellowstone National Park after a morning thundershower. The air was pristine. I traveled through the park, stopping at various locations to enjoy, the geyser, Old Faithful, and El Capitan, the iconic rock formation on the north side of the park—an incredible experience that just flooded my senses.

After a week in Sturgis, I returned to Irvine to prepare myself for the medical procedure I scheduled for September. While playing golf with Steve Williams, who was an anesthesiologist and a good friend, he said to me, "Before you have your procedure, I want you to schedule an appointment with a friend of mine, Dr. Kenneth Tokita, a radiation oncologist."

After an appointment with Dr. Tokita and having discussed the extent and state of my prostate cancer, I decided on permanent prostate brachytherapy. This involved placing radioactive seeds within the prostate. The seeds emit radiation that kills the cancer. It's an outpatient procedure, and I was playing golf in a couple of days. The radiation seeds become inactive after about ten months.

I did have some complications. I couldn't completely empty my bladder. Well, you do what you have to do. I inserted a sixteen-inch catheter each time I had to urinate. Sounds painful, but it wasn't. I kept a catheter in my car, my golf bag, and in my briefcase. When you have to go, you have to go. I did this for fourteen months and then had a surgical procedure that enabled me to empty my bladder without the catheter. Dr. Kenneth Tokita had saved my life. For that, I will always be grateful. You also realize that when you face adversity, you face it head on and move on. I had a life to live and experiences to enjoy.

Upon hearing of my departure from Oakley, numerous individuals and companies contacted me. They wanted to "rent my rolodex." I had great relationships in the sports business, and they were willing to pay me for a conversation and a point of view and my opinion. That started a business, Pegasus Sports Marketing. I had a variety of projects with a variety of brands that included Levi Strauss, Outback Steakhouse restaurants, NASCAR, AAA, and Under Armour.

As numerous individuals reached out to me, I decided to look at opportunities at a variety of corporate brands. The Coca-Cola Company, a longtime competitor, seemed like an obvious place to start. My history with their brand was from a distance, but I felt my skillset, contacts, and negotiating expertise would be an asset for their brand. After numerous conversations with a variety of their management executives and their human resources, we scheduled a visit and a series of interviews.

Earlier that year, PepsiCo and the Coca-Cola Company were both making a run to acquire the Quaker Oats Company. Their primary focus was to acquire the crown jewel, Gatorade. Years earlier, the management group of the Quaker Oats Company reached an agreement with the Coca-Cola Company in a joint project called "Cardinal." Its primary goal was to explore opportunities with a joint taskforce to evaluate mutual business objectives. We all thought it would be the beginning of an acquisition by the Coca-Cola Company. We shared all our company information, contracts, production and distribution schedules, product development, and our research. Those of us involved with the project signed nondisclosure agreements. I made a special trip to Washington DC to meet with Barbara Allen from FAME to make Michael Jordan aware of the project and possible acquisition by the Coca-Cola Company.

The acquisition never happened. There were those of us that felt the Coca-Cola Company received all our information, then just moved on. The word was that "synergies weren't efficient," and the project was dropped.

During the time of the competition to acquire the Quaker Oats Company by PepsiCo and the Coca-Cola Company in the summer of 2001, I received an interesting phone call. "Hello, Bill, this is Peter." It was Peter Ueberroth, my former boss at the 1984 Los Angeles Olympics and Major League Baseball Commissioner. "I'm at a Coca-Cola Company board meeting, and we're discussing the acquisition of the Quaker Oats Company. Warren"—as in Warren Buffet—"thinks $16 billion is too high of a price for the company. Now, Bill, it's a given that should we acquire Gatorade, you'll be back running the sports marketing. So tell me what they don't do well." That's what made Peter, Peter. He would ask questions in a way that nobody else would.

I said, "Gatorade uses a broker system for its distribution, and with the Coca-Cola Company's distribution, you could double the business in less than five years. I also assume you'd sell off the businesses in the Quaker Oats portfolio of brands that provided no synergies."

Peter thanked me and went back to the Coca-Cola Company board meeting. I'm assuming that Warren Buffett stood firm on his opinion, and the Coca-Cola Company was outbid by PepsiCo in August 2001. I'd like to think that Warren Buffett, in hindsight, might have regretted not doing that deal.

My trip to visit the Coca-Cola Company had been confirmed. It was coincidently after the PepsiCo acquisition had been announced. The morning of my scheduled flight, I received a phone call from my longtime friend, Spanky Stevens. It was 5:30 a.m. on the West Coast.

He said, "What are you doing?"

I said, "I'm preparing for my flight from John Wayne Airport this morning to Atlanta."

He said, "You're not going anywhere, turn on your TV." It was September 11, 2001. I watched in horror as everyone did that day.

My interview was later rescheduled for December 7. I should have taken that as an omen. I made the trip and met with a variety of junior management personnel. None of the individuals I interviewed with had any influence nor were they decision-makers. A few worked on the Powerade brand, and it was apparent to me that someone thought it would be a good idea to interview our competitor's brand's former sports marketing executive. Another fact-finding mission for the Coca-Cola Company. There was no follow up or mentioning of employment.

I relocated to Knoxville, Tennessee, in 2001. I went to Knoxville in September of 2001 to watch the University of Tennessee versus Florida football game. I bought a house that was under construction that weekend. It was on the Parade of Homes and had visitors for three weekends before I moved in late October.

A friend of mine, Dr. Buck Jones, was the head of the sports management program at the University of Tennessee, Knoxville. He provided me an office, and I became an Adjunct Professor in his department. I taught a graduate class for five years, titled "The Financial and Economic Aspects of Sports." I also was a guest lecturer on occasion at the James Haslam School of Business.

While teaching, I still worked on consulting. I received a call from my dear friend, Phil Marineau, then CEO of the Levi Strauss Company. He said, "We've decided to enter into a sponsorship with the San Francisco Giants Baseball team. We don't have anyone here within the company that's qualified to negotiate the deal. I want you to do the deal."

He outlined what the Levi Strauss Company budgeted and defined their signage objectives. One of the "must haves" was the 501 distance sign to clear center field. Levi Strauss manufactured a "501 Jeans," and the chairman of Levi Strauss wanted to put "Levi" above the sign. It was the final item that I negotiated into the contract.

There were a variety of signage proposals that started at $4 million and went as high as $7 million. Levi Strauss settled on a sponsorship of an area in right field to be named "Levi's Landing." It also included the last two rows of seats that would be used for Levi Strauss promotions and for employees. Payout was $2.1 million per year for five years. During that five-year period, the SF Giants hosted an MLB All-Star game and two World Series. The television exposure more than paid for the sponsorship.

I was later asked to assist the Docker's brand at Levi Strauss to sign a professional golfer. I narrowed the field to three PGA Tour golfers—Arron Oberholser, Lucas Glover, and Vaughn Taylor. The endorsement would be a "head-to-toe" apparel deal. They selected Arron Oberholser. He was from the San Francisco Bay area and had won the prestigious AT&T Pebble Beach National Pro-Am in February of 2006, a great-looking guy who looked great in their apparel. The Docker's ad campaign was titled, "Docker's, you can wear them to work, after work, and to play." It was a great campaign and Arron was perfect for it.

There were a few companies that employed me that were in Knoxville, Tennessee. AAA (the American Automobile Association), WVLT-TV, the CBS affiliate television station, and A3, a professional NFL and NBA players' representative agency. I was hired to develop marketing strategies, management staffing, CEO coaching, and media training. This was very rewarding, and it also enabled me to hire a few students from my classes in positions where I was able to pay them. For WLVT-TV, I was also the on-site producer for a weekly segment titled "Our Town." I loved it!

There was still a desire in me that wanted to pursue a professional sports management position. I was qualified to do more than consult and teach. I targeted several NFL football teams. I sent my resume to Wayne Huizenga, owner of the Miami Dolphins and Arthur Blank, the owner of the Atlanta Falcons. In both cases, I stated that in my opinion, their teams were undermarketed, and given my experience, I could be a value-added resource to their organization.

I received a phone call from Robert Henninger, Executive Vice President of Huizenga Holdings. He said, "Mr. H will be flying to Knoxville, Tennessee, to meet with you on Friday. You'll meet him at TAC Air at McGhee Tyson Airport, and you have only fifteen minutes of his time." He would be flying to Knoxville from Linville, North Carolina, where he owned a home.

Huizenga Holdings made me curious, so I researched what holdings Mr. Huizenga had in his portfolio of businesses. It was listed as a private money management firm. He had owned AutoNation, Waste Management, Blockbuster Videos, as well as the Miami Dolphins and part ownership of the Florida Panthers, an NHL team, the Florida Marlins, an MLB team, and hotels, resorts, and golf courses listed under Boca Resorts. The group of hotels included the Hyatt Pier 66 Hotel, Boca Ratan Resort and Golf Club, and the Bahia Mar Hotel and Marina. It was obvious that Mr. Huizenga's Miami Dolphins were but a small property in his holdings. The bulk of his investments were in real estate with hotels, golf clubs and marinas.

On the day of the scheduled meeting, I arrived at the TAC Air facility thirty minutes before Mr. Huizenga's arrival. I had a dozen Krispy Kreme doughnuts and two cups of coffee that I delivered to the conference room on the second floor. Checking with TAC traffic, Mr. H's flight had landed, so I went to the front office and awaited his plane's arrival.

A beautiful white Gulfstream V with a Miami Dolphins logo on its tail slowly moved into the covered area, except for the tail. It was too high. Everyone within the facility was abuzz when they saw the Dolphins' logo. Hell, you couldn't miss it. I met Mr. Huizenga as he entered the lobby of TAC Air. I introduced myself and directed him to the conference room on the second floor. I handed him a Styrofoam cup of coffee and opened the box of Krispy Kreme Doughnuts. He grabbed one and asked me, "Tell me a little about yourself."

I remembered that he was from Chicago and started in the garbage collection business, like his grandfather. I shared my humble beginnings as well as mentioning we shared the same birthday, December 29. He was impressed with my work career and experiences. The meeting that I was told would last ten minutes lasted an hour. He asked all the questions about what I thought about his team and the Miami Dolphins organization. My response that got his attention was, "Mr. Huizenga, from the outside, it appears that your team is undermarketed. The Miami market opportunities haven't been capitalized by your organization." Even though I'd been with him for an hour, I wasn't comfortable calling him "Mr. H."

He led the way downstairs to the lobby where numerous people were taking pictures of his plane and the Miami Dolphins' logo on its tail. He said, "Join me on my plane." To say the interior was impressive is an understatement. He said, "Have a seat."

I said, "Mr. Huizenga, I want to thank you for the time today."

He said, "Call me Mr. H." He sat in the aisle across from me. At a quick count, it appeared the plane could accommodate about twenty people. There were two in the flight crew and one female flight attendant. This at the time was the biggest private jet manufactured with a flight range of over 7,000 miles.

He said, "I want you to come to Miami and review our practice facility and offices in Davie, Florida, and Pro Player Stadium in Miami Gardens, Florida. After your report and findings, we'll work on getting you to Miami to be President of the Club."

I felt that we connected on a variety of levels, and I knew I could work for this gentleman and his organization. Also, don't ever discount the importance of a dozen Krispy Kreme doughnuts.

Within a week, I flew to Miami on a commercial flight and was greeted by a private car owned by Mr. H's holdings. The driver said, "Mr. H said to take you anywhere you wanted to go."

I started with the Miami Dolphin facilities in Davie where I toured the layout and spent three hours meeting with staff and personnel. The facility manager said, "Mr. H said to be open and fulfill any and all your requests."

I then went to Pro Player Stadium after stopping for lunch at a fast-food drive-thru. The driver was amused by this. He said, "This is something Mr. H would do." I spent four hours there with the stadium manager. Given my observation skills and attention to detail, there were noticeable opportunities for additional signage and sponsorships. I took litigious notes and photos.

Upon returning to Knoxville, I assembled my report and findings and sent it on to Mr. Henninger at Huizenga Holdings. I followed up with a phone call. Mr. Henninger said, "Mr. H was pleased with your analysis and will be moving forward with you and the project."

Two weeks went by, and I knew Mr. H was busy because I followed in the news his negotiations to get Ricky Williams, University of Texas star running back and Heisman Trophy winner, to return to the Miami Dolphins. Ricky Williams had been suspended by the NFL for testing positive for marijuana on numerous occasions.

Williams had gone to Asia and wasn't responding to efforts to get him back to Miami.

I eventually called Mr. Henninger. He was polite but direct. "Mr. Huizenga has decided to sell the Miami Dolphins." He thanked me for my efforts. I assumed he was tired of babysitting overpaid athletes and wanting to spend more time with his wife, who had been diagnosed with cancer. I watched when the ownership changed. My submitted plan had been implemented by the new ownership staff. It's not like it was rocket science. It was my marketing expertise and attention to detail formulated into a detailed action plan. They just implemented it. It confirmed my opinion, findings, and next steps.

There was an appreciation of what Mr. H saw in me and the responsibility he was ready to entrust to me. It confirmed there were opportunities with the NFL teams.

A week later, I received a call from the Atlanta Falcons. They were responding to the similar letter I had sent to Mr. Huizenga. In this instance, I addressed my letter to Falcons owner Arthur Blank. The call was from their Human Resources Department. They were calling to coordinate my visit/interview with the Atlanta Falcons at their facilities in Flowery Branch, Georgia.

Arthur Blank's business background was impressive. He was the co-founder of Home Depot and had a net worth of $5 billion in 2006. The Atlanta Falcons, like the Miami Dolphins, in my view, were undermarketed. Mr. Blank was exceptional at the "Big Box Store" but seemed to lack the marketing expertise in his organization to capitalize on the Atlanta market. The Falcons invited me for an interview to explore how I could help. I went with an open mind and cautious optimism.

My interviews with the Atlanta Falcons were noticeably different in tonality and purpose. I never felt like they were recruiting me for how or where I could help their team or fit into their organization. I met with their General Manager, Rich McKay, son of legendary USC coach and the first coach of the NFL expansion team, the Tampa Bay Buccaneers. At the time, he was viewed as a rising star in the NFL community. I was not overwhelmed by his skillset or his communication skills. He was a young attorney, and I felt he was better suited to dealing with player personnel and negotiating contracts than he was in marketing an NFL team and putting people in the seats.

After three other interviews with various senior staff personnel, I was asked by Rich McKay, with his staffers present, "What do you expect this position to pay?" I learned that it was better to not express my opinion regarding salary during an interview. I wanted to make them aware of what expertise I offered, then wait for their initial offer and negotiate from there. Mr. McKay continued to press the issue. It was then that I realized they had no interest in me.

The odds of me joining the Atlanta Falcons organization were slim to none. Now with my current clients, I was making over $250,000 a year. I knew it would take more than that to have me fold up my shop and move to Atlanta, Georgia. I also knew that this was also a fact-finding trip for me. I wasn't impressed with their front office administration, and my intuition told me this wouldn't be a good fit for me.

Reluctantly, I said, "$275,000."

The first words out of Mr. McKay's mouth were, "For marketing?" Then I realized he and the organization were inept not only in marketing but in assessing talent and one's potential to the organization. End of interview. No follow up by me or them. I did follow up with a letter thanking them for the opportunity and their time. Enclosed were also my expense receipts for the trip.

I continued to cultivate my relationships and servicing clients through 2012 when I retired. In 2014, I officially closed Pegasus Sports Marketing. As in Greek mythology, "Pegasus was regarded as a symbol of inspiration." I was inspired and hopefully inspired others along the way.

CHAPTER 37

FOR THE RECORD

In the history of the Summer Olympic Games, there have been eight Olympic medals won in the men's and women's javelin by the United States of America. There have been twenty-nine Summer Olympic Games scheduled, and three were canceled due to war.

America's first Olympic javelin medal, a gold, was won by "Babe" Didrikson Zaharias in Los Angeles in 1932 (143 feet, 4 inches). It was the first time that women competed in the javelin throw at the Olympic Games. She also won a gold in the 80-meter hurdles and a silver in the high jump. She was an all-around athlete who competed in golf, basketball, and baseball. After the 1932 Los Angeles Olympics, she became a professional golfer and won ten LPGA major championships. She is in the Golf Hall of Fame.

The first American male to win a medal in the javelin throw in the Olympic Games was Eugene Oberst in Paris, 1924. He won a bronze medal (190 feet). He was a Notre Dame football player who played for Knute Rockne. Legend has it he was walking by track practice, picked up a javelin that had been thrown by another individual, and threw it back. The rest is history.

At the London Olympic Games in 1948, Steve Seymour won a silver medal (221 feet, 7 inches). He had traveled to Finland to learn the Finnish technique of throwing the javelin in 1947. Born Seymour Cohen, he changed his name to Steve Seymour in his twenties to avoid "the strong anti-Semitism of post-war America."

In the 1952 Olympic Games, the United States had its best results in the men's javelin throw in Helsinki, Finland. Cyrus "Cy" Young won the gold medal (241 feet, 10 inches), and Bill Miller won the silver medal (237 feet, 7 inches). Toivo Hyytiainen, from Finland, the favorite, finished third.

When I was competing in Finland in 1985, I was at a small grocery store and noticed a photo on the counter of Janus Lusis, renowned Russian javelin thrower, standing with another gentleman. I asked the clerk, "Who's the guy with Janus Luis?"

She said, "That's my husband. He was the bronze medalist in the javelin at the Olympics in 1952."

Tom Jennings, our Pacific Coast Track Club manager, said, "This is Bill Schmidt. He was the Bronze Medalist in the javelin at the Munich Olympics in 1972."

The wife of Toivo closed the store and took us in her car to her home to meet her husband. I had a memorable day at Toivo Hyytiainen's home where he had walls of display cases full of the silver trophies he had won. It was most impressive. The javelin throw is the national sport in Finland, and he was one of their best ever.

At the Munich Olympics in 1972, I stunned the world, winning a bronze medal (276 feet, 11 inches), the USA's first Olympic medal in twenty years. Kate Schmidt, no relation, also won a bronze medal in the women's javelin throw (196 feet, 7 inches). In 1976, at the Montreal Olympics, Kate Schmidt would win another bronze medal (209 feet, 10 inches).

In the board game, Trivial Pursuit, the answer to this sports question, "What American male and female both won bronze medals in the javelin throw at the same Olympics and share the same last name?" Kate and Bill Schmidt, Munich Olympics, 1972. What they didn't know was that we also shared the same birth date, December 29.

Kate Schmidt was the last American women's javelin thrower to win a medal, and I'm the last American male to win a medal, fifty years ago. Where did all the time go?

EPILOGUE

My relocation to Knoxville, Tennessee, has been great. As an adjunct professor at the University of Tennessee, I was able to continue to consult as President of Pegasus Sports Marketing. In addition, I remained current on the news and trends in the sports business industry. The students kept me challenged, and I tried to have the "giants" in the industry speak at our annual sports marketing conference. When possible, I also employed a few students to assist in some of my Pegasus projects.

When asked, I also assisted the University of Tennessee's athletic department regarding their marketing proposals. I really wanted to be the athletic director at the University of Tennessee, and I applied when the position came open twice. It was political, and certain people felt you had to have been an athletic director. As a business executive who managed a 250-million-dollar budget and negotiated multimillion-dollar contracts in the sports business industry who was an Olympic athlete and an Olympic organizer, I felt that I was more than qualified. It is about fundraising and building your brand. something I felt certain that I could do.

Having been "self-taught" in learning the javelin, I felt obligated to share that knowledge when asked. I worked as a board member with the National Athletics Sports Foundation (NASF) and conducted javelin clinics for them in Chapel Hill, North Carolina, for five years. I loved coaching those high school athletes.

Kim Hamilton, a two-sport All-American in softball and in the javelin who competed for Kent State University relocated to Knoxville for my coaching. Kim was very talented and progressed quickly. In 2012, she finished third at the US Olympic Track and Field Trials in Eugene, Oregon. throwing 190 feet, 5 inches, her best throw ever.

She was from Oregon and was able to have her family there to witness her success. Normally, the top three athletes in each event qualify for the US Olympic Team. That's if you have made the Olympic "A" standard. Kim hadn't thrown the "A" standard distance and therefore wasn't on the USA Olympic Team headed to London, England.

As part of the interview process for the javelin candidates for the NASF Program, I met with Madison Wiltrout and her family when I was in Canonsburg, Pennsylvania, for a Fourth of July celebration. She was quite an athlete. She played point guard for the Connellsville High School girls' basketball team. Her family later declined on having Madison joining the NSAF program but asked me if I'd coach her.

She was raw but extremely talented. After seeing her in her first workout with me, I told her mother that she'd break the national high school record for the girls' javelin and receive a full scholarship to college. She had thrown 153 feet at this point in her career. Her mother, Amy, didn't believe me. I traveled to Pennsylvania on a regular schedule, at my own expense, to train her. Madison became a four-time Pennsylvania state champion and set a new national record throwing 185 feet, 8 inches. She also received a full scholarship to the University of North Carolina where she's been an All-American, ACC Champion, and UNC record holder.

My coaching of boys' javelin throwers had been mainly at clinics and not over an extended period of time. I have recently coached two decathletes who are in college. It's amazing what a little technique training can do. With the basics, an individual can improve ten to twenty feet. It's all relevant, and greater improvement comes with greater commitment by the athletes. I don't see myself writing daily workouts for any additional athletes in the future. Would I consult with them or their coaches at a throwing session? Absolutely.

When I decided that teaching in graduate school for five years was enough, my thoughts turned to traveling the world. I eventually completed my quest to have traveled to all fifty states. I've been to the Black Hills Rally in Sturgis, South Dakota, seven times on my Harley. I then traveled on long flights to faraway places across the world.

I visited the head waters of the Amazon River where I stayed in a straw hut and explored the Amazon Rainforest. That trip also included visiting Iguazu Falls, the most beautiful waterfalls in the world, located on the border between Argentina and Brazil.

Although I'm not a hunter, I booked an African safari. There was no hunting involved, just sightseeing. My travel included stops in Cape Town and Johannesburg, South Africa, and safari experiences in Kruger National Park and Sabi Sabi Private Game Reserve. My visit to Zimbabwe included visiting and staying at Victoria Falls. My trip lasted two weeks—incredible animal sightings and educational settings.

My AAA travel agent, Susan Redmond, has been exceptional. She convinced me to take a "Round the World Cruise" on Princess Cruise Lines. It was awesome. It was for 109 days. My departure was out of Fort Lauderdale, Florida, and ended in Rome, Italy. I visited thirty countries on six continents and traveled through the Panama and Suez Canals. There were forty-four ports of call that included Easter Island, New Zealand, Australia, Papua New Guinea, Japan, Korea, Shanghai, the Great Wall of China, Hong Kong, the Valley of the Kings and the Pyramids in Egypt, Jerusalem, Athens, Istanbul, Monaco, Barcelona, and Venice, to name a few. Great trip. There were 700 passengers on the *Royal Princess*, and the cruise was in four segments, and 424 of us did the entire cruise. My dog, Bogie, didn't recognize me when I returned home.

My latest excursion was a river cruise with TAUCK Travel. They are the experts when it comes to travel. TAUCK also booked my travel for the African safari. The river cruise was from Amsterdam, the Netherlands, to Budapest, Hungary, for a total of sixteen days. We traveled through Germany, Austria, and Slovakia. Great cities, history, and food. Highlights included a dinner at the Royal Palace in Vienna and two extra days touring Buda and Pest, the two cities that making up Budapest, Hungary. I've already planned my next TAUCK trip, to Antarctica, the only continent I haven't visited.

Retirement is great. I play golf twice a week and work out at the gym four days a week. I sold both my Harley Davidson motorcycles and purchased a convertible. East Tennessee and the Smoky Mountains have beautiful sights with four distinct seasons, the best being spring and fall. I get my sports fix by attending the University of Tennessee athletic events and still occasionally guest lecture in the Sports Management Program.

My travel has also taken me back to my hometown of Canonsburg, Pennsylvania. I've lost my older brothers, Michael and Edward. My twin brother, Bob, and I have invested in our hometown's town park to enhance and provide activities for the youth there today and in the future, much like it did for us while growing up. Mayor David Rhome and my good friend and former employee at Gatorade, John Somsky, have shepherded these projects for us.

There were exceptionally talented people working with me during my fifteen years on Gatorade and at the Quaker Oats Company. Starting with the first employee I hired, Hank Steinbrecher, and including Delores Kennedy, Greg Via, John Somsky, Kim Frabotta, Pattio Jo Sinopoli, Dawn Wantuck, Suzie Cruz, Kathy Maddis, John Marovich, Jackie Harris, Tom Fox, Greg Bradshaw, Jeff Price, Scott Paddock, Cindy Alston, Cindy Sisson, Patti Sus, Anna Gallup, and Jackie Leimer.

There's no doubt that I couldn't have achieved any level of success without these team members. It was a small integral group that could handle any issue or challenge and execute a strategy and plan with perfection.

They say there's a woman behind every successful man. That woman for me was Christine Grzybowski. Her title might have been administrative assistant, but she was much more than that. She was my chief operating officer and my chief of staff. She had the greatest skillset to communicate with everyone, regardless of job title or seniority, and make them feel significant and important. Her communication skills were exceptional. She was also the conscience of our sports marketing group. Thank you, Christine.

I'd be remiss if I didn't mention a few people that provided me with information and knowledge that rounded out my business acumen. The advertising agency of Bayer Bess Vanderwarker's employees, Bernie Pitzel, Sr. Vice President and Group Creative Director and the genius behind the "Be Like Mike" commercial; Steve Seyferth, Sr. Vice President, Account Director; Jane Richtsmeir,

Vice President, Account Supervisor; John Fraser, Vice President and Account Director; and Danny Shulman, Group Creative Director.

From John LaSage, CEO of Chicago based Burson-Marsteller, the public relations firm, I learned crisis management and media management. He was absolutely the best in the business. He managed the Tylenol crisis and Gatorade's California tainted product crisis. I will be ever thankful for the many occasions I was his and Irv Seaman's guest at Augusta National Golf Club. Working with John was Ken Trantowski, one of the very best in every facet of public relations. His expertise helped Gatorade on a variety of fronts and made us proactive in public relations as we launched any marketing campaign. John LeGear of Timothy Communications provided me all the knowledge and the importance of the athletic training community.

I worked along with Peggy Dyer, Vice President of Marketing, Gatorade, and Matt Mannelly, Director, Consumer Gatorade, to execute the "Be Like Mike" campaign. Our President of Grocery Specialties Group was Peter Vitulli. It was a group effort that everyone takes great pride in its success. I was Vice President of Gatorade, Sports Marketing at the time.

In one's journey of life, many people pass through our lives. The person who has had the biggest impact on my career and my life has been Phil Marineau. He provided me an opportunity and friendship that I will forever be grateful. Bill Smithburg, Chairman and CEO of the Quaker Oats Company, had faith in me and supported me in some of the most challenging times. He understood how I planned and executed Gatorade's sports marketing programs.

For years, people were saying, "Bill, you should write a book. You have a unique and compelling story to tell." Then I realized if I didn't tell my story, no one would. I originally thought of a ghostwriter or a contributing author. When I interview several writers, they said, "No one can tell your story like you." So here it is, after three and a half years of work and research.

My hope is that you find it entertaining, motivational, and educational. My life has been a series of events and stories. I'm extremely proud and humble to be sharing these with you.

Enjoy!

Appendix A

Professional Positions/Accomplishments/Honors:

- Three-time All-American Javelin thrower.
- 1971: World Military (CISM) Recordholder and Champion, Javelin.
- 1972: Olympic Bronze Medalist in the javelin, Munich Germany.
- 1975: Second in World University Games, Javelin, Rome, Italy.
- 1978: USA National Champion, Javelin Throw.
- 1982: Director of Sports, 1982 World's Fair, Knoxville, Tennessee.
- 1984: Vice President of Sports at the Los Angeles Olympics.
- 1988: Inducted into University of North Texas Sports Hall of Fame.
- 1985–1999: Vice President of Gatorade Worldwide Sports Marketing.
- 1994: Named in "The 100 Most Powerful People in Sports" by *The Sporting News* (Ranked #56).
- 1995: Named in "The 100 Most Powerful People in Sports," by *The Sporting News* (Ranked #81).
- 1997: Inducted into the Pennsylvania Sports Hall of Fame.
- 1999: CEO Oakley, eyewear and apparel company.
- 2000–2005: Adjunct professor, University of Tennessee, Knoxville, Tennessee.
- 2000–2013: President of Pegasus Sports Marketing.

- 2013: Inducted into the Greater Knoxville Sports Hall of Fame.
- 2014: "Champions Award" recipient presented by *The Sports Daily/Global Journal* as "A Pioneer and Innovator in Sports Business."
- 2014: Inducted into the Knoxville Track Club Hall of Fame.
- 2015: Retired.

APPENDIX B

Letter to Coach Bill Parcells, Head Coach of the New York Giants, dated January 7, 1987, regarding the "Gatorade Dunk."

Quaker

The Quaker Oats Company, Merchandise Mart
Plaza, Chicago, Illinois 60654
January 7, 1987

Mr. William Parcells
Head Coach
New York Giants
Giants Stadium
East Rutherford, New Jersey 07073

Dear Coach Parcells:

We at the Quaker Oats Company, makers of GATORADE® Thirst Quencher realize that due to the year-long "GATORADE dunking" you have been receiving, your wardrobe has probably taken a beating.

The enclosed should help remedy this problem; after all, we do feel somewhat responsible for your cleaning bill.

Wishing you the best of luck this weekend.

Sincerely yours,

Bill D. Schmidt
Director, Sports Marketing

About the Author

An Olympic medalist, Olympic organizer, educator, entrepreneur, and a pioneer in sports marketing, Bill Schmidt served as director of sports at the 1982 World's Fair; vice president of Sports at the 1984 Los Angeles Olympics; vice president of Gatorade Worldwide Sports Marketing; and CEO of Oakley, the eyewear and apparel company.

He was instrumental in growing Gatorade from $80 million to a 1.8 billion-dollar brand. He has negotiated multiyear and multimillion-dollar contracts with the NFL, NBA, NHL, NASCAR, and Major League Baseball and signed Michael Jordan as the brand's spokesperson. The Sporting News named him in the "100 Most Powerful" people in sports, #56 in 1994, and #81 in 1995. In 2014, the *Sports Business Daily/Global Journal* recognized him with their "Champions Award" as a pioneer and innovator in sports business.

As president of his own sports business agency, he developed strategic plans, staffing and organizational reviews, contract negotiations, sponsorship reviews, and CEO coaching with clients that included Levi Strauss, Dockers, NASCAR, Under Armour, CBS, and AAA. At the University of Tennessee, Knoxville, Tennessee, he was an adjunct professor in the College of Education/Sports Management and taught a graduate class, "The Financial and Economic Aspects of Sports."

Bill was an All-American in track and field at the University of North Texas, Denton, Texas, captain of the track team, and the last American male to have won an Olympic medal, a bronze, in the javelin throw at the Munich Olympics in 1972.

CPSIA information can be obtained
at www.ICGtesting.com
Printed in the USA
LVHW111251250123
737445LV00001B/1

9 781684 984459